Contents

A
R
rj

PI
Saran Palmer

PAGE DESIGN:
Craig Lamb
Kriele Ltd
design_lamb@btinternet.com

COVER DESIGN:
Kelvin Clements

REPROGRAPHICS:
Paul Fincham
Jonathan Schofield

ADVERTISING:
Craig Amess
camess@mortons.co.uk

PUBLISHERS:
Steve O'Hara
Tim Hartley

PUBLISHING DIRECTOR:
Dan Savage

COMMERCIAL DIRECTOR:
Nigel Hole

MARKETING MANAGER:
Charlotte Park
cpark@mortons.co.uk

PRINTED BY:
William Gibbons and Sons,
Wolverhampton

ISBN:
978-1-911276-46-3

PUBLISHED BY:
Mortons Media Group Ltd,
Media Centre,
Morton Way,
Horncastle,
Lincolnshire
LN9 6JR.
Tel: 01507 529529

COPYRIGHT:
Mortons Media Group Ltd, 2018
All rights reserved.

All pictures marked * are published
under a Creative Commons licence.
Full details may be obtained at
http://creativecommons.org/licences

MR 4F 0-6-0 No. 43924 and guest locomotive LMS 'Black Five' 4-6-0 No. 44871 stand in Haworth yard on the Keighley & Worth Valley Railway as the snow falls on the evening of December 29, 2017. No. 44871, which is owned by Bury engineer Ian Riley, hauled Santa the train over the festive season that year, and was also booked to appear in the line's 2018 spring steam gala, along with another guest, Somerset & Dorset Joint Railway 7F 2-8-0 No. 88 from the West Somerset Railway hauled the Santa train, and also guest locomotive Oliver Cromwell. ANDREW RAPACZ

BRONTE STEAM
50 years of the
Keighley & Worth Valley Railway

COVER PICTURE: Ivatt 2MT 2-6-2T No. 41241 and USA 0-6-0T No. 30072 being prepared for the reopening special in Haworth yard on June 29, 1968. BARNARD LUMB

No part of this publication may be produced or transmitted in any form or by any means, electronic or mechanical, including photocopying, recording, or any information storage retrieval system without prior permission in writing from the publisher.

KEIGHLEY & WORTH VALLEY RAILWAY
A LINE OF IMAGINATION

During my English degree course, a friend and I became so enraptured by Emily's Bronte's classic novel Wuthering Heights, backed up by a series of excellent lectures, that we vowed on that very cold and snowy winter's day, we would make a pilgrimage one day to Haworth to walk over those wild and windy moors to Top Withens, the ruined farmhouse said to be an inspiration for the home of Heathcliff and Cathy Earnshaw, so we could immerse ourselves in the atmosphere that had inspired the writer.

For one reason or another, it never happened, and it would be another 20 years before I ventured into the Worth Valley. That was when my career path led me into railway journalism, and between Keighley and Oxenhope, I found a heritage railway the magic of which, for me, equalled or even bettered anything that the Bronte sisters came up with.

There are around 120 heritage lines in the UK today, and in the sector of standard gauge, the Keighley & Worth Valley Railway at 4¾ miles is one of the shortest. Yet here I discovered a railway in a million.

Mile by mile, yard by yard, I do not know of any similar railway with so much to offer and discover over such a comparatively short distance. Every station has its own individual appeal and attractions and is worth a visit in itself; the magnificent variety of the steam and diesel locomotive and carriage fleets is truly awe-inspiring. Furthermore, it is home to three significant and associated groups in the Vintage Carriages Trust, the Bahamas Locomotive Society and the Lancashire & Yorkshire Railway Trust.

This railway is a treasure of national, and yes, even international, rather than merely regional, significance.

The revival of the closed Oxenhope branch by local people began not with the aim of creating a preserved railway, but to restore services that had been snatched away. Of course, history records that the KWVR did emerge as a market leader in the heritage sector, but local residents still use it for transport along the valley.

In this special publication to mark half a century of public services on the KWVR since it reopened on June 29, 1968, I have endeavoured to place it in the long and winding story of the evolution of the railway sector. It was not the first heritage line by any means, but the KWVR broke new ground and blazed trails for others to follow, not least of all the purchase of the branch from British Rail. Indeed, the KWVR is unique in that it is still the only heritage line to have bought – rather than leased – the entire length of its original branch including the operational main line connection at Keighley. The KWVR does lease its section of Keighley station and the track through the station to the mainline from Network Railway.

The many-faceted ground-breaking heritage line that we have today is the result of herculean efforts by a multitude of volunteers including both enthusiasts and local residents over nearly six decades. It would take a telephone directory to credit them all, and their achievements were undoubtedly helped by the publicity that followed the release of EMI's big-screen production of The Railway Children, for which the line provided location filming, in 1970. As with the Bronte sisters' novels, Haworth and its district became a meeting point of imagination and reality, and the railway still retains a unique romantic

Ralph Povey, whose letter to a local newspaper proved to be the foundation stone of the movement to revive the Worth Valley branch. KWVR

> Remember
> **Ralph Oliver Thomas Povey**
> **1923 - 2007**
> K&WVRPS President 1978 - 1999
> Whose quiet genius inspired the saving of this railway for future generations
> "...all things are possible for those who believe"

charm as immortalised in Lionel Jeffries' blockbuster movie.

However, there are two people without whose vision we would not have this magnificent railway today. The first is Ralph Povey, an Oakworth resident who had been calling for organised volunteer-led railway revival schemes since 1959 and two years later suggested in a letter to the Bradford Telegraph and Argus that the Worth Valley branch

The late Bob Cryer MP, the first Keighley & Worth Valley Preservation Society chairman. KWVR

> In Memory of
> **GEORGE ROBERT CRYER MP BSc(Econ)**
> **1934 - 1994**
> K&WVRPS Chairman 1962-1972
> whose idea it was ....
> 'If you seek his memorial, look around you'

Camilla, Duchess of Cornwall, visited the KWVR on Friday, February 16, at their start of their 50th anniversary year celebrations and met staff and volunteers before taking a special 'royal train' from Haworth to Oxenhope. KWVR

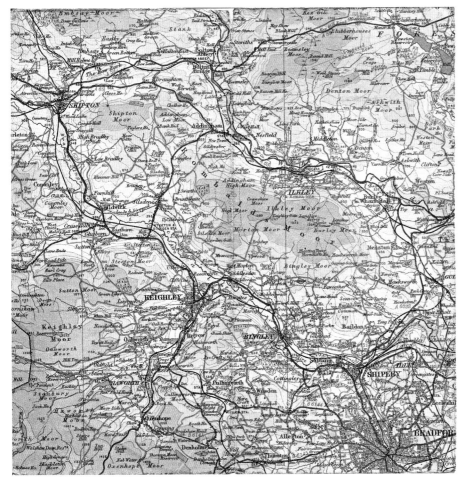

A half-inch to the mile map of 1939 showing the position of the Worth Valley branch in relation to the surrounding rail network. ROBIN JONES COLLECTION

should be preserved. That letter led to what we see today.

Ralph served as president of the Keighley & Worth Valley Preservation Society from 1978-99 and passed away in 2007 aged 84, having spent his last years with his wife Marion in a cottage near Oxenhope station.

The second is Bob Cryer, a University of Hull economics graduate who was determined that the Worth Valley branch would not go the same way as the adjoining Great Northern line from Keighley to Bradford. He attended the first meeting of the revivalists and served as society chairman from 1962-72, being re-elected annually by members, and under him the railway ascended to the pinnacle of excellence that it is today. He was a qualified steam driver on the line until the late Seventies and became the society's vice-president.

Bob served as a Labour MP for Keighley from February 1974-83 and represented Bradford South from 1987-94. A Eurosceptic, he was MEP for Sheffield from 1984-89.

However, tragedy struck on April 12, 1994, when the car Bob was driving to London overturned on the M1 near Watford and he was killed.

His wife Ann, whom he married in 1963, survived the crash and went on to become an MP in her own right, representing Keighley from 1997-2010. She is president of the society having also been a member from its early days.

In his tribute to Bob at his memorial service in St George's Hall, Bradford, on April 22, 1994, society chairman, Graham Mitchell, said: "The Worth Valley Railway has always been neutral territory, a classless society where a person's age, sex, race, income, religion… or politics have never signified very much. But integrity has always been significant. No-one could ignore, or fail to admire, Bob's total sincerity; always completely honest and straightforward, a man of boundless optimism and enthusiasm, he was a lifelong supporter of public transport.

"Five thousand society members have lost a great man; a true friend and a loyal champion. We owe him an enormous debt. I hope that the KWVR will be seen as one of his lasting memorials. For all that you have done for us, thank you Bob."

Ralph and Bob were no mere railway revival pioneers. They are giants in the story of UK transport heritage, and it is to them that this 50th anniversary publication is dedicated with immense gratitude.

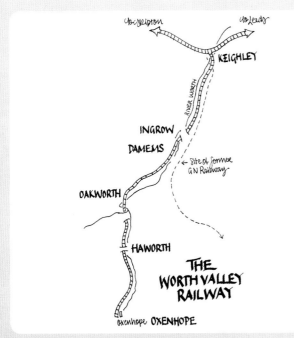

A system diagram of the Worth Valley branch. SARAH PALMER

Ingrow West is the first station after leaving Keighley. The original building had fallen into decay and following a hugely successful appeal to members, was replaced with one from Foulridge, which closed in 1959, on the Skipton to Colne line. The station now houses two award-winning museums, the Vintage Carriages Trust's Museum of Rail Travel and Ingrow Loco, home of the Bahamas Locomotive Society, plus the VCT Rail Story learning coach.

The next station, Damems, is a request stop and Damems is only long enough for one coach making it the smallest 'full-size' station in Britain. The current booking office and waiting room are new structures based on the Midland Railway original. A winner many times of the Best Restored Station competition, Oakworth was just a small country station with a goods shed and yard serving the nearby village until it soared to worldwide fame in the 1970 EMI big-screen version of The Railway Children.

Haworth has the largest station and goods yard on the railway, and has a large locomotive works and a shop. It is the base for the railway's engineering needs.

Oxenhope, the terminus, is also the home for operational coaches. It contains the exhibition shed, which is used for storing coaches that are less well-used and long-term out-of-use locomotives, and is open to the public. The vehicles inside are very regularly changed according to operational needs.

Chapter 1

An early 20th-century view of Haworth village. ROBIN JONES COLLECTION

Bronte Falls on Haworth Moor. Charlotte Bronte wrote: "There rises some low rock, All wet with surge's spray." ROBIN JONES COLLECTION

DREAM WEAVERS OF THE WORTH VALLEY ...FIRST TIME ROUND

Haworth and its wild untamed moors became world famous in the 19th century through the literary works of three sisters, who would never have guessed that history would be repeated more than a century later, when another author's novel would bring crowds flocking to the Worth Valley.

In 1820, Irish priest and author Rev Patrick Bronte accepted the post of curate of St Michael and All Angels' Church in Haworth in the Worth Valley and moved there with his young family.

Nearly three decades later, three of his daughters, Charlotte, Anne and Emily had produced some of the greatest masterpieces of English literature before their lives were cut short by illness at relatively early ages.

The wild and rugged moorland setting around the village in which they spent their adolescence provided a fertile ground for their imaginations.

Led by Emily Anne, the three conjured up a fantasy island called Gondal, which became the basis for a series of poems written at first for their own amusement, and later published with all references to the imaginary land removed. Weaving together strands of English Romanticism, the Gothic tradition, shadows of Shakespeare's The Tempest, but most of all, the substance and raw energy of the landscape of their own environment, Emily produced what many consider to be the finest piece of all 19th century prose in the novel Wuthering Heights. It was published in

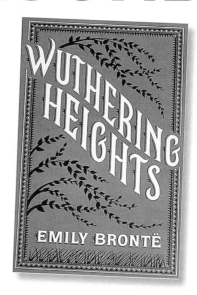

WUTHERING HEIGHTS

EMILY BRONTË

1847, a year before her untimely death from consumption at the age of 30 on December 21, 1848.

Emily never spelled out exactly which real buildings, if any, inspired her only novel. As the work snowballed in popularity over the decades that

followed its publication under the pseudonym, Ellis Bell, many pointed to the ruined farmhouse of Top Withens near the Brontes' home of Haworth Parsonage, although it does not match the description in the book.

Top Withens was first suggested as the model by Charlotte's friend Ellen Nussey, when she spoke to Edward Morison Wimperis, an artist commissioned to illustrate the Bronte sisters' novels in 1872.

The sisters' older brother Branwell had been appointed as assistant clerk for the Leeds & Bradford Extension Railway in 1840 – only to be sacked 18 months later when he was held responsible for a default in the books.

Emily did not live long enough to see the railway encroach upon her wild

Sir Laurence Olivier and Merle Oberon in the 1939 film Wuthering Heights.

Out on those wild and windy Haworth Moors, as depicted in an early 20th century postcard. ROBIN JONES COLLECTION

LEFT: Capitalising on the fame of its former residents in the early 20th century was Haworth post office. ROBIN JONES COLLECTION

and windy moors: the line from Leeds reached Keighley in 1847, six years before the last of the family, Charlotte, author of Jane Eyre, died during her first pregnancy along with her unborn child.

Branwell Bronte died at Haworth parsonage on September 24, 1848, most likely from tuberculosis aggravated by delirium tremens, alcoholism, as well as laudanum and opium addiction, apparently worsened by a failed relationship with a married woman, bringing the family's short railway connection to an end.

Critics were divided about Wuthering Heights when it was first published. However, both it and novels by Charlotte and Anne Bronte soared in popularity over the decades that followed their publication.

In the early 1860s, engineer John Landsborough, in response to clamour from Worth Valley mill owners, drew up a plan for a branch line in the Worth Valley.

He outlined the multiple benefits that a railway connection would bring to the valley… and also, almost as an afterthought mentioned the possibility of tourists being brought in by train to see for themselves the moorland landscapes in which the Bronte works had been set.

The Brontes have been big business for more than a century in Haworth; with gift shops, restaurants and even a caravan site named after them, such

A portrait made by Branwell Bronte about 1833: sources disagree as to whether this image is of Emily or Anne Bronte.

is the legacy of this talented family, not to mention Haworth Parsonage itself, which is now the Bronte Parsonage Museum.

Wuthering Heights has inspired adaptations, including film, radio and television dramatisations, a musical, a ballet, operas, and in 1978, a

hit by Kate Bush, which launched her career. The most famous adaptation of all was 1939's American movie Wuthering Heights, starring Laurence Olivier (Heathcliff) and Merle Oberon (Cathy Earnshaw) directed by William Wyler and produced by Samuel Goldwyn.

However, the drawing together of divergent ideas and influences and the blending of them into a new whole to create something magical, a unique and perfect fusion of fantasy and reality, far greater than the sum of its components, and with worldwide appeal, did not perish in these parts along with Haworth's great literary family.

The Worth Valley was to come alive once more a century after John Landsborough first made his appearance there.

It would involve no less than an entire community working together to save their local branch line, with more than a little help from a writer who lived around half a century after the Bronte sisters, and her classic children's novel that the Worth Valley 'borrowed' and immortalised with no less resounding impact.

In 1962, in 1968 and 1970, as we shall see in the chapters that follow, the fertile mills of the dream weavers of the Worth Valley were back in full production, and their steel wheels are turning to this day!

One of the infamous tame sheep of Haworth Moor stands in front of the ruined farmhouse known as Top Withens, which may have been the inspiration for Wuthering Heights. TJ BLACKWELL*

Grade I listed Haworth Parsonage, where the three Bronte sisters spent most of their short lives, is now the Bronte Parsonage Museum. It is maintained by the Bronte Society, a registered charity. The parsonage was used as a location in the 1970 EMI film The Railway Children, where it became the home of Dr Forrest. DEFACTO*

Chapter 2

STEAMING INTO
THE LAND OF
ROMANCE

Running into the heart of Bronte Country, the branch from Keighley to Oxenhope
was built not so that literary fans could visit the moors made famous by the
three sisters – but to facilitate the growth of industry in the Worth Valley.
Tourism came much later.

Midland 0-6-0T No. 1823 with early bogie stock passes what is now Damems loop in 1920.

Back in the mid-19th century, the Worth Valley was a hive of industry with its landmark woollen mills, and for a long time local mill owners had been calling on the valley to join the railway revolution.

As local wool was lacking in both quantity and quality, they needed to bring in more from outside, principally from Leicestershire but also from the Cotswolds.

A line was needed to serve the valley, but local mill owners lacked the knowledge as to how to go about it. They need a man who could – and found it in draper's son John McLandsborough.

Born in Otley in 1820 he went on to train as a civil engineer. He became a member of the Institute of Civil Engineers, a fellow of the Royal Geographical Society and a fellow of the Royal Astronomical Society.

The greater part of McLandsborough's professional practice was taken up with drains and sewerage engineering but he had experience of railway building with the Otley & Ilkley Joint Railway. While he lived in Otley, his business moved to Bradford in 1856, and he became frustrated at the lack of a rail link between the towns.

He lobbied the Midland Railway to build a line from Bradford to Otley and Ilkley.

This was a 6½-mile line linking the three towns, built to bring wealthy Ilkley residents to their place of work in Bradford, to give access from Bradford to Otley for the agricultural traffic, but also, and very importantly, to keep the North Eastern Railway out of Bradford and the Aire and Wharfe valleys, which gave an easy direct route to the west coast, much easier and cheaper to work than the arduous trans-Pennine Stainmore route.

The Ilkley to Otley line was owned and managed by the Midland and North Eastern railways, but the section forming the middle of that route (Menston/Burley-in-Wharfedale) to Bradford was entirely Midland. The North Eastern had its own route into Leeds from Otley and used running powers into Bradford for a limited Harrogate to Bradford service. This also gave the Midland access to Harrogate from London. The route opened to passenger traffic on August 1, 1865 and freight several months later.

In 1861, McLandsborough visited Haworth and described himself as "a pilgrim at the shrine of Charlotte Bronte" and was surprised at the locality's lack of a rail link.

McLandsborough and his friend, the Midland's Sir Matthew William Thompson, who was also a Bradford brewer and banker, drew up a 'package deal'. They would promote, build and work the line, in return for the interest paid on its building.

Keighley station had been opened in March 1847 by the Leeds & Bradford Extension Railway, and was rebuilt on its present site in 1883.

The Leeds & Bradford (Shipley-Colne Extension) Railway Act of June 30, 1845, was strongly opposed by commercial interests in the Worth Valley, because it gave Keighley an advantage over them. It was only when the Leeds & Bradford agreed to include a branch to Haworth (Springhead, not Bridgehouse as was eventually built) did they agree to withdraw opposition and support the project.

In July 1846, Leeds & Bradford Railway was leased to the Midland Railway, which it later absorbed on July 24, 1851.

The first section of the line ran from Shipley, at a triangular junction with the Leeds & Bradford Railway, to Keighley. The section opened on March 16, 1847 and included a 151-yd tunnel at Bingley.

A second section from Keighley to Skipton opened on September 7, 1847, at first single track, it had doubled by the end of the year. The final section between Skipton and Colne opened on October 2, 1848.

At Colne, it made an end-on junction with the East Lancashire Railway's Blackburn, Burnley, Accrington & Colne Extension Railway, after that line opened on February 1, 1849. By April 2 that year, the line had become part of a through route between Leeds and Liverpool but most passenger trains were local services between Skipton and Colne. Eventually, Keighley found itself on the Midland's main line route from London to Glasgow.

McLandsborough designed a route as far as Oakworth (named the Keighley & Vale of Worth Railway), with the route south of there to be determined.

Spinning machines at Bradford Industrial Museum, Bradford. LINDA SPASHETT*

THE FIRST CHAIRMAN

Holden was born into a poor family in Hurlet, a village between Glasgow and Paisley. Nonetheless his father did his best to buy him an education. He was apprenticed for a short period as a draw boy for two hand weavers, but attended grammar schools and became a pupil teacher. He then tried to become a Wesleyan minister, before teaching at schools in Slaithwaite and Leeds.

In 1830 he moved to become a bookkeeper at Townsend Brothers' worsted factory in Cullingworth near Bingley. Transferring to the technical side and becoming a manager, he sought to improve the process of combing wool.

Holden left Townsends in 1846 to set up a factory making Paisley shawls at Pit Lane in Bradford. When the business failed two years later he formed a partnership with Samuel Lister.

Holden and Lister worked together to develop the square motion wool-combing machine, which was patented by Lister in 1848, although Holden had drafted the patent. The origins of the machine became the subject of a lifelong dispute between the two men.

Trading as Lister & Holden, in 1848 Isaac Holden set up a factory at St Denis near Paris, where over the next few years he perfected the square-motion machine. He then set up two more factories in France and after buying out Lister and renaming his firm Isaac Holden et Fils, he and his sons, Angus and Edward, set up an experimental factory at Penny Oaks in Bradford. In 1864 they opened the massive Alston Works at Bradford.

Holden's factories in England and France had, by the 1870s, become the largest wool combers in the world. He celebrated his success by building a large Italianate mansion at Oakworth near Keighley. Holden, a devout Wesleyan, also pledged £5000 to build 50 chapels in London.

In 1865, Holden was elected to Parliament as Liberal member for Knaresborough and in 1885 became MP for the Borough of Keighley; a seat he held for a decade.

In the late 1870s he personally bought all the debt owed by the KWVR, and then sold it on to the Midland Railway at a considerable profit. He was also the major shareholder so for several years, and in effect owned the KWVR.

His fellow directors owned most of the balance of the shares and much of the debt, and were very relieved to be rid of both.

The Midland was desperate to avoid the branch falling to the Great Northern, which was trying to buy it for its route into Keighley from the valley for 150% of the face value of the capital plus a huge payment, equal to a 5% return on the capital since it was first created, but which had never been paid.

When Holden sold out to the Midland he made a very considerable profit, however, his fellow directors and the minority holders did not lose out, as they

Isaac Holden, as painted by Samuel Sidley.
BRADFORD MUSEUMS GALLERIES & HERITAGE

were paid face value by him.

During his political life he campaigned for electoral reform, church disestablishment and Irish Home Rule. In 1893, at the age of 86, he was created a Baronet, of Oakworth House in the County of York.

Holden died in August 1897, aged 90. Oakworth House burned down in 1907 and in 1927 its grounds were given by the family to the people of Oakworth as a public park, named Holden Park.

We are jumping a decade or two ahead here though, because most importantly to us, Holden became a pivotal figure in the early life of the branch.

THE MAKING OF OXENHOPE

Oxenhope as a village did not exist until the railway came. In legal terms it was a 'hamlet' and a 'parish' (from 1848). The name is derived from Old Oxenhope Hall, where there was also a small mill of the same name, on the edge of the moor, far above the valley where the railway was eventually built.

The decision to build the branch to Haworth (Bridgehouse) came as a result of Richard S Butterfield putting up the money to do so, in opposition to the Cravens and Merrels who wanted the line to go to Haworth (Springhead). Only when that route was agreed was McLandsborough asked to survey a route to what then was known as Lowertown, a part of the hamlet and parish of Oxenhope where the Feather family had a mill at the side of the proposed terminus.

They put up £5000 and William Oates Greenwood, who owned Old Oxenhope Hall and mill, a further £5000. However, they fell out over the location of the terminus, as planned it would be alongside Feather's Lowertown Mill, but Greenwood's was about a mile away

high on the moor, putting Feather at an advantage. Therefore, the terminus was put at an equally inconvenient point for both of them ("corner of Mill Lane & Weasel Lane") and as the nearest building was Old Oxenhope Hall, it was called Oxenhope. Had it gone to Feather's, it was to have been called 'Lowertown'. Indeed for a good while, the line's name was the 'Keighley & Lower Town Railway'.

It was only when all this had been agreed, in October 1862, that the present name, Keighley & Worth Valley Railway was agreed. No-one knows why, as the Worth Valley goes off to Springhead at Oakworth so half the line is not in the Worth Valley; the river being the Bridgehouse Beck. The Midland was foreseen to have no objection: after all, it had a monopoly on goods taken to and from the Worth Valley because they all had to be unloaded at Keighley, and a branch line from there would not harm the existing main line trade in any way – in fact, it was quite the opposite.

McLandsborough's vision for the Worth Valley was by no means original. The Railway Times of October 18, 1845,

carried an advertisement asking for the subscription of £350,000 of capital for the Manchester, Hebden Bridge & Keighley Junction Railway, which was to run through Haworth with a branch to Oakworth. Like many schemes proposed during the height of Railway Mania, this line was never built.

However, the fact that a large number of people were ready to promote the scheme indicated demand and enthusiasm for a rail connection.

Nothing concrete happened until October 1861, when a delegation of businessmen from the Worth Valley met with Midland officials, who told them that the railway would support a branch from Keighley to Oxenhope, and would also operate it in return for half the receipts.

That autumn, the Keighley & Worth Valley Railway Company was launched with 22 provisional directors, most of them local mill owners or their family members. Investors were told that the line would cost £36,000 (around £3 million by today's standards) to build.

A total of 3134 shares worth £10 each were issued, and directors, bankers, solicitors and engineers were elected. McLandsborough was appointed acting engineer; while John Sydney Crossley of the Midland Railway was appointed consultant engineer.

On June 30, 1862, the Keighley & Worth Valley Railway Act was passed in the House of Commons, and subsequently 200 individuals subscribed to provide the necessary finance to build it. However, in the event most did not pay up and the line had to be built with much more borrowed, rather than share capital, than was envisaged.

The following November, John Metcalfe of Bradford, a very close friend of McLandsborough and someone also known to Sir Matthew, was awarded the contract to build the branch. Notices were then served for the demolition of property and fields taken.

Shrove Tuesday, February 9, 1864, saw the first sod cut by Isaac Holden, the chairman of the Keighley and Worth Valley Railway Company. He stepped in as necessary to offer guidance and also to safeguard his own financial interests.

To the left can be seen the damage to the Wesley Place Methodist church in 1865.

A WESLEYAN CHAPEL UNDERMINED

Less than a year before he cut the first sod, Holden had presided over the ceremony when the foundation stone was laid for the new Wesley Place Methodist chapel at Ingrow, which was to stand above the railway, and was to pass under nearby Halifax Road through a cut-and-cover tunnel. Holden performed this role as chairman of the chapel trustees.

Work on the tunnel began, but only a few yards in, the workmen encountered unstable wet sandy soil.

The engineering solution was to drive piles to hold the walls of the cutting element of the 'tunnel', officially known as 'Ingrow Covered Way' creating, in effect, a very long bridge, on top of which five roads converge. There is only about two feet of cover over the tunnel crown, which is almost entirely brick.

However, the loss of a large quantity of quicksand, which held water that had

percolated from the moors, combined with vibrations from the piling operation to cause structural damage to the chapel overhead.

Lawyers acting on behalf of the chapel trustees handled a claim for compensation from the railway, and it was decided to dismantle the building and re-erect it. After nearly £3500 compensation was awarded, the new chapel opened in November 1867. It caused the railway company to go into what amounted to receivership.

The earliest-known image of Haworth station. KEIGHLEY DIGITAL ARCHIVE

Did a member of the Midland Railway's 29-strong 156 Class of 2-4-0 tender engines, designed by Matthew Kirtley and built at Derby Works between 1866-74, haul the test train over the newly completed Worth Valley line? Nobody knows for certain, but the type operated out of Leeds and Bradford to Ilkley at the time of the contractor's trial run to Oxenhope for which he borrowed a locomotive from the Ilkley line. This class was the one that operated what are now the electrified services from Leeds and Bradford to Ilkley and Skipton in the last years of the 19th century. In September 1930, the LMS recognised the significance of the class and No. 156 was earmarked for preservation. But LMS Chief Mechanical Engineer William Stanier, who made it clear he had no time for history and conservation, ordered it to be scrapped two years later. No. 156 was based at Bradford at the time the Worth Valley line was opened, and could well have headed the test train. The sole-survivor is No. 158A, which is in static display at the Midland Railway-Butterley. ROBIN JONES

TEST RUN AND THUNDERSTORM

McLandsborough organised a test run along the branch once it was completed, using a locomotive borrowed from the Ilkley line on November 1, 1866. It was almost certainly Midland No. 101, 118,119 or 162, a 2-4-0 of the 75 or 'large 70' class.

A wagon was fitted out with planks to provide seats for McLandsborough, the Keighley stationmaster and his staff.

The outward journey from Keighley to Oxenhope took two hours, because frequent stops had to be made to remove debris from the line. However, the return trip took just 13 minutes.

The next step was to install lineside fences.

However, disaster struck when violent thunderstorms hit the locality on November 14. The storm was so severe that Apperley Viaduct between Leeds and Shipley collapsed. The branch, by comparison 'got off lightly', with just 40 yds of embankment washed away with

its track left suspended in mid-air. Compounded by minor damage elsewhere, the storm preceded a five-month delay in opening the line. That was the reason given out in public, but it was not the real one, as not a great deal of damage had, in fact, been done. The real reason was that the Midland had not told its Chief Mechanical Engineer, Matthew Kirtley, that the line was ready for opening, or more correctly, the KWVR had not told the MR, so Kirtley was unaware.

Kirtley learned this only in October 1866, but had no suitable locomotives. He hurriedly converted five locomotives into well tanks, the first being ready in March 1867, hence the opening in April that year.

As it was, the storm damage, combined with unforeseen costs, helped triple the cost of building the line. The prospectus had asked for £36,000 in subscriptions, but the total cost ended up at £111,422 17s 10d.

OPENING DAY

The line opened on a dull wet Saturday on April 13, 1867. The first train comprised a tank engine, one of Nos. 213, 214 or 215, seven coaches and a guard's van. Another two locomotives were converted later that year, bringing the line's fleet up to the stipulated five.

The opening train slipped to a halt on the 1-in-58 gradient south of Keighley. It climbed the gradient at the second attempt, but stopped again between Oakworth and Haworth.

The VIP guests were treated to a celebratory dinner in the Mechanics Institute in Haworth.

At the opening-day dinner, the speeches made it quite clear that the line's purpose was to carry goods, with passengers as a side line.

Speaker after speaker spoke of the pending coverage of the valley with mills. There were very few before 1867 and those already there were small affairs, employing fewer than 50 people and usually reliant on water power.

After 1875, and the coming of the railway, there was a mill-building boom

RIGHT: A later view of Haworth station, showing how much development had taken place around it. KEIGHLEY DIGITAL ARCHIVE

MIDLAND RAILWAY

KEIGHLEY & WORTH VALLEY BRANCH.

TIME-TABLE OF TRAINS

From JUNE 1st, 1869,

AND UNTIL FURTHER NOTICE,

The Midland Company's Trains run between KEIGHLEY and OXENHOPE in connection with their Main Line Trains, as under:

This Table shews the times at which the Trains may be expected to arrive at and depart from the several Stations, but their arrival or departure at the times stated is not guaranteed, nor does the Company hold itself responsible for delay or any consequence arising therefrom.

Miles from Keighley.	FARES FROM KEIGHLEY. Single Journey. 1st Class	2nd Class	3rd Class	GOV	Return. 1st Class	2nd Class	The classes of Trains shown on this Table refer to Stations between Keighley and Oxenhope only.	WEEK-DAYS. 1w	2w	3w	4w	5w	6w	7w	8	SUNDAYS. 1w	2w	3w	4w
								a.m.	a.m.	a.m.	a.m.	p.m.	a.m.	Runs on Saturdays only.		a.m.	a.m.	p.m.	p.m.
..	..	..	..	..	..	..	LONDON (St. Pcrs.) dep.	..	..	6 15	9 0	10 0	11 45		..	..	..	..	..
..	..	..	..	..	..	..	LEEDS "	7 5	8 55	1 15	2 30	4 5	5 50		..	6 0	8 0	1 0	5 30
..	..	..	..	..	..	..	BRADFORD "	7 35	9 30	1 45	3 0	4 50	5 55		..	6 20	8 40	1 20	6 30
..	..	..	..	..	..	..	Shipley "	7 45	9 41	1 56	3 12	5 1	6 6		..	6 37	8 50	1 35	6 45
..	..	..	..	..	..	..	Bingley "	7 55	9 53	2 8	3 21	5 11	6 28		..	6 45	9 0	1 45	6 55
..	..	..	..	..	..	..	KEIGHLEY arr.	8 6	10 3	2 18	3 30	5 20	6 36		..	6 55	9 11	1 56	7 6
..	..	..	..	..	..	..	Lancaster dep.	..	8 0	11 5	..	2 20	..		..	..	8 20	..	..
..	..	..	..	..	..	..	Colne "	6 15	8 40	1 0	..	3 50	..		..	..	9 15	..	4 15
..	..	..	..	..	..	..	SKIPTON "	8 0	9 35	1 40	..	4 27	..		..	..	10 5	1 0	6 40
..	..	..	..	..	..	..	Kildwick "	8 13	9 48	1 53	..	4 4[illegible]	..		..	..	10 18	1 13	6 57
..	..	..	..	..	..	..	KEIGHLEY arr.	8 29	10 3	2 8	..	4 55	..		..	..	10 32	1 27	7 13
								1 2 Gov.	1 2 3 Class.	1 2 3 Class.	1 2 3 Class.	1 2 3 Class.	1 2 3 Class.	1 2 3 Class.	..	1 2 Gov.	1 2 3 Class.	1 2 3 Class.	1 2 3 Class.
								a.m.	a.m.	p.m.	p.m.	p.m.	p.m.	p.m.		a.m.	a.m.	p.m.	p.m.
..	..	..	..	..	..	..	KEIGHLEY dep.	8 40	10 15	2 30	3 40	5 30	6 40	8 30	..	7 50	10 40	2 5	7 20
1¼	0/3	0/2	0/1½	0/1	0/6	0/4	Ingrow	8 45	10 20	2 35	3 45	5 35	6 45	8 35	..	7 55	10 45	2 10	7 25
2	0/5	0/3	0/2	0/1½	0/9	0/6	Damems	8 48	..	2 38	..	..	6 48	..	..	..	..	..	..
2¾	0/6	0/4½	0/3½	0/2½	0/10	0/8	Oakworth	8 50	10 25	2 40	3 50	5 40	6 50	8 40	..	8 0	10 50	2 15	7 30
3¾	0/8	0/6	0/4½	0/3¼	1/2	0/10	Haworth	8 54	10 29	2 44	3 54	5 44	6 54	8 44	..	8 4	10 54	2 19	7 34
4¾	0/11	0/8	0/6	0/4½	1/7	1/2	OXENHOPE arr.	9 0	10 35	2 50	4 0	5 50	7 0	8 50	..	8 10	11 0	2 25	7 40

Miles from Oxenhope.	FARES FROM OXENHOPE. Single Journey. 1st Class	2nd Class	3rd Class.	GOV	Return. 1st Class	2nd Class	The classes of Trains shown on this Table refer to Stations between Oxenhope and Keighley only.	WEEK-DAYS. 1w	2w	3w	4w	5w	6w	7w	8w	SUNDAYS. 1w	2w	3w	4w
								1 2 Gov.	1 2 3 Class.	1 2 3 Class.	1 2 3 Class.	1 2 3 Class.	1 2 3 Class.	1 2 3 Class.	1 2 3 Class.	1 2 Gov.	1 2 3 Class.	1 2 3 Class.	1 2 3 Class.
								a.m.	a.m.	a.m.	p.m.	p.m.	p.m.	p.m.	p.m.	a.m.	p.m.	p.m.	p.m.
..	..	..	..	..	..	..	OXENHOPE dep.	8 0	9 30	11 10	1 5	3 0	4 25	6 0	7 10	8 35	1 0	6 35	8 5
1¼	0/3	0/2	0/1½	0/1	0/6	0/4	Haworth	8 4	9 34	11 14	1 9	3 4	4 29	6 4	7 14	8 39	1 4	6 39	8 9
2	0/5	0/3½	0/2½	0/2	0/9	0/6	Oakworth	8 8	9 38	11 18	1 13	3 8	4 33	6 8	7 18	8 43	1 8	6 43	8 13
3	0/7	0/5	0/3½	0/2½	1/0	0/9	Damems	8 12	..	11 22	..	..	..	6 12	..	..	..	..	..
3½	0/8	0/6	0/4½	0/3½	1/2	0/10	Ingrow	8 15	9 43	11 25	1 18	3 13	4 38	6 15	7 23	8 48	1 13	6 48	8 18
4¾	0/11	0/8	0/6	0/4½	1/7	1/2	KEIGHLEY arr	8 20	9 50	11 30	1 25	3 20	4 45	6 20	7 30	8 55	1 20	6 55	8 25
..	..	..	..	..	..	..	KEIGHLEY dep.	..	10 3	..	1 32	4 22	..	6 28	..	9 11	1 56	7 6	..
..	1/8	1/3	..	0/8½	2/10	2/1	Kildwick arr	..	10 16	..	2 31	4 40	..	6 41	..	[illegible]	[illegible]	[illegible]	..
..	2/7	1/11	..	1/1	4/6	3/3	SKIPTON ..	..	10 30	..	1 50	4 41	..	6 55	..	9 40	2 25	7 35	..
..	4/7	3/4	..	2/0½	7/9	5/9	Colne "	..	11 5	..	3 40	5 35	..	[illegible]	..	10 30	..	..	..
..	..	..	..	..	..	..	Lancaster "	..	12 50	..	[illegible]	6 11	..	9 0	..	..	..	..	..
..	..	..	..	..	..	..	KEIGHLEY dep	8 29	10 3	11 41	1 35	3 45	4 55	..	7 36	10 32	1 27	7 13	8 37
..	1/7	1/4	..	0/7½	[illegible]	2/0	Bingley arr	[illegible]	[illegible]	11 50	[illegible]	[illegible]	[illegible]	..	[illegible]	[illegible]	[illegible]	[illegible]	[illegible]
..	2/1	1/6	..	0/10½	3/6	2/6	Shipley ..	[illegible]	10 25	12 0	[illegible]	4 0	5 11	..	[illegible]	[illegible]	[illegible]	7 35	9 0
..	2/5	1/8	..	1/1½	[illegible]	2/10	BRADFORD ..	9 0	10 35	12 10	2 40	4 30	5 25	..	8 20	11 5	2 0	7 50	9 10
..	2/7	[illegible]	..	1/9	6/0	4/6	LEEDS "	9 33	11 3	12 40	2 20	4 35	6 40	..	8 35	11 30	2 30	8 20	9 30
..	35/6	26/3	..	16/7½	59/3	43/9	LONDON (St. Pncrs.) ..	4 0	6 40	6 40	8 35	10 45	..	..	4 20	..	10 0	..	4 20

Derby, 1869. JAMES ALLPORT, General-Manager.

LEFT: A branch poster of 1869. KEIGHLEY DIGITAL ARCHIVE

when the huge 'landmark woollen mills' were built.

Regular passenger services began on Monday, April 15, 1867, but freight had to wait until July 1.

The first timetable had six trains on weekdays but only two on Sundays. Journey times took a modest 16-17 minutes.

The contractor was responsible for maintaining the line for a year, after which it became the owning company's responsibility.

Unlike several other 'rural' short lines opened around the same time, the railway appeared to do well. One big factor, of course, was the worsted trade from local mills. Secondly, the population of the valley was increasing. Thirdly, the valley now had the stirrings of the beginning of a small tourist trade, fuelled by the growing popularity of the Bronte sisters; however, the local vicar actively discouraged tourism.

At first, tourism by train to the valley was limited to those who could afford to travel and have time off work, hence the high proportion of first-class accommodation on the trains. Indeed, the first excursion to Haworth was for the last services in the old church in 1879, 12 years after the branch opened.

When the line opened, the last of the Bronte sisters had only recently died, but as their works increased in popularity, so the visitors came. Eventually, thousands of visitors arrived at Haworth by train. The Bronte Society ran a special train to Haworth on May 18, 1895.

Haworth station, looking towards Oxenhope with the platform end level crossing removed, a new footbridge and original turnout into the goods yard moved south. The small goods shed was by then replaced by the current larger structure. KEIGHLEY DIGITAL ARCHIVE

THE CRASH OF 1875

At 6.13am on September 27, 1875 an empty stock train left Keighley behind a tank engine, moving the coaches to Oxenhope for the first Up service. It comprised six goods wagons, five coal wagons, five empty carriages and two brake vans.

Next to Oakworth goods yard, the train stopped and Keighley porter, John Wigglesworth, who was on board, was told by the guard, Abraham Welch, to screw down the handbrake in the rear van while he applied the other brake – but ignoring the rule that stated that a sprag – a piece of wood – had to be placed between the spokes of wheels when a train was left on the main line.

Welch rode on a wagon after it was uncoupled and shunted it into the goods yard by the train engine. To his horror, he then saw his train move of its own accord.

In scenes that might have well come straight from a Keystone Cops silent movie, he tried to shut the stable door after the horse had bolted by throwing a sprag into one of the wheels. It was no use, and so he climbed aboard the engine, which then set off in pursuit of its train, while he fervently sounded its whistle.

Under normal circumstances, the train should have derailed at Ingrow, but the porter in charge, 21-year-old Jermiah Laycock, misinterpreted the whistling as a signal that a normal train was to pass through, and so set the catch points accordingly.

At Keighley, the runaway train collided with a stationary Bradford to Colne train. The Keighley signalman had seen what was coming, and station staff managed to persuade many of the passengers on the main line service to alight.

A total of 14 passengers on the main line train escaped with minor injuries, but Wigglesworth was the most fortunate of them all. Knocked unconscious by the impact, he woke to find his brake van beneath the back coach of the main line train.

Despite ignoring basic safety rules, Welch kept his job. However, Laycock left the Midland's employment a few weeks later, reportedly as a result of the shock. Some of his descendants work on the heritage line today.

Damems – the smallest station on the line then, and not dissimilar to how it is now. KEIGHLEY DIGITAL ARCHIVE

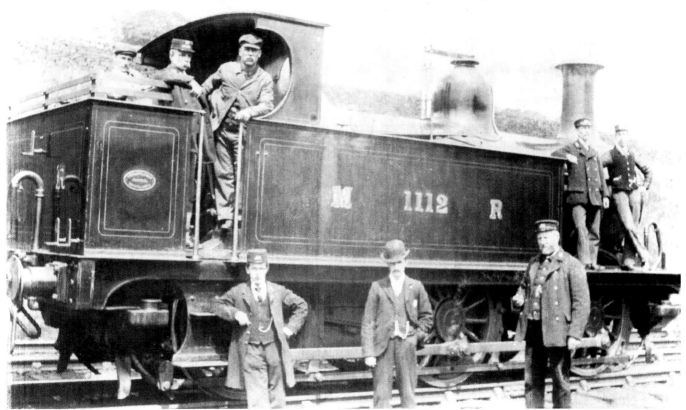
A Midland Railway Class 1377 0-6-0T stands at Oxenhope in the 1890s.

MIDLAND TAKEOVER

On July 1, 1881, the Midland Railway, which had operated the branch from the start, gained complete control by means of a lease, taken out purely to prevent the Great Northern taking over the KWVR as part of its route from Bradford to Keighley, then being built.

The Keighley & Worth Valley Company remained in existence for a further five years until it was dissolved under the Midland Railway Act 1866.

The takeover was necessitated by the need for the Midland Railway to spend money on the branch, in order to accommodate the Great Northern Railway at Keighley. The GNR was completing its line from Halifax and Bradford via Queensbury and needed a junction with the KWVR. If the Midland had not taken over the KWVR at that stage, it may have been that the GNR would have done so, and diverted its trains to an independent Keighley station.

To avoid any prospect of that happening, the Midland provided a new station at Keighley and doubled the first three quarters of a mile of the branch south from Keighley to what became Keighley GN Junction. The new station was built on the opposite side of Bradford Road and opened on May 6, 1883. The Worth Valley line ran the first services into the new station. The 12.30pm from Oxenhope arrived at about 12.55pm. Later the same year the GNR line was extended into Keighley.

The new station had two platforms to serve the main line and two others curving off at an angle for Worth Valley and GNR trains. The old station was flattened to make room for an expanded goods yard. It is now a supermarket car park.

The Haworth station gardens in Midland times. KEIGHLEY DIGITAL ARCHIVE

A Midland-era view of Oxenhope station. KEIGHLEY DIGITAL ARCHIVE

Private-owner wagons jostle with Midland Railway counterparts in Oxenhope yard. The branch was built primarily for freight. KEIGHLEY DIGITAL ARCHIVE

A TUNNEL FOR MYTHOLMES

As built, the line south of Oakworth crossed the Vale Mill Dam on a timber trestle viaduct, a cheaper option than building a stone structure.

It was known from the outset that such viaducts would have only a limited life, and speed restrictions were imposed across it. Indeed, many people were scared to travel over it. The Midland Railway decided that rather than replacing the viaduct, a deviation would be built around it.

So the company ordered the construction of a tunnel, five bridges as well as a considerable embankment at a

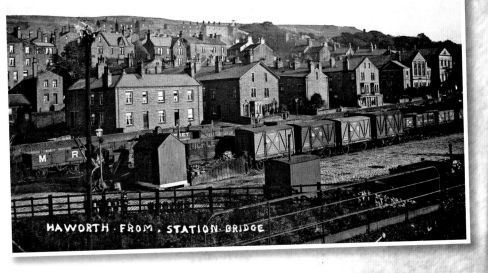

HAWORTH FROM STATION BRIDGE

LEFT: Haworth yard as seen from the footbridge in Midland Railway days.
KEIGHLEY DIGITAL ARCHIVE

cost of £25,000. On Sunday, November 6, 1892, the 7.25am service from Oxenhope passed over the old viaduct.

The track was then reconnected at either end to the new line, which was ready to take the 10.50am from Keighley. Extra coaches were added to that train, because of the large number of people who wanted to be first through the tunnel. The viaduct was retained as standby.

The site of the new Keighley station as seen in the 1870s.

LOCOMOTIVES AND TRAIN WORKING

The practice for working the branch was to start the first train of the day at Oxenhope, not Keighley. At first, the empty coaching stock was attached to a northbound goods train.

The locomotives used were well tanks, of which the Midland had about 20. They were Nos. 213 to 217, starting a trend for the MR and later BR, of providing five locomotives especially for the branch as they were built. It is suspected that these did not have adequate water capacity for peace of mind, so they were replaced in 1875 by five Samuel Johnson 1102 class 0-6-0Ts; Nos. 1134, 1135, 1136, 1137 and 1138. Called the "South Wales tanks" they were not vacuum fitted so when the branch trains received vacuum brakes, these locomotives were replaced by new vacuum-brake-fitted machines.

They were replaced by five Class 1377 0-6-0Ts in 1883, Nos. 218, 219, 1397, 1398 and 1399.

Midland Railway locomotives were originally liveried dark green throughout including the underframes. Around 1876 the colour was changed to a much lighter green and about six years later, a brick-red colour was introduced.

Demand for services slowly but surely intensified, and by 1880, the number of trains had risen to eight on weekdays and five on Sundays. Many 'early bird' passengers were workmen who, after 1883, were entitled by law to travel at lower fares provided their destination was reached by 8am.

Some freight workings were made at night because of the absence of passing loops. However, at Haworth in 1900 a double-ended siding was installed to allow Oxenhope to be shunted without closing the whole branch to traffic. That year, signalling on the line was greatly improved.

Like everywhere else, the busiest period on the branch covered the first two decades of the 20th century. By then, services had doubled to 16 departures from Keighley on Mondays to Saturdays with two extra trains on Saturday, and seven on Sundays.

In 1921, the branch ran a maximum of 21 trains per day.

Oxenhope station staff pose for the camera, date unknown. KEIGHLEY DIGITAL ARCHIVE

An early postcard view of Oakworth station with an empty gasometer in the foreground.
KEIGHLEY DIGITAL ARCHIVE

Photographs of trains working on the Worth Valley branch in its early years are extremely rare. This view of a typical Midland 1860s/1870s branch train headed by a Kirtley well tank and comprising Kirtley coaches appears to have been taken on the similar Nailsworth branch in Gloucestershire around 1877.
MIDLAND RAILWAY SOCIETY

After 1924, there were four signalboxes on the line: Keighley West, GN Junction, Oakworth and Haworth. Before that, there had been five; there being two at GN Junction. All were open seven days a week.

In July 1932, a 'motor train' push-and-pull service was introduced using Midland 0-4-4T, there then followed in a slight drop in the number of services, owing to a decline in traffic.

Haworth station had two men and two women clerks in the booking office, and by then a pair of ticket collectors were hard pressed to attend to the increasing number of passengers drawn to the village by the romance of the Brontes.

George Breadmore and his horse and cart were kept busy all day delivering the parcels arriving by train, and two clerks, a foreman, a checker, four

porters and a weighbridge man were part of a freight team that amounted to around two dozen people.

Each month, up to 5000 tons of coal arrived by train. Industrial coal from Haworth yard was carted to Bridgehouse Mill, Hattersley's Mills, Merrall's Mills and Haworth Gasworks. In return, Merrall's despatched six vanloads of cloth by rail to Bradford every week.

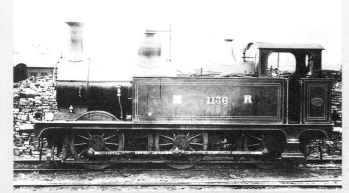

Class 1102 0-6-0T No. 1136, a 'South Wales tank', which ran on the Worth Valley line, and was painted in Midland red livery. MIDLAND RAILWAY SOCIETY

LEFT: The first Railway Children on the branch? What may have been an excursion train passes Donkey Bridge between Oxenhope and Haworth. KEIGHLEY DIGITAL ARCHIVE

Was this the locomotive that hauled the first train to Haworth? This well tank was converted from a tender locomotive in March 1867 as No. 215, a month before the line opened. The date of the conversion has led some historians to conjecture that it hauled the first passenger train. It is seen here as No. 2038A, having become No. 2038 in March 1873, two years before it left the KWVR in 1875. It is pictured here after 1892 with a Johnson design of Class B boiler, chimney, dome and safety valve trumpet. It was withdrawn as a well tank in 1906. It is quite possible (indeed likely given the conversion date, which is one month before the KWVR opened) that this is THE locomotive that hauled the first train to Haworth, but we can never be certain. MIDLAND RAILWAY SOCIETY

Chapter 3

CLOSED BEFORE THE
BEECHING
AXE FELL

While railways revolutionised society everywhere in the 19th century, it was road transport that acquired the upper hand in the 20th. The result was the closure of many branch lines, cross-country and secondary routes, as cars, buses and lorries replaced trains. The Worth Valley branch to Oxenhope was no exception, going to the wall a year before Dr Beeching swung his infamous axe.

Despite a widespread misconception among the general public, Dr Richard Beeching did not invent rail closures, despite his name becoming synonymous with them.

Indeed, rail closures began more than a century before he came on the transport scene. In 1851, the Newmarket & Chesterford Railway closed its Great Chesterford to Six Mile Bottom section after opening a more viable length linking Six Mile Bottom straight to Cambridge.

The First World War saw a comparatively small number of rural railways closed, with their tracks lifted for use on the Western Front military lines, never to reopen again. These included the Bideford, Westward Ho! & Appledore Railway, and the GWR line from Rowington to Henley-in-Arden, which had been superseded by the North Warwickshire Line between Tyseley, Henley-in-Arden and Stratford-upon-Avon. However, these were very much small fry in the overall scheme of railways.

The 1930s, however, saw a swathe of closures of many 'rural fringe' lines, the like of which had been empowered by the 1896 Light Railways Act. Some, including the GWR-operated Welshpool & Llanfair and Corris railways, lost their passenger services but remained open for freight, while others, such as the Lynton & Barnstaple, by then part of the Southern Railway, the Welsh Highland Railway and the Leek & Manifold Valley Railways, closed outright.

Regarding standard gauge, the Charnwood Forest Railway in Leicestershire ceased running passenger trains in 1931, and Birmingham's Harborne branch closed to passengers in 1934 in the face of direct competition from trams and motor buses.

The Weston, Clevedon & Portishead Railway, the only direct route of any description between those three Somerset coastal towns, ran its last public train in 1940.

None of these can be regarded as anything like mainstays of the railway network; indeed, regardless of their historical or romantic appeal, it is debatable whether some of them should have been built at all, and had road vehicles provided a creditable alternative at the time, it is all but certain that they would not have been.

Ivatt 2-6-2T No. 41273 heads a local branch train at Keighley in 1959. Built at Crewe in September 1969, this ideal branch line locomotive was based at Royston, Skipton and Farnley Junction sheds, and was with withdrawn in December 1963, prior to scrapping the following g March, after just 13 years' service. Such was the fate of so many perfectly-serviceable steam locomotives made redundant by branch line closures and dieselisation. COLOUR-RAIL

Ivatt 2-6-2T No. 41327 pulls into Oxenhope in the snow in the 1950s. VIC DRAKE

WHY THE WORTH VALLEY BRANCH WENT INTO DECLINE

Keighley Corporation introduced its first omnibus road services to Oakworth, Haworth and Oxenhope just before the First World War. In this case, it was their appearance that marked the start of the railway's decline.

Oakworth and Oxenhope were incredibly well served by trolleybuses, albeit not all services were successful. Then buses came along. They offered the advantage of far greater flexibility and versatility than the often more expensive rail alternative.

There was always a problem at Haworth in getting buses up the main street and the hills. Most services until the 1970s terminated by the railway station so Haworth was always reasonably busy with commuting traffic, mainly comprising engineers wanting to get to the factories around Keighley station.

However, all other traffic went to the buses as these went to the middle of Keighley and were much more convenient, unless you needed a connecting train.

It was the strange topography of the valley as much as anything else, with the villages on top of hills and the railway in the bottom that more or less killed off the branch's passenger traffic.

Although the line boasted around 150,000 commuters a year, BR was keen to be rid of it as it was making a loss as well as being an operational

A Midland Railway Johnson 0-4-4T, which was built in 1892, at Oxenhope in the Fifties. B AKINSON

inconvenience. An agreement with the bus operator was the main reason for its closure. In short, BR said would close the line if the bus company would guarantee services.

Both sides kept their bargain, and to this day, the Worth Valley is one of the best-served areas for public transport anywhere in the UK.

As we have seen, the primary reason for building the branch had been the expansion of the milling industry.

However, the years after the Second World War saw individual electric motors for looms, which destroyed the need for stationary steam engines in the mills, and with it destroyed the market for coal, which had been brought in by rail.

After the First World War, there was a fresh spirit of entrepreneurship among the soldiers returning from the Western Front. Large quantities of road vehicles were sold off as military surplus, and many were eagerly bought up by those wishing to launch their own haulage businesses.

Accordingly, freight was switched slowly but surely from rail to the

BRANCH ON STRIKE!

Industrial action is said to have twice diverted traffic from rail to road. No trains were run from Keighley or over the Worth Valley branch during the General Strike of May 1926. Train crews went on strike and the only trains that the unions were allowed to run carried urgent food supplies.

When the strike was over, railwaymen reporting for work were told to stay at home until they were required. So the nine days' stoppage became a fortnight, even though the dispute had been settled.

The trains may have stopped during the strike, but not so the private buses. The dispute had shown the public that railways were no longer the be-all and end-all of public transport, for passengers or freight.

The General Strike was not the first dispute to have stopped trains on the Worth Valley. On August 17, 1911, the four railway unions of the day had called a strike in support of a demand for better conditions. The next day, the morning trains along the branch did not run, but officials managed to get a reduced service operating by the afternoon. The strike ended on August

20. Everything was back to normal the following evening, and without a serious competitor to rail in Edwardian times, traffic resumed.

Jumping to the rock-n-roll era, a similar but greater and more widespread impact hit Britain's railways as a result of the 1955 national rail strike.

During the 1950s, as the austerity years mellowed and the British economy boomed, trade unions became stronger. Backed by the threat of strike action, unions found themselves able to demand better wages and working conditions for their members.

Days after Anthony Eden's Conservative government won a General Election victory, ASLEF, the Associated Society of Locomotive Engineers and Firemen, the union representing train drivers in Britain, called a strike over a pay dispute, demanding a rise that amounted to the price of an extra packet of cigarettes a week.

The strike lasted from May 28 to June 14, and brought British industry to a standstill, although locomen who belonged to the National Union of Railwaymen continued to work. British Railways still managed to convey

a quarter of its normal passenger traffic and a third of its freight, but the damage in the minds of the public was irreparable.

The strike signalled a mass switch by both passengers and freight customers from rail to road. They were forced to do so by necessity during the strike, and in a world where road transport was now far more commonplace than it had ever been before, many customers did not return after it ended.

A compromise was eventually reached with the union, but the dispute cost around £12-million in lost revenue. Five years later, the British Transport Commission accepted the findings of a government-commissioned investigation into railway pay levels, the Guillebaud Report, which led to higher wages and a shorter working week.

The merits of the 1955 national rail strike were questionable: few predicted the severity of the outcome. However, in global terms, the strike was but a little local factor in rail decline, for countries across Europe and North America were also closing swathes of short lines and branches that could no longer compete with road transport.

A BR engineers' saloon enters Keighley's Platform 4 after inspecting the Worth Valley in May 1958. P SUNDERLAND

cheaper, and more versatile, road alternative. In turn, local authorities began build more roads to cater for the increase in traffic. The growth of road haulage meant that the railways' profit margins began to suffer. Road hauliers could offer significantly lower prices than the railways, while offering the benefits of door-to-door delivery, while the railways were hampered by their original charters of the 1840s and 50s to act as common carriers, and legally were unable to refuse unprofitable cargoes and thereby lower their transportation costs accordingly.

The short nature of the Worth Valley branch meant that it was easier from the start for local traffic to use road transport, once the use of motor lorries became widespread.

Hence the 'marginal' local traffic, so important to so many railway lines, was never much in evidence on the Worth Valley branch and door-to-door lorries merely destroyed what little there was.

BOOM YEARS TO BUST
The late Thirties were halcyon times for the Keighley to Oxenhope branch.

The summer of 1938 showed the best timetable ever for the branch, with 21 weekday departures from Oxenhope and 19 from Keighley (two of them in each-way Saturdays only) and six trains on Sundays.

The journey took 16mins, or 17mins if a train called at Damems. The 11.10pm from Oxenhope to Keighley was advertised to run non-stop in just 10mins.

The use of push-pull trains helped enormously by allowing turn-round times to be cut to just three minutes.

However, the services were reduced

No. 41273 in the platform at Oxenhope with a push-pull train from Keighley in the Fifties.
RICHARD GREENWOOD

Ivatt 2MT 2-6-2T No. 41326 crosses Mytholmes Viaduct with a three-coach service for Oxenhope in the Fifties. P WILSON

during the Second World War, and those lost were never to be replaced.

Sunday trains had ended in 1947, and in 1948, the first year of British Railways, there were nine weekday trains each way and 12 on Saturdays.

Damems station, the smallest on the line by far, which was used by half the services, closed in May 1949.

The reduction in freight rather than passenger services meant that there no was need for the passing loops and signalboxes at Oakworth and Haworth, and these closed in early 1956.

The loops were never used for timetabled trains, but on an as-required basis for goods services. There were only two timetabled freight trains a day but many ad hoc ones, using the three goods locomotives pottering round the branch using the loops and

Midland Railway Johnson 1F-A 0-6-0T No. 1726 worked the branch in the 1920s.
MIDLAND RAILWAY SOCIETY

yards as refuges to get away from the passenger trains. The loss of most goods traffic other than day-old chicks from Oakworth and domestic coal, resulted in there being no need for them.

Further cutbacks came with the early 1950s introduction of a three-carriage corridor push-pull set, allowing the train guard to issue tickets at stations, over and above the 'motor train' sets introduced in 1932. As a result, Ingrow and Oxenhope lost their staff, while Oakworth retained its staff just for the level crossing.

One stationmaster was placed in charge of the entire branch, and he was based at Haworth.

Sadly, none of Johnson's 167 1P-D 0-4-4Ts of 1881 survived into preservation. This one, No. 58066, was a regular performer on the Worth Valley line before being withdrawn on October 31, 1959, and its subsequent scrapping. It was fitted with motor train apparatus for use on the branch in 1948. MIDLAND RAILWAY SOCIETY

THREE YEARS TO CLOSE THE LINE

April 1959 saw reports that a proposal by BR to close the branch was to be referred to the Transport Users' Consultative Committee, a body that had been created under the Transport Act 1947 to represent users of the railway, although the transport minister was not bound to follow any of its recommendations.

A new procedure was set out for the closure of railway lines, requiring that British Railways gave at least six weeks' notice of its intention to close a line and to publish this proposal for two successive weeks in two local newspapers in the area affected. The notice would give the proposed closure dates, details of alternative transport services (including services that BR was to lay on as a result of closure) and inviting objections to a specified address.

In July 1959, Keighley Borough Council passed a resolution to make representations to the TUCC (Transport Users Consultative Committee) and local Labour MP Charles Hobson after BR announced its intention to close the line. Mr Robson raised the issue in the House of Commons and asked for BR to take economy measures to turn the branch's losses into a profit.

The TUCC met to consider the BR application on September 1, 1959, and after the borough council presented a strong case, the TUCC also urged BR to develop the Worth Valley branch rather than close it.

The Mayor of Keighley called a public meeting to discuss the closure threat on September 21, 1959, and all the points raised were used to prepare a strong case for a meeting with British Transport Commission representatives in Keighley on October 26.

The TUCC looked at the issue again in early December 1959 at a meeting

A Metro-Cammell diesel multiple unit at Haworth station in 1961. Dieselisation of branch services did nothing to deter British Railways from closing the branch the following year. P SUNDERLAND

RIGHT: A notice posted at Oakworth on August 19, 1959, proposing closure of the branch. JOHN A PITTS

also attended by the mayor and his delegation. TUCC officials were impressed, and BR was urged to think again.

In the Fifties, Diesel Multiple Units and railcars had been introduced on many branches in a bid to effect economy measures. The measure may be regarded as a long time coming, for the Great Western Railway had successfully introduced diesel railcars two decades previously.

On December 1, 1954 British Railways unveiled its blueprint for the future in a report known as Modernisation and Re-Equipment of the British Railways, or the Modernisation Plan for short, which set out to combat the threat presented to the railways by road transport. The

BELOW: A DMU runs north of Haworth in 1961, with the village in the background. P SUNDERLAND

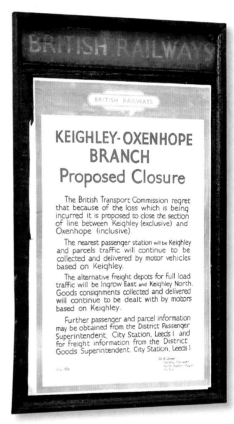

BRITISH RAILWAYS

BRITISH RAILWAYS

KEIGHLEY-OXENHOPE BRANCH
Proposed Closure

The British Transport Commission regret that because of the loss which is being incurred it is proposed to close the section of line between Keighley (exclusive) and Oxenhope (inclusive).

The nearest passenger station will be Keighley and parcels traffic will continue to be collected and delivered by motor vehicles based on Keighley.

The alternative freight depots for full load traffic will be Ingrow East and Keighley North. Goods consignments collected and delivered will continue to be dealt with by motors based on Keighley.

Further passenger and parcel information may be obtained from the District Passenger Superintendent, City Station, Leeds 1. and for freight information from the District Goods Superintendent, City Station, Leeds 1.

The last BR train on the branch was also the first organised by the Keighley & Worth Valley Railway! LMS 3F 0-6-0 No. 43586 heads up Keighley bank after departing from Platform 3 at Keighley on June 23, 1962. P SUNDERLAND

aim was to increase speed, reliability, safety and line capacity, while making services more attractive to passengers and freight operators. The most notable aim was the complete phasing out of steam locomotives by diesel and electric alternatives.

DMUs made their debut on several lines in and around Yorkshire, replacing steam-hauled trains, but the Worth Valley missed out until June 13, 1960. It was then that a new DMU service offered 15 return trips on weekdays and 20 on Saturdays, but still no Sunday services. The introduction of the DMU services came about in the wake of the TUCC meetings.

However, it was to no avail, and BR reported that the DMU services had not stemmed the losses on the branch.

In late February 1961, TUCC members inspected the branch on a special train before making a final decision.

BR would get its own way, for in October 1961, notices were posted saying that the branch would close to passengers on Saturday, December 30, and the pick-up freight in June the following year.

THE LAST TRAINS

Snow blanketed the valley on the last day of BR services, creating a white landscape of the same kind that had inspired the Bronte sisters.

Most of the passenger services comprised a four-car DMU. The last train left Keighley at 11.15pm with the mayor and mayoress of Keighley, the Keighley stationmaster and around 150 other passengers on board.

Driver Jim Clarke was in charge of the DMU, which also had two guards on board.

It was a Saturday-only service, which under normal circumstances would return to Keighley as empty stock.

A Fifties scene sees Ivatt 2-6-2T No. 41273 attack Keighley Bank on the west side as used today by KWVR trains. B AKINSON

Ivatt 2-6-2T No. 41324 at Oxenhope in the Fifties. B AKINSON

However, on this day, return tickets were issued and the otherwise non-stop service called at all stations on the way back. That evening, the Platform 4 sign at Keighley, indicating the Worth Valley arrival platform, crashed to the ground for no discernible reason.

In the last year of its operation, 130,000 tickets were sold, and the branch continued to serve its purpose as a feeder to the main line right to the end. Still, the London Midland Region insisted that cuts had to be made. After all who would miss such a short line when buses could readily provide an alternative?

Just as the freight services were being withdrawn, a final BR steam special was run on June 23, 1962, hauled by Midland Railway Johnson 0-6-0 No. 43586.

This was the first train organised by the Keighley & Worth Valley Railway Preservation Society.

Eight months later, on March 27, 1963, British Railways chairman Dr Richard Beeching published his report The Reshaping of British Railways. In it he called for the closure of one-third of the country's 7000 stations and the withdrawal of passenger services from around 5000 route miles.

By then, the powers that were had long realised that drastic action was needed to save Britain's railways, as more people switched to buses and private car ownership soared.

British Railways' annual working deficit in 1956 was £16.5 million: by 1962 it had reached £100 million. The inability of the 1955 Modernisation Plan to claw back the promised £85-million a year, coupled with a desire to prevent the country ever being held to ransom again by the unions, saw the emphasis of government transport policy finally shift from rail to road, paving the way for Beeching.

However, the Worth Valley branch did not survive long enough to be included in Beeching's 1963 report.

Midland 3F No. 43586 accelerates along Oxenhope Straight on June 23, 1962, with the last passenger train run by British Railways over the branch. Sadly, this locomotive, built by Kitson in 1899, did not survive into preservation, for six weeks later it was withdrawn from traffic, and was scrapped on August 20 that year. RICHARD GREEENWOOD

The headboard placed on the rear of the June 23, 1962 'Worth Valley Special' farewell train at Bradford Forest Square, the fireman stands by. DENNIS WHITFIELD

Midland Johnson 3F 0-6-0 No. 43586 shunts coal wagons in Haworth yard in the 1960s. P SUNDERLAND

The locomotive that started the railway preservation movement: Canterbury & Whitstable Railway 0-4-0 *Invicta* is displayed, cosmetically restored, inside the Canterbury Heritage Museum.
ROBIN JONES

THE LONG ROAD TO
OXENHOPE

While the Keighley & Worth Valley revivalists broke much new ground in reopening the branch, they were building on the foundations of a railway preservation movement that can be traced back to Victorian times.

Railway preservation could be deemed to have its roots in 1839, just nine years after the opening of the Liverpool & Manchester Railway, the world's first inter-city line, and two years after Queen Victoria came to the throne.

It was then that *Invicta*, the 20th locomotive built by Robert Stephenson & Co in Newcastle-on-Tyne for the Canterbury & Whitstable Railway, which in 1829, was next off the production line after *Rocket*, was placed into storage after failing to find a buyer. The locomotive had been rendered redundant in 1836 by retro-technology, in that the Kent line replaced locomotive haulage with stationary steam engines and cable haulage.

Set aside, *Invicta* came into the ownership of the Southern Eastern Railway and was exhibited at the Golden Jubilee of the Stockton & Darlington Railway in 1875 and at the Newcastle Stephenson Centenary six years later. *Invicta* is now safely inside the Canterbury Heritage Museum.

However, setting an antique locomotive aside for posterity is a long way from volunteers and enthusiasts taking over a complete railway.

In 1929, efforts to save Suffolk's 3ft-gauge Southwold Railway attracted the attention of the national press, and had they been successful, it is likely that it would have been Britain's first heritage line.

After the First World War, financial depression caused a general decline in the fortunes of the line. Up to 1925 it had showed a profit, but when the end came,

Sharp Stewart 2-4-2T No. 1 *Southwold* heads a typical Southwold Railway train. The eight-mile line between Halesworth and Southwold closed in 1929 after having nearly become the first in the UK to be taken over by local people. ROBIN JONES COLLECTION

it was sudden. It fell victim to the motor buses, which in 1928, were allowed to pick up from within the town itself. The directors gave up and decided to cut their losses by closing the line rather than investing in an already outdated railway, which had become the butt of music hall jokes.

On April 11, 1929, after one week's notice, the line closed. So abrupt was the closure that the line had to carry on for a further 10 days to clear the goods backlog.

Two separate plans to reopen the line quickly divided support, bringing an end to any hopes of a revival. However, the company existed for many years and no one was able to do anything about the line. Scrap metal recovery during the Second World War provoked a last-ditch attempt to save it but it came to nothing, and in July 1941 the line and engines were cut up for scrap, realising the grand total of £1500.

The idea of building private railways for enthusiasts was not new.

The roots of such ventures go back much further. Sir Arthur Heywood had a 15in-gauge line built on his Duffield Bank estate in Derbyshire in 1874, with the idea of selling it to a wider audience (of rich estate owners) and in 1895 he built a similar system at Eaton Hall for the Duke of Westminster. At this stage, such miniature railways were intended purely for private estates and to highlight the potential of trains running on such a small gauge.

Wenman Joseph Bassett-Lowke, the most famous modelmaker of the early 20th century, and miniature locomotive engineer Henry Greenly formed a company, Miniature Railways of Great Britain, in 1904, to develop such lines.

After Heywood died, Bassett-Lowke and his friends bought up much of the Duffield Bank equipment.

In 1915, he converted the derelict 3ft-gauge Ravenglass & Eskdale Railway to 15in gauge and ran miniature steam engines, and followed it up a year later with a similar conversion of the 2ft-gauge Fairbourne Railway, at that time a horse-worked passenger and local freight concern.

These railways could not in their day by any stretch of the imagination be described as 'heritage' lines, because they were merely using often newly built scale replicas or types based on contemporary state-of-the-art main line locomotives. Neither were they primarily rebuilt to serve local communities, with the main focus being on visitors to the areas concerned.

Tennis Ground station on Sir Arthur Heywood's 15in-gauge Duffield Bank line as seen in 1898. While such ventures were aimed at wealthy estate owners who had an interest in railways, they were also the forerunners of 20th-century seaside miniature railways.

Ellis D Atwood built the Edaville Railway (pictured on July 1, 1959) as a line to serve his cranberry estates, using secondhand locomotives and rolling stock, and it slowly took off as a tourist attraction. Its trains were certainly in the 'heritage' category, but it was a newly built line, unlike the Talyllyn Railway, which is almost universally recognised as the first heritage line in the world. RICKPILOT 2000*

Some observers have pointed to the Edaville Railway in South Carver, Massachusetts, as being the world's first full-size heritage railway.

However, the Edaville was not a heritage railway, but an all-new line that used locomotives, rolling stock and equipment from the Maine 2ft-gauge system that closed in 1941, originally developed by Boston pioneer George E Mansfield, who had been impressed by a trip on the Festiniog Railway and had founded the USA's first 2ft gauge line, the Billerica & Bedford Railroad, in 1879.

In 1948, cranberry producer Ellis D Atwood bought up locomotives, rolling stock and track following the closure of the Maine line in order to build a line specifically to serve his estates, while preserving some last vestiges of the 2ft empire for posterity, with a small railroad museum. He deployed his cranberry growers to tracklaying and train crew duties and by 1948 he had laid more than seven miles of track, on which secondhand Vulcan and Baldwin locomotives and luxury coaching stock ran. It was a far cry from what you might expect on an industrial concern serving

a cranberry bog, and soon local people and groups began asking it they could take a ride on it, and its tourist trade slowly took off from there.

The Edaville Railway was, in effect, laid on a green-field site, or more accurately, a red cranberry bog, but it was, by and large, the creation of an enthusiast, not an existing line.

INTERESTING SUGGESTION

The concept of volunteers taking over an existing railway and running it, without such wholesale modifications, was mooted in the letters column of the January 1941 issue of The Modem Tramway, the journal of the Light Railway Transport League.

Headed 'An Interesting Suggestion', Manchester reader Arthur E Rimmer, concerned at the Welsh Highland Railway's imminent prospect of having its track lifted for the war effort, wrote that the line, which closed to passengers in 1936 and freight the year afterwards, had proved its value during the First World War in carrying timber and slate, while a passenger service could be reintroduced to save petrol supplies.

If the reinstatement of the Welsh Highland on commercial grounds was found to be not possible, he continued, would it be practicable for clubs and societies supplying free labour to tackle such a scheme?

The biggest watershed in the history of preservation came in spring 1951, with the takeover of the Talyllyn Railway by volunteers. It marked the giant leap from the arbitrary preservation of classic locomotives by those in authority to ordinary people running a full-scale railway by themselves.

When Britain's railways were nationalised on January 1, 1948, the Talyllyn Railway was one of the few operating lines not included, but the slate traffic on which it had depended had vanished, the infrastructure had severely deteriorated yet its owner, Sir Henry Haydn Jones, vowed it would not close while he was alive.

On July 2, 1950, Sir Henry died and closure of the 2ft 3in gauge line seemed inevitable, but it continued to operate for the remainder of the summer season, ending on October 6.

It would, however, not be the end, but the start of something that would, as we now know, become very big indeed.

On September 2, 1949, an anonymous letter appeared in The Birmingham Post, headed, 'Breakdown on Talyllyn Railway'.

The writer said that Dolgoch, by then the line's sole operating locomotive, had suffered a fractured frame and had to be withdrawn from service, leading to the then two-days-a-week passenger service being suspended.

A reply in the newspaper's letters column came on September 9 from renowned transport author Tom Rolt, who in 1935 had helped found the Vintage Sports Car Club, and in 1947, had prevented the GWR from effectively closing the northern section of the Stratford-upon-Avon Canal, by exercising his right of passage at a dilapidated lock in Kings Norton, Birmingham.

Tom Rolt congratulated the writer, but disagreed with his demand that the government or British Railways should step in to save the Talyllyn from closure.

Instead, Tom argued, ordinary people should take the initiative themselves.

He called a public meeting on at the Imperial Hotel in Birmingham on October 11 that year to consider the future of the Talyllyn Railway, and 36 people turned up, electing a committee, which met for the first time on October 23, and became known as the Talyllyn Railway Preservation Society.

Through the generosity of Sir Haydn's widow, the society was effectively given the line in February 1951 - and members ran their first train on May that year, with initial services running between Tywyn Wharf and Rhydyronen. Regular

Welsh Highland Railway flagship Hunslet 2-6-2T *Russell* heads north through the Aberglaslyn Pass in the 1930s. In the early 1940s, it was suggested that railway clubs and societies could reopen the closed trans-Snowdonian line to provide a community service, but nothing came of it. FR

Preservation pioneers: Tom Rolt alongside No. 2 *Dolgoch*, being driven by David Curwen at Tywyn Wharf on May 14, 1951 when the Talyllyn Railway Preservation ran its first trains to Rhydyronen. TR

Tom Rolt's landmark book on the volunteer takeover of the Talyllyn, Railway Adventure was a major inspiration for The Titfield Thunderbolt.

trains began to run on June 4 and continued through the summer.

The takeover of the Talyllyn by volunteers was the inspiration for the successful 1952 Ealing Studios comedy The Titfield Thunderbolt about a group of villagers attempting to run a service on a disused branch line after closure.

The success at Tywyn was followed by the saving of the Festiniog Railway (the two 'f's in the current title was added later in the preservation era).

Festiniog passenger services ended on September 15, 1939, with slate trains running three days a week during the war, until they too finally ended, on August 1, 1946. By then, the company was so short of money that it could not afford an Act of Parliament to provide the statutory powers necessary to close the railway and lift it.

The revival of the Festiniog may have been sparked off by teenager Leonard Heath-Humphreys whose letter about the line's potential for restoration was published in the January 1951 edition of the Journal of the British Locomotive. He made contact with the Festiniog company in July 1950 and suggested launching a society to reopen the line.

The big breakthrough came when businessman Alan Pegler – the future saviour of A3 Pacific No. 4472 *Flying Scotsman* – attended a meeting of the nascent Festiniog Railway Preservation Society at the Great Northern Hotel at King's Cross in January 1953, and came on board.

Detailed negotiations ended with Alan and his nominees taking over control of the Festiniog board on June 24, 1954. And on July 23, 1955, after a formal Ministry of Transport inspection, a passenger service ran from Porthmadog Harbour station across the Cob to Boston Lodge, behind *Mary Ann*, a 1917-built four-wheeled Motor-Rail Simplex First World War trench railway locomotive that the railway had bought in 1923.

ENTER MADGE BESSEMER

Ground-breaking global landmarks in the field of preservation as they were, the saving of the Talyllyn and Ffestiniog railways were a world away from the aim of saving a line not for enthusiast or tourist purposes, but to maintain existing public services. In Britain, there was no direct or immediate threat

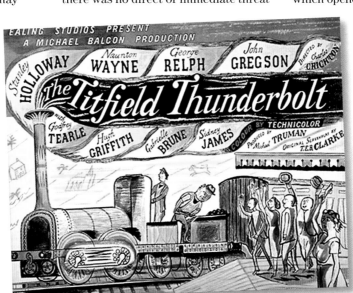

Poster for the Ealing comedy The Titfield Thunderbolt.

to main line steam when the Talyllyn takeover took place, but branch line closures were happening nonetheless, as they had been since the Thirties, if only involving the withdrawal of passenger services and leaving rural backwaters open for freight.

In The Titfield Thunderbolt, the villagers set out to save their local transport link, not run steam engines for posterity.

That is exactly what Sussex spinster and battleaxe Madge Bessemer, grand-daughter of Henry Bessemer, inventor of Bessemer Converter for converting pig iron into steel, aimed to do.

Her father, Henry William Bessemer, a chartered accountant, and his wife Rose lived on the Burchetts estate at North Chailey, a stone's throw from the LBSCR's Lewes-East Grinstead line, which opened on August 1, 1882. Their 14-bedroom mansion house was built in 1905 and they bought the freehold of the estate in 1911.

Mrs Bessemer reached an agreement with the railway to have a private gate built to access the footpath alongside Newick and Charley station, providing a quick access route for the family.

Madge Bessemer became heavily involved in local community life, teaching at a village school and serving as a parish councillor, she was also a Girl Guide captain and commandant of the local branch of the Red Cross.

A lover of wildlife, it has been theorised that

Early Ffestiniog Railway preservation-era livery to the fore as No. 2 *Prince* passes the permanent way department's Wickham trolley at Harbour station in the late Sixties. NF GURLEY/FR

while picking spring flowers on the embankment near her estate she may have come up with the nickname of the 'Bluebell Line'.

Madge Bessemer's finest hour came when the British Transport Commission posted notices announcing that it would close the lossmaking Lewes-East Grinstead line with effect from May 28, 1955. She was determined from the start to stand in the way.

Studying key documents from the line's history, she reread the small print in the Act of Parliament, which had given powers for its building. It required the owners to run four trains each day.

It was the just loophole that she needed. Aided by local MP Tufton Beamish, she forced British Railways to reinstate the service, which it very begrudgingly did in August the following year.

Locals dubbed it the 'sulky service' as BR had to comply with the law, but did so begrudgingly. The statutory four services were mostly restricted to just a single coach, which did not stop at Barcombe or Kingscote, because those two stations did not appear in the original Act. Also, the restored services appeared to be deliberately timed so that they would be of little use, arriving at East Grinstead after the start of normal working hours and departing before the end of the working day.

But history records it was a major victory, in view not only of what happened in Sussex but its ramifications for the entire country – including West Yorkshire!

Madge Bessemer had won a reprieve for the line until BR obtained the statutory powers it needed to revoke the terms of the original Act. Services were again withdrawn between Lewes and East Grinstead on March 16, 1958, but this time she could do nothing.

Her stalwart efforts had attracted national media attention, however, and when the final train ran, the unduly large number of passengers and sightseers proved that the public at large really did care about rail closures, and would fight to save their local lines.

STUDENT POWER

On that final day, Madge Bessemer encountered Carshalton Technical College student Chris Campbell, who shared his many recollections of travelling on the line while spending school holidays with relatives. Inspired by her efforts to save the line, Chris, then 18, wondered if it might be possible that he could take up the cause.

Elsewhere, Martin Eastland, 19, a telecommunications engineering student of Haywards Heath, David Dallimore, a student at the London School of Economics, from Woodingdean, and Brighton-based Alan Sturt, 19, who was studying at the Regent Street Polytechnic, had mooted the idea of setting up a Lewes and East Grinstead Railway Preservation Society, drawing on the examples of the Welsh narrow gauge lines.

They sent a letter to interested parties highlighting Madge Bessemer's campaign and the unexpected public support that it had generated.

They initially hoped to save the entire route from Lewes to East Grinstead, reopening it in stages at a time, acquiring a GWR railcar for regular use and using steam during the summer months. Incidentally, the preservation of GWR railcar W4W by Swindon Railway Museum in 1958 may be held to mark the start of diesel preservation.

In December 1958, Chris told a journalist on the East Grinstead Observer about the possible formation of a preservation society, leading to the headline: 'Bluebell Line Sensation – May Be Run Privately'.

During a December walk along the disused track to Newick & Chailey station they had lunch within the sight of Madge Bessemer who was picking flowers on the lineside opposite. It was then that Chris met Martin for the first time and decided to call a public meeting to officially launch the society.

The founders' meeting was held on March 15, 1959, at the Church Lads' Brigade Hall in Haywards Heath. It was chaired by Bernard Holden, 51, a signalling assistant in the general manager's office at Liverpool Street, because the students were minors in the eyes of the law as they were all under 21 and were, at that time, legally barred from holding positions. Bernard had been born in Barcombe station house where his father Charles was stationmaster.

A collection raised £6 for society funds, and a meeting with the assistant general manager of the Southern Region was arranged to take place at Waterloo.

The preservationists were hardly taken seriously, probably because of their age if not their lofty ambitions. A price of £55,000 for the purchase of the line between Horsted Keynes (then still in use as the eastern end of the electrified Ardingly branch) and Culver Junction was quoted, and the society was given just a month's option to purchase.

Eventually, however, an affordable £2500 per annum five-year lease on the four-mile Horsted Keynes-Sheffield Park section was agreed.

The first Bluebell train ran on August 7, 1960. The entire route had not been saved, but a different animal appeared in the form of a heritage railway, which would not see the lost public services restored, but would showcase the glories of the steam era and the travel of yesteryear on a comparatively short section of track.

When all but the entire Midland & Great Northern Joint Railway system between the East Midlands and Norfolk was closed on February 28, 1959, revivalists similarly expressed an aim to take over the whole lot and restore public services throughout. They did not stand the slightest chance of saving the whole system, but edited their dreams to saving the most scenic section of the route, which is now the North Norfolk Railway.

Had the Bluebell Railway not started in operations in 1960, the first time that a redundant section of the national network had been reopened by volunteers, its shining example would not have been there for others to follow. If the preservation movement had taken several more years to reach that stage, how many now-priceless examples of classic steam locomotives and rolling stock would have been lost forever?

It was to be another eight years before the next former BR line, the Keighley & Worth Valley Railway, would run public trains.

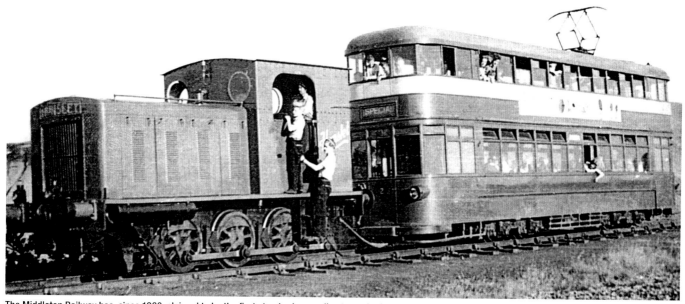

The Middleton Railway has, since 1960, claimed to be the first standard gauge line to run heritage trains, although it was never part of British Railways as the Bluebell had been. Here, diesel shunter No. 1697 hauls a redundant Swansea & Mumbles Railway tramcar on the line's first heritage-era services.

YORKSHIRE LEADS THE WAY

The Bluebell was not the first private standard gauge railway to run trains. It was beaten by several weeks by the Middleton Railway at Leeds, which started operating public services on June 20, 1960 a few weeks earlier. In doing so, it kept alive the Middleton's proud boast of being the world's oldest railway in continuous operation, having been founded in 1758.

However, they were very different animals. The Bluebell revivalists had set out to keep a route open, whereas their Middleton counterparts had initially wanted a line on which they could run historic trams, not trains.

Furthermore, the first Middleton heritage-era train – and therefore the first in British standard gauge preservation – was hauled not by a steam locomotive, but by a diesel!

Leeds University Union Railway Society had been seeking somewhere to home the historic Leeds street tramcars that it had managed to preserve.

In September 1959, it was suggested that a suitable railway should be acquired, or even built, on which to run them.

Student Chris Thornburn then suggested that the Middleton Railway could be instead used for this purpose. The decision by the National Coal Board to switch from rail to road the bulk of the shipments of coal from Broom Pit had left much of the historic line redundant.

The Middleton Railway Preservation Society was founded in December 1959 as a separate organisation. The prime mover was lecturer and society president the late Dr Fred Youell, who fought and won a seemingly impossible

battle against all odds to make it happen.

He obtained agreements for the use of the line, the majority of which was owned by Clayton, Son & Co Ltd, and by the following June, during university rag week, everything was in place.

The first train comprised Hunslet diesel shunter No. 1697 (later named *John Alcock*) which had worked on the LMS in 1932 and was therefore the very first preserved main line diesel locomotive in Britain, hauling Swansea & Mumbles Railway tramcar No. 2, which had been obtained following the controversial closure of what was the world's first public passenger-carrying line in January that year.

That first week of services saw around 7700 passengers carried, showing that a heritage railway could become an attraction.

The dawn of former British Railways' standard gauge preservation: LBSCR A1X 'Terrier' 0-6-0T No. 55 *Stepney* leaves the crowded platforms at Sheffield Park with the first public Bluebell Railway passenger train on August 7, 1960. Hayling Island branch veteran *Stepney*, one of the characters in Rev W Awdry's Thomas the Tank Engine series, was the fledgling line's first locomotive. BLUEBELL RAILWAY ARCHIVES

SAVING THE WORTH VALLEY BRANCH

Oakworth station as seen on September 13, 1965, before the revivalists moved in. Nature had already reclaimed the tracks.

While the Bluebell and Middleton railways were founded by youthful enthusiasts, the Keighley & Worth Valley Railway had very different origins.

As we have seen, early hopes of restoring the entire Lewes-East Grinstead route and reinstating timetabled public – as opposed to tourist or enthusiast – trains were beyond wildly optimistic, just like the early schemes to save the entire Midland & Great Northern system.

However, at just 4¾ miles, the Worth Valley branch was by comparison 'doable', even at the still embryonic stage of the standard gauge preservation movement in the early Sixties.

Here was a classic Titfield Thunderbolt case of a community coming together to save its line, standing up against the powers that be who seemed to care little for the effect its closure would have on local people. In that respect, what happened on the Worth Valley was far more true to the Ealing comedy than its inspiration, the Talyllyn Railway, had been.

It was local residents, not railway enthusiasts, who saved the branch, not to keep steam alive but to save their local services, and this point cannot be overstated.

Their actions may have been inspired by many of the principles of the preservation movement that went before, but here their initial and primary aim was loud and clear – to save the railway for the local community it was built to serve.

In September 1959, Oakworth resident, Ralph Povey, who worked in Bradford and used a combination of bus and train to get there, had a letter published in Trains Illustrated calling for a "National Federation of Railway Preservation Societies" to direct volunteer labour and finance to lines where it could do most good.

In November 1961, Ralph wrote a letter to the Bradford Telegraph and Argus newspaper suggesting that a preservation society for the branch should be formed.

Another local resident, Bradford-born University of Hull graduate Bob Cryer, who worked as a teacher and lecturer had, in 1960, written to local newspapers calling for the Great Northern line from Keighley to Bradford to be saved. The line by then was already overgrown and his calls fell on deaf ears, but he was determined that the adjoining Worth Valley branch should not suffer the same fate.

On January 24, 1962, three and a half weeks after the last passenger train, a meeting was called at the Keighley Temperance Hall, from which a committee emerged to explore the possibilities of local people taking over the line.

A second meeting at the Temperance Hall on March 1, called by Bob Cryer and attended by more than 100 people, led to the formation of the Keighley & Worth Valley Railway Preservation Society, and a provisional committee was set up, with Bob as chairman.

By the end of 1962 there were 266 members.

No time was wasted in making contact with BR officials, for time was of the essence. In those times, tracks were often lifted within days of a line's closure, never to be relaid.

The society sought to create a company to buy the line outright, lease access into Keighley station and operate a regular public service.

Their primary aim was not to preserve steam locomotives, but to save the railway that had served their towns and villages so well for so long, and reintroduce regular services.

It was hoped that the freight services on the branch could be saved, and timetabled diesel trains could run for local people on weekends, with steam-hauled services run by volunteers at weekends.

Haworth station was rented as a headquarters and a small museum of railway relics was set up there, as a focal point of the revival bid.

It would take six years of negotiations and repair work to reopen the line.

During that time, the freight that the branch had carried switched to road and 150,000 local passengers found other means of transport – so would a traditional public service have paid its way?

Hardly likely in the circumstances, but a very different animal was set to emerge in phoenix style – one of the world's greatest heritage railways.

TAKING THE FIRST STEPS

The society needed to show the public it meant business, and what better way to do this than to run a special train?

As we saw in the last chapter, Saturday, June 23, 1962 saw a six-coach train hauled from Bradford Forster Square to Oxenhope and back by Midland 35 0-6-0 No. 43586, a veteran of the branch goods.

However, the last freight train over the Worth Valley branch had run the week before the special train, and BR ceased track maintenance thereafter. Accordingly, BR banned any more special trains. It would be another six years before any more public trains would run over the branch.

Looking at the Bluebell blueprint, the society offered to lease the branch from BR. However, BR was having none of it – stipulating that the line had to be sold if it was not to be torn up.

In 1962, BR asked for £34,000 for the four miles from GN Junction to Oxenhope. The section from GN Junction to Keighley was still used by occasional coal trains to Ingrow East on the GNR line.

While local businesses had shown some enthusiasm for the reopening of the branch, when it came to putting their money where their mouths were, they suddenly fell silent. Likewise Keighley Corporation, which had opposed BR's closure, declined to help the revivalists.

The society considered the idea of a public share issue to raise the necessary finance to reopen the line, or approaching potential rich benefactors with an interest in railways. However, the last option was not pursued, because of fears that one individual might have too much control and act in a contrary manner to the wishes of the volunteers and local community

It seems that the society was getting nowhere very fast, and membership dropped off to just 140 by March 1964. To many supporters, the revival began to seem like 'pie in the sky', and the achievement of the Bluebell looked to be a world away.

Unwanted, unloved, but within a few years it would be on the global stage: Ingrow West station, as seen on September 13, 1965 from the north end.

Tiny Damems' single-coach platform viewed from the north end in March 1964. DENNIS WHITFIELD

August 1963 saw BR issue a threat to begin lifting the track if no progress was made on lodging a bid to buy the line. However, hopes were raised following a meeting with BR officials at York on October 4 that year.

The society offered to buy the line on a 'hire purchase' basis over 49 years. BR insisted on 25 years, but offered to sell at the abovementioned price plus interest.

In September the following year,

the society announced that the branch revival was very much on again, and services were intended to resume at Whitsun 1965.

As highlighted in Chapter 5, the first locomotive arrived on the line in January 1965, and BR permitted the society to maintain the track. The following month, the society issued the first issue of its members' quarterly magazine, Push and Pull.

General view of the approach to Oxenhope station from the road, on September 13, 1965.

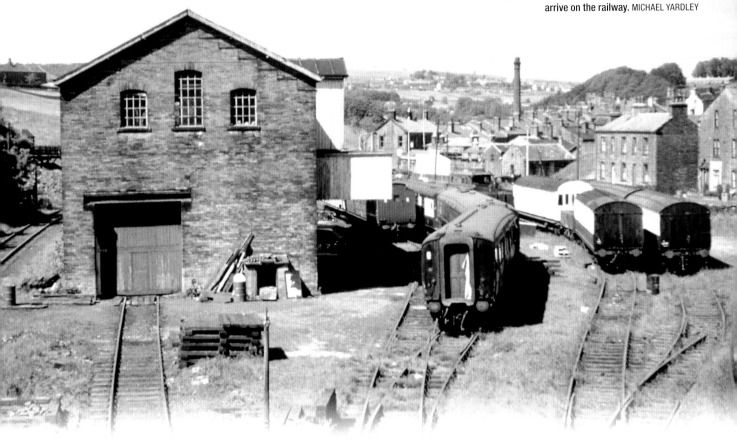

Haworth yard, as seen from Bridge 26 on June 29, 1966, with some of the early items of rolling stock to arrive on the railway. MICHAEL YARDLEY

A WELCOME CLOSURE!

However, there would be no public trains in the spring of 1965. Indeed, the detailed terms of the sale of the line were not agreed until January 1966.

On February 8, 1966, Keighley & Worth Valley Railway Light Railway Limited was incorporated as a company with a share capital of £10,000 authorised. While some individuals bought shares, most were acquired by the society itself out of its own funds raised via subscriptions, retail sales or other initiatives. This move had very positive ramifications for the future, because it ensured that the KWVR would always remain in the hands of its supporting society.

The report by BR chairman Dr Richard Beeching, The Reshaping of British Railways, which had been published on March 27, 1963, called for railways to continue doing what they did best, and to accept that road transport could in other circumstances do better than rail. It heralded the end of the pick-up goods and the mass closures of goods yards, in favour of bulk container traffic: indeed, Freightliner was one of Beeching's big success stories.

Accordingly, the last coal train ran to Ingrow East in June 1965. While they had spent years trying to reverse the closure of the Worth Valley branch, society members were jubilant at this particular closure.

Rendering the section of line from GN Junction to Keighley redundant would mean that the society would not have to pay BR rent to operate over this section.

BR told the society it would include the three-quarters of a mile of track in its sale offer, but the price would go up to £45,000.

However, BR officials were unsure of the exact boundary of the land to be sold at Keighley, and it was not until December 1966 that the BR board finally approved the sale of the branch.

A formal agreement was signed that allowed the company to buy the entire branch apart from Platform 4 at Keighley, which was to be leased for 25 years.

The revivalists paid the £45,000 in six-monthly instalments with interest over the following 25 years, the last being made in 1992 . However, taking inflation into account, BR to all intents and purposes gave the line to the KWVR. The comparatively low sale price was down to the high number of bridges over a short distance.

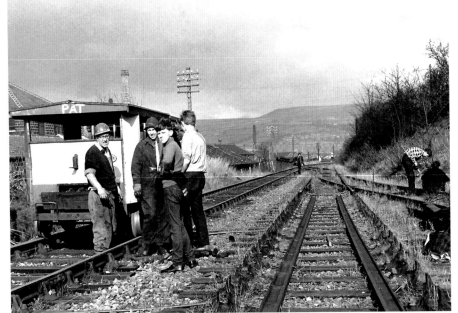

In March 1967, before the opening of the line by the society, members are attending to the GN Junction trackwork before it was lifted, aided by the line's Wickham trolley.

The first train through Oakworth under KWVR management comprised a stock delivery in March 1965. RALPH POVEY

A Sixties view of trackwork underway in the Ingrow area.

Haworth station, as seen before the toilet block (now admin block) was built

STATUTORY POWERS

The next big steps were administrative and legal. The company needed to acquire the statutory powers to operate the line.

The company drew on the provisions of the 1896 Light Railways Act, which facilitated the building of railways in rural outbacks 'on the cheap', with a maximum speed limit of 25mph. This limit applies to virtually all heritage railways today.

The company applied for a Light Railway Order to operate the branch, but still under the control of BR. It then needed a Transfer Order to acquire the running powers outright from BR. The local bus company, which was

half owned By Keighley Corporation, objected, fearing that the railway might undercut its fares. That issue was settled with an agreement that the railway would not do so.

The British Railways (Keighley & Worth Valley) Light Railway Order came into force in October 1967.

The Transfer Order came through on May 27, 1968.

The Keighley & Worth Valley Railway had broken new ground through the purchase of the freehold of it line. It was the first to buy a former BR line, and in drawing up a blueprint for the procedures involved, blazed a trail for other revival schemes to follow.

With the purchase agreed and statutory powers obtained, all that was needed to start running public trains again was for the branch to be inspected by the Department of Transport.

Saturday, June 8, saw inspector Col J R H Robertson of the DoT give the green light.

After six years of long hard slog, the KWVR revivalists found themselves standing at the top of a mountain that had proved far more difficult to climb than had been anticipated, on the verge of transport history being made by local people who were determined that their railway should not go the way of the others closed before, during and after the Beeching Axe.

Chapter 5

THE FIRST
LOCOMOTIVES
ARRIVE

With the operation of the branch in its sights, the Keighley & Worth Valley Railway Preservation Society needed motive power and coaching stock. From humble beginnings, help came from several quarters, and soon what had begun as an arbitrary collection became one of Britain's finest historic locomotive fleets.

The famous pocket-money priced Airfix plastic kit to make a Lancashire & Yorkshire Railway 'Pug'.

Lancashire & Yorkshire Railway 'Pug' 0-4-0ST No. 51218, the first locomotive to arrive on the Keighley & Worth Valley Railway as a heritage line with Pullman coach in Platform 3, at Keighley station during an empty coaching stock move in the winter of 1966. KWVR

BELOW: June 5, 1965, saw LYR 'Pug' No. 51218 haul the first heritage-era passenger train at Haworth station. CHRIS BRAY

The first engine to arrive on the moribund branch at Haworth on January 7, 1965, via a Pickfords low-loader, was diminutive Lancashire & Yorkshire Railway 'Pug' 0-4-0ST. It was representative of one of the smallest steam locomotive types on British Railways' books, working at many allocations including Bristol and Swansea East Dock.

It had been bought directly from British Rail in 1964 by the Lancashire & Yorkshire Railway Saddle Tanks Fund (now the Lancashire & Yorkshire Railway Trust) and was looked after by the revivalist society's Rochdale Group. It was the first locomotive on the branch for more than two years.

At this very early stage of the preservation society, the method of watering was a hosepipe.

Anyone who had a model railway at the time, or indeed in the ensuing decades, will be familiar with the 'Pug' for it became the subject of a pocket-money price OO-gauge polystyrene kit made in the 1960s by Kitmaster. The moulds were subsequently sold to Airfix then passed on to Dapol, which still manufactures the former Airfix plastic kit range. Various

manufacturers made motorising kits for them, and Hornby brought out a ready-to-run model.

Indeed, among schoolboy modellers, the little black 'Pug', kit price half a crown (2/6 or 12½p), was probably as famous as *Flying Scotsman*!

The class originates in the purchase of three saddle tank locomotives made by Vulcan Foundry in 1886. LYR Locomotive Superintendent John Aspinall then ordered more locomotives to a modified design, with 17 built at Horwich Works. His successor, Henry Hoy, ordered another batch of 10, and Hoy's successor, George Hughes, ordered 30 more in two batches. A total of 57 were produced between 1891 and 1910. They were specifically designed for shunting tightly curved sidings on the LYR's dock lines and goods yards.

As LYR No. 68, the engine emerged from Horwich Works in 1901, was given the number 11218 at the Grouping of 1923 and clocked up 63 years' service before being withdrawn in Neath, South Wales in 1964.

Splendid little shunters, the early KWVR conjectured that its 'Pug' could also haul one or two carriages as a passenger train and was therefore fitted with vacuum brakes.

On June 5, 1965, the 'Pug' hauled what amounted to the first heritage-era passenger train on the KWVR, comprising Southern Railway 'Matchboard' coach No. 3554. Rides were offered out of Haworth Yard, under Bridge 26 and a short distance along Haworth loop.

No. 51218 left Haworth on February 10, 1967 by road for display at Rochdale Fire Station in connection with the Roch Valley Railway Society's exhibition. Three days later No. 51218 was taken to Newton Heath shed where it was off loaded in the former Dean Lane coalyard and taken on shed by No. 46506.

On Sunday February 19, No. 51218 made three trips on the line from Rochdale to Whitworth with four brake vans.

No. 51218 moving empty stock through Damems on March 19, 1966. IAN HOLT

THE PRIVATE PURCHASE PIONEER

In 1959, the late Cpt Bill Smith became one of the first people to buy a British Railways' locomotive to be privately preserved, in J52 0-6-0ST No. 68846. His action set the ball rolling for other locomotives to be bought from BR, notably *Flying Scotsman*.

Built for the Great Northern Railway in 1899 as J13 No. 1247, it is the sole survivor of a class of 85. Its new owner had the locomotive repainted into Great Northern Railway livery with its original number 1247. He always spoke of it as "the Old Lady". The type was designed by Henry Ivatt for shunting and general freight work and was built by Sharp Stewart. The locomotive was best known for its role as the pilot engine in King's Cross 'Top Shed' where it hauled A3 and A4 Pacifics not in steam around the yard. Bought straight out of service, it arrived at Keighley from Doncaster on March 6, 1965, in what was the KWVR's first delivery by rail.

No. 1247 became the first locomotive to work over the branch for nearly three years when it hauled Lancashire & Yorkshire 'Ironclad' 0-6-0 No. 957 and coaching stock from Keighley to Haworth.However, its stay on the KWVR did not last long. Cpt Smith demanded facilities for it that the line could not offer and it departed before the reopening.

In 1980, he found that the cost of operating No. 1247 was too expensive. It was the first donation of an operating standard gauge locomotive to the NRM. In recognition, he was made the first honorary life member of the Friends of the National Railway Museum.

Retired naval commander Cpt Smith had, on January 6, 1962, been elected as the first chairman of the Railway Preservation Society, the forerunner of the Association of Railway Preservation Societies, an umbrella group to look after the newly emerging heritage lines. The organisation evolved into what is now the Heritage Railway Association.

No. 1247 is currently out of ticket and is on static display at York.

The 'Pug' remained at Newton Heath shed until Wednesday, April 5, when, in steam but coupled to WD 2-8-0 90625, it travelled via Phillips Park, Gorton and Chorlton Junction to reach Trafford Park. Here it passed along the Trafford Park Road to the premises of Brown and Polson where it was in regular daily use while its loco, a large Barclay, received attention. It was used on a joint LCGB/RVRS brake van trip round the private Trafford Park Estate.

No. 51218 was employed with No. 67 on a railtour on September 14, 1969 to commemorate the 75th anniversary of the opening of the Manchester Ship Canal. No. 51218 then returned to Haworth after an absence of 2½ years.

No. 51218 was chosen to appear in the 1975 Shildon Cavalcade to celebrate the 150th anniversary of the opening of the Stockton & Darlington Railway. In scenes that could have come straight out of a Thomas the Tank Engine story, this little shunter was hobnobbing with far more glamorous engines such as *Flying Scotsman*, *Evening Star* and *Clan Line*.

The mid-1990s saw the first major overhaul of No. 51218 since 1963, taking place at Rileys of Bury and the East Lancashire Railway, with a return to steam in late 1997 as BR No. 51218 complete with a replacement saddle tank. Once back in steam, it visited several other heritage lines and at times masqueraded as Percy in the Thomas the Tank Engine series.

The boiler tubes lasted well beyond the expected five years but were eventually condemned in early 2006. No. 51218 will not run again until the boiler has had a 10-year overhaul, which is scheduled to begin as soon as the rebuild of LYR Class 23 0-6-0ST No. 752 is complete.

Sister LYR No. 19 (LMS No. 11243), built in 1910, was sold by the LMS into industry in 1931 and was acquired by the trust from the United Glass Bottle Manufacturers Ltd at Charlton in 1967. It was found to be in poor mechanical condition and was later placed on static display pending overhaul, most recently at the Ribble Steam Railway at Preston Docks.

Cpt Bill Smith's GNR J52 0-6-0ST No. 1247 heads a trial train above Haworth on June 11, 1966. IAN HOLT

A LOCOMOTIVE THAT BUILT MAIN LINES

The second locomotive arrived on January 19, 1965, and was also brought in by a low loader.

It was a small industrial tank engine, but one with an impeccable main line pedigree.

For Leeds-built Manning Wardle 0-6-0ST No. 1210 of 1891 *Sir Berkeley* had worked for contractors on the building of much of what became the Great Central Railway.

It was supplied new to Logan & Hemingway, a firm of engineering contractors which, during the latter half of the 19th century and the first third of the 20th century worked mainly on railway and associated constructions.

It became No. 30 in the company's fleet and was used to help build the Manchester, Sheffield & Lincolnshire Railway (which became the GCR). It also worked on the excavation of the Nottingham GCR/GNR joint station site that became Nottingham Victoria.

Rationalisation of the firm's fleet saw it become No. 10. More GCR work followed: Wath Concentration Sidings (1905-07) and the Doncaster Avoiding Line (1908-09), Frodingham Viaduct infilling, then the Keadby Deviation Line construction (both 1910-15).

No. 10 was next used at Thoresby Colliery in Nottinghamshire branch line construction in 1925-26, the Crofton Tunnel widening at Barnt Green near Birmingham for the LMS in 1926-27 and the Hattersley Widening between Mottram and Godley Junction (east of Manchester) for the LNER. In 1930 No. 10 undertook its last railway contract; the GWR Westbury and Frome cut-offs.

In 1935 Logan & Hemingway went into liquidation and the locomotive was sold to the Cranford Ironstone Company of Kettering where it received the nameplate *Sir Berkeley* from a scrapped Manning Wardle engine. At Cranford it hauled short rakes of loaded ore wagons from the quarry face to the storage sidings, or from there up an incline to the LMS

Manning Wardle 0-6-0ST *Sir Berkeley* was used on many railway construction projects including the Manchester, Sheffield & Lincolnshire Railway, later the Great Central. Current owner the Vintage Carriages Trust has loaned it to the Middleton Railway. VINTAGE CARRIAGES TRUST

interchange sidings. Between 1943 and 1947 it was loaned to the Pilton Quarry in Rutland.

During 1957, *Sir Berkeley* underwent a complete renovation, during which the original weatherboard was replaced by an open-backed cab. It also had a Wakefield mechanical lubricator fitted, a new sheet-steel sandbox was fitted on the right-hand side and the original wooden dumb-buffers were removed.

At the end of 1957 Cranford Ironstone acquired a Hudswell Clarke 0-6-0ST to replace *Sir Berkeley*, after which it saw scant use. It was moved to associated Byfield Quarries in 1959, and worked there for a year. It then spent two years in a siding before formal retirement in 1963, and the

following year, it was saved from the scrapman after being bought in the nick of time by enthusiast Roger Crombleholme.

At the KWVR, the original weatherboard was refitted, having been found at Cranford.

When its boiler ticket ran out, it was sold to the Vintage Carriages Trust, which eventually restored it. Running again, it toured heritage railways throughout Britain and even visited the Dutch National Railway Museum and the Middleton Railway at Leeds, which is its present location.

The engine was repainted in early 1998 to a light apple green livery, similar to the one it carried at the Cranford Ironstone Quarry.

Sir Berkeley's 10-year boiler certificate ran out in 2001. With the help of

£50,000 Heritage Lottery funding and donations from hundreds of individuals, a new boiler was built by Israel Newton of Bradford and *Sir Berkeley* returned to service at the Middleton Railway on April 14, 2007. Too small for regular KWVR traffic, it remains there.

To mark the 50th anniversary of the arrival of the first two coaches on the KWVR in 1965, on January 10, 2015, *Sir Berkeley* headed three Ingrow-to-Keighley specials comprising those vehicles. They were 1876-built Manchester, Sheffield & Lincolnshire Railway tri-composite carriage No. 176 and 1924-built Southern Railway brake corridor third No. 3554 (built in July 1924 by the Metropolitan Carriage, Wagon & Finance Company for the Southern Railway).

LYR 0-6-0 No. 957 stored in Keighley carriage sidings with the Midland six-wheeled coach on March 6, 1965. IAN HOLT

BELOW: LNER B1 4-6-0 No. 61151 is seen bringing Midland Railway six-wheeled coaches, Nos. 957 and 4744 to the railway on February 26, 1965. The photograph was taken from Guiseley Junction signalbox and clearly shows the former Great Northern line from Shipley (Windhill) climbing away from and diverging from the Midland line. ROBIN LUSH

THE GREEN DRAGON

Lancashire & Yorkshire Railway 0-6-0 No. 957 was brought to the branch behind B1 4-6-0 No. 61151, on February 26, 1965. Sadly, the B1 did not make it into preservation, but Great Northern Railway N2 0-6-2T No. 4744 and the Midland Railway six-wheel coach, which were also part of the consist, did.

Designed by W Barton Wright as the standard goods locomotive for the LYR in 1876, the class eventually numbered 280 examples.

No. 957 was one of the final batch of 50 examples and left the Beyer Peacock works in Manchester in 1887.

Taken into LMS stock at the Grouping, when it was based at Goole shed, it was renumbered 12044 and became No. 52044 at Nationalisation. It survived until withdrawal from British Railways' service at Wakefield in May 1959.

Enthusiast Tony Cox followed in the footsteps of Cpt Smith and bought it straight out of BR service. At first he kept it kept at Retford, but when he became secretary of the Keighley & Worth Valley Railway he relocated it there.

Within a few years, it would acquire world fame with the fictitious name *The Green Dragon*, but more of that later.

It was taken out of traffic in 1975 and remained sidelined on static display in Oxenhope museum until a bequest came to the locomotive's rescue.

Now owned by the Bowers 957 Trust, the locomotive returned to full working order in 2002 following a $150,000 overhaul, which saw it repainted into BR black as No. 52044, before reverting to its LYR livery two years later.

On withdrawal at the expiration of its boiler certificate in January 2013, No. 957 went back on static display at Oxenhope before being moved to Haworth in July 2016. At the time of writing, its latest overhaul was underway.

USA 'dock tank' No. 30072 shunting at Guildford yard in May 1963. HUGH LLEWELLYN*

USA 'dock tank' No. 30072 in Haworth loop on February 25, 1968. IAN HOLT

YANKEE SWITCHER

One of the most eye-catching locomotives on the embryonic KWVR came from "across the Pond".

Carrying No. 72 in the KWVR fleet, it was a S100 class 0-6-0T built for the United States Army Transportation for use in the Second World War.

Designed by Col Howard G Hill in 1942, a total of 382 were turned out by a series of manufacturers in the USA.

Painted USATC black with white numbering and lettering 'Transportation Dept' on the tank sides, they arrived in the UK in 1943 in anticipation of D-Day, after which most were shipped to the continent.

A few remained in store at Newbury racecourse having seen little use. Like other Big Four companies, the Southern Railway found itself short of locomotives after years of wartime austerity and sought to replace its E1, B4 and D1 tanks used in Southampton Docks.

The locomotives needed to have a short wheelbase to negotiate the tight curves found in the dockyard, but also be able to haul heavy freight trains as well as full-length passenger trains in the harbour area.

SR Chief Mechanical Engineer Oliver Bulleid ran the rule over the S100s, and recommended that 14 were bought, plus another one for spares. Other S100s went to the National Coal Board, the Longmoor Military Railway and Austin Motors.

Of the 15 acquired by the Southern Railway, 13 were built at the Vulcan Iron Works in Wilkes-Barre, Pennsylvania in 1942, with the other two coming from HK Porter of Pittsburgh.

Once in Southern hands, they were fitted with steam heating, vacuum ejectors, sliding cab windows, additional lamp irons and new cylinder drain cocks.

Further modifications became necessary once the locomotives started to enter traffic, including large roof-top ventilators, British-style regulators (as built they had US-style pull-out ones), three rectangular cab-front lookout windows, extended coal bunkers, separate steam and vacuum brake controls and wooden tip-up seats.

Radios were later installed on the footplate to improve communication on the vast network of sidings at Southampton.

It took until November 1947 for the entire new class – which became known as 'Yankee tanks' – to be ready for work.

Before Nationalisation, the locomotives were painted in Southern black livery with the word Southern in sunshine yellow lettering. The lettering on the tank sides was changed to British Railways during 1948 as a transitional measure. Finally, class members were painted in BR departmental malachite livery, with BR crests on the tank sides and numbers on the cabsides.

Thirteen of the locomotives were renumbered in a single sequence from 61-73 by the Southern Railway but No. 4326 retained its earlier War Department number instead of being renumbered 74. The locomotive used for spares was not numbered.

After 1948 they were renumbered 30061-30074 by BR. Six examples were transferred to Departmental use in 1962-63 and renumbered DS233-DS238.

They were used for shunting in Southampton Docks for 15 years and as such were usually referred to as 'dock tanks'. They were powerful, economical to operate and at first relatively easy to maintain. However, because they were basic machines turned out as cheaply as possible during the years of wartime austerity, age took its toll more quickly than might be expected.

Their steel fireboxes rusted and fatigued quickly and by 1951 several

USA 0-6-0T No. 72/30072, long owned by Richard Greenwood and an icon of the Keighley & Worth Valley Railway, was transferred to the Ribble Steam Railway for restoration after being been sold to Andy Booth, who has a fleet of hire locomotives. It is pictured inside the KWVR's Oxenhope museum before its move to Lancashire. ROBIN JONES

needed new ones. At the docks, they were replaced with British Rail Class 07 diesel-electric shunters, in 1962, when the first member of the class was withdrawn. Nine examples remained in service until March 1967 and five of these survived until the end of steam on the Southern Region that year.

Examples of the class were the last locomotives in steam on the Southern Region. Although the official date for the end of Southern steam is given as July 9, 1967, two S100s soldiered on until September that year in use at Ashford wagon works.

The Kent & East Sussex Railway bought Nos 30065/DS237 and 30070/DS238, which had got no further than Tonbridge on their way to Woodhams Bros' scrapyard because of a number of axleboxes that had run hot. They remained on the site of the former locomotive shed until resold to the KESR in August 1968. Two others survive: No. 30064 and 30072. Both were moved to Salisbury. No. 30064 was purchased by the Southern Loco Preservation Co Ltd and now resides on the Bluebell Railway, while No. 30072 was bought by Richard Greenwood for use on the KWVR. No. 30072 eventually arrived at Ingrow after a rather eventful journey by road from Salisbury in early 1968.

Many were bought by the railways of countries in which they served following D-Day, joining locomotive fleets of railways in France, Greece, Hungary, Turkey, Czechoslovakia, Yugoslavia and Iraq. Around 100 were bought by China and two ended up in Israel. The KWVR example was manufacturer's number 4446 of 1943, and also carried the number 72 in Southern service, working at Southampton docks, and No. 30072 in BR service.

It was Guilford Shed pilot from the mid-1960s until July 9, 1967 when it made the journey to Salisbury light engine. In August 2015, the locomotive was bought by Andy Booth, who also owns Lancashire & Yorkshire Class 27 No. 1300. It's currently at the Ribble Steam Railway, and once completed, Andy has said he intends for it to return to the KWVR on loan.

UNIQUE 'HOME-GROWN' SURVIVOR

Bellerophon hauls a passenger train on the snow-covered Foxfield Railway, in December 2009.

Built in 1874, Haydock Foundry 0-6-0 well tank *Bellerophon* screams Victorian magnificencefrom every orifice.

One of the oldest working steam engines in the world, it was one of six almost identical locomotives built for the Haydock Collieries around St Helens between 1868-87, and is also the sole survivor. Unusually for the time the locomotives had outside motion with a further revolutionary aspect being the use of piston valves, nearly two decades before the Stephenson/Gooch type of valve gear is generally recognised as being in use.

The Haydock collieries and foundries' individual sites were all interconnected by 60 miles of private railways with links to the London & North Western Railway and the Liverpool & Manchester Railway. Locomotives were needed to haul heavy trains over severe gradients.

Engineer Josiah Evans, a member of the family who owned the complex, made the foundry capable of supplying the needs of the colliery and its rail network. It was he who came up with the idea of a 'home-grown' locomotive fleet.

Bellerophon made two daily runs alternately between Haydock and Northwich and Golborne and Edge Green collieries and the Haydock shunting yards. Both of these involved running over main lines, the West Coast Main line between Earlstown and the Evans' private coal yard at Warrington. This arrangement continued right up to Nationalisation in 1947.

In the 1880s it was fitted with a cab, and used alongside Lancashire & Yorkshire Railway locomotives to haul the firm's annual trips to Blackpool for its workers and their families.

Bellerophon and its sisters *Amazon, Golborne, Hercules, Makerfield* and *Parr* proved superbly reliable machines. *Amazon* was withdrawn in 1935 but the other five made it to Nationalisation and National Coal Board ownership.

In 1957 *Bellerophon* received its last overhaul at Haydock but it continued to operate until 1964. The longest survivor of the six, it was last employed at Lea Green Colliery, which closed that year.

Earmarked for scrapping, the NCB offered it to Liverpool City Museum,

but there was no space and turned it down. After several enquiries by the KWVR, the NCB agreed to donate the locomotive to the railway provided that the railway remove the locomotive from the site at Lea Green colliery at no cost to the board. Another gem to the KWVR's growing fleet. However, it was not considered to be of much use to the revivalists because of its limited capabilities, and run-down mechanical condition. November 1966 saw it placed on static display in Haworth Yard where it did receive some cosmetic attention. In 1981 *Bellerophon* was bought from the KWVR for a nominal £1 by the Vintage Carriages Trust and restoration work commenced.

As work progressed it was found that the locomotive was worn out, but a small restoration team soldiered on, with the help of a 50% grant from the Science Museum towards the cost.

It was steamed for the first time in preservation on May 1, 1985. On October 5 that year, it hauled its first passenger train and it was officially renamed in a ceremony that December.

In 1986, *Bellerophon* won the NCB's Steam Heritage Award, and three years later, carried off the Institution of Mechanical Engineers' Heritage Hallmark Award.

Since its restoration, it has worked on both the KWVR (off-peak services) and other heritage lines, and has also visited Belgium and The Netherlands.

Bellerophon is considered too small for regular KWVR work, and so the VCT has placed it on long-term loan to Staffordshire's Foxfield Railway, where it can be seen in an authentic industrial railway environment. One of its first visits elsewhere in 2018 was to the Severn Valley Railway for its March 16-18 spring steam gala.

Haydock Foundry 0-6-0WT *Bellerophon* leaves Lea Green Colliery at St Helens on November 4, 1966.

The smoke and steam emitting from the boiler of No. 41241 in the yard at Bridgnorth on December 3, 2016, is a sure sign that it is close to being ready for return to Haworth and reuniting with its bottom half, so it can be completed in time for it to take part in the KWVR's 50th anniversary celebrations in 2018. PAUL APPLETON

AN IDEAL WORTH VALLEY BRANCH LOCOMOTIVE

March 1967 saw the arrival of a locomotive that was historically appropriate for the branch, in the form of LMS-designed light passenger 2-6-2T No. 41241.

Although built in the Crewe workshops of the former LMS to H G Ivatt's design, No. 41241 was one of 100 constructed by British Railways, after the Nationalisation of the railways in 1948. This batch was followed by a run of 30 locomotives, the 84000 class, which were built to a very similar design. Many examples of both classes were motor-fitted for push-pull working, and the type worked over the Worth Valley branch until June 1960 when they were replaced by diesel railcars.

No. 41241's first allocation was Bath Green Park, and it subsequently served at Bristol Barrow Road, Wellington in Shropshire, Leamington Spa, Bangor, Croes Newydd and Llandudno Junction. before finally ending its BR days at Skipton.

No. 41241 was purchased by two pioneering members of the KWVR, Ron Ainsworth and W H Foster directly from British Railways shortly before the closure of Skipton shed, with ownership eventually passing to The Society in the early Seventies.

This locomotive, although it was never motor-fitted, possibly represents the most typical branch-line engine of all KWVR stock, making it ideal motive power for the heritage railway. When the engine arrived on the Worth Valley the owners decided that it was to be painted maroon, reflecting the colour of the company for which the type was

originally designed. It also represented the KWVR at the 150th anniversary of the opening of the Stockton & Darlington Railway in Durham in 1975. Following a later full overhaul, No. 41241 was re-painted in authentic BR lined black, that being the only livery the engine carried while in everyday service with British Railways.

It was withdrawn from traffic when its 10-year boiler certificate expired in 1988, and was placed on display in the museum at Oxenhope for a few years before another full overhaul was undertaken by a combination of volunteers and contractors. Upon expiry of that 10-year boiler ticket, the society decided that it would like to have No.

41241 overhauled and running for the 50th anniversary of the heritage line's first public trains in 2018. It was known that No. 41241's boiler would require a new copper inner firebox, a public appeal was launched to attempt to raise sufficient funds to cover the cost of the overhaul. The contract for the overhaul of the boiler was awarded to the Severn Valley Railway, which completed the work in late 2017. Having passed its hydraulic test, a fire was lit and the boiler steam tested in the first week of December in the yard at Bridgnorth, with the overhauled boiler mounted on the SVR's 'boiler test' well wagon. The boiler was then returned to the KWVR, for the final assembly of the locomotive.

Ivatt 2-6-2T No. 41241 hauling a works train at Oakworth bottom point on March 25, 1967. IAN HOLT

GRESLEY'S LAST TANK ENGINE

Mention the name Sir Nigel Gresley, and you immediately think of the magnificent A3 and A4 Pacifics that once ruled the East Coast Main Line. However, he also designed smaller classes – but only one of his tank engines survives.

The Great Northern Railway N2 0-6-2T was introduced in 1920. Further batches were built by the LNER from 1925. Some locomotives were fitted with condensing apparatus for working on the Metropolitan Railway Widened Lines between King's Cross and Moorgate.

No. 4744, which was built by the North British Locomotive Company in Glasgow in 1920, entered traffic in February 1921 as No. 4744, and in 1949 became No. 69523.

It was based at King's Cross from 1921 until May 1962, and was reallocated to Peterborough New England shed, from where it was withdrawn on September 16, 1962.

It was purchased for preservation by the Gresley Society in October 1963, and moved from Doncaster Works to Harworth Colliery in Bassetlaw for storage.

After steaming at the colliery, it was moved to the KWVR, on February 25, 1965. However, after running in traffic for several years, a boiler tube failure necessitated considerable boiler work.

BELOW: Former Worth Valley engine GNR N2 No. 1744 takes on water at Loughborough on the Great Central Railway on May 11, 2014. ROBIN JONES

GNR N2 0-6-2T No. 4744 at Oxenhope undertaking stock movements on March 19, 1966. IAN HOLT

The Loughborough-based Main Line Steam Trust eventually offered to do the job as the N2 was ideal for the Great Central Railway, and the locomotive moved to Quorn & Woodhouse on November 21, 1975. It entered GCR traffic on April 16, 1994.

It is now based on the North Norfolk Railway, where it is earmarked for future running over the main line into Cromer once the mandatory equipment is fitted.

Joem climbs up to Beck Hole on the North Yorkshire Moors Railway on May 5, 2013. PHILIP BENHAM

A MOONLIT FLIT DOWN THE EAST COAST MAIN LINE

The smallest of today's North Eastern Locomotive Preservation Group steam fleet but by no means any the less popular is J72 0-6-0T No. 69023, which was the given the name *Joem* when it began its heritage-era career on the KWVR.

The J72 class is particularly remarkable in that it was designed by William Worsdell for the NER with the first examples appearing as the E1 class in 1898, yet they were still being built by British Railways in 1952. *Joem* is the sole survivor.

The first batch of engines was built at Darlington North Road Works by 1899.

Nigel Gresley reclassified the engines as J72s and had a further batch built at Doncaster in 1925. British Railways had more built at Darlington, 20 in 1949 and eight in 1951, bringing the total to 113. The last batch were nearly identical to the originals but had a vacuum brake, steam heating and sanding gear to allow them to be used on empty passenger stock workings.

They were used in shunting yards, docks and coal staithes and on station pilot workings all over the North East. Again somewhat remarkably, all 113 remained in service until 1958, when they began to be replaced by diesel shunters.

Only two had not been scrapped by 1964. These were Nos. 69005 and 69023, which were taken into Departmental Stock as No. 58 and No. 59 and used at North Blyth and Heaton for de-icing. No. 69005 was scrapped but No. 69023 became the only survivor when it was purchased by enthusiast Ronald Ainsworth for preservation, and moved from Holbeck shed to the Keighley & Worth Valley Railway on October 16, 1966.

Three days earlier, in the middle of the night, it was driven down the East Coast Main Line through Newcastle, Durham, Darlington, York and on to the shed. This 'moonlit flit' was the longest journey that the little engine would ever have made, and British Railways' staff had even made up a wooden extension to the coal rails to increase the capacity.

At Keighley, it was professionally repainted in NER livery, and named *Joem*. The key to the name was once carried on a small brass plate on the cabside which read: "This locomotive, *Joem*, is preserved in memory of Joseph S Ainsworth (50 years LNWR), his wife Emmeline, by their son Ronald". The first two letters of Ronald's parents' names make up the name *Joem*.

BR-built J72 No. 69023 *Joem* heads a branch centenary special at Ingrow on April 4, 1967. IAN HOLT

Small locomotive timetable trials on April 21, 1968, saw industrials Nos. 1999 and 2226 leaving Keighley. IAN HOLT

On the KWVR, *Joem* was used on Santa specials and other duties between 1968 and 1970. *Joem* left the KWVR in the early 1970s for other railways.

It was sold in 1977 to the Derwent Valley Light Railway at York. There, after several years of inactivity, it was retubed and used to start up a new steam passenger service on this private line.

It was even passed for main line running for scenes in Harrogate station in the film, Agatha, starring Dustin Hoffman and Vanessa Redgrave.

However, the Derwent Valley Light Railway, which had been built for carrying agricultural produce, wanted to close its line and sell off the land for development. The former owner's son Paul Ainsworth exercised the family's

option to buy back the J72 and moved it to the National Railway Museum for storage before the sale.

It was offered for sale by Sotheby's in London on December 4, 1981, but failed to reach the reserve price of £25,000. It seemed that heritage railways were deterred by its limited haulage capacity.

NELPG officials then met Paul Ainsworth and negotiated the sale price down to £10,250. The sale was completed on November 20, 1982, after which it moved to the North Yorkshire Moors Railway in January 1983 and was steamed within four months.

Since then, *Joem* has undergone two overhauls and visited many other railways. NELPG hires it out because it is too small for NYMR services at peak periods.

In the early years of the KWVR small locos such as No. 31, No. 67 and *Joem* did a fair amount of passenger mileage either on their own or double-headed. For many years a steam service wasn't run during the winter, just the Santa services in December and a shuttle service between Oxenhope and Haworth, where these small locos were usually rostered with a couple of coaches.

Even No. 1999 undertook some, but not many, of these services, but only with a single coach. No. 31 and *Joem* often doubleheaded on some full line services.

Manchester Ship Canal Hudswell Clarke 0-6-0T No. 67 in the rain at the Middleton Railway in June 2007. THOMAS H TAYLOR*

INDUSTRIAL TANKS AS 'STEPPING STONES'

Many of today's standard gauge heritage lines began their steam operations using industrial locomotives that were historically inappropriate for a main line setting, while waiting for bigger former BR and Big Four engines to be ready.

Peckett 0-4-0ST No. 1999 of 1941 was built for the Southport Gas Company. Midland Railway livery was specified by the customer, together with the Southport Corporation Crest.

In 1958, No. 1999 was transferred to Darwen Gas Works where it worked until it was replaced by a diesel locomotive in 1963. After lying derelict for three years in an open siding, it was acquired by the KWVR in September 1966 for a nominal sum and moved to Haworth where it was restored to working order.

However, its small size limited its use for passenger traffic on the line, and so it was loaned to the now-closed Steamport Museum at Southport. It ran there in the Seventies and Eighties, and in March 1999, it was bought from the KWVR by the Ribble Steam Railway where it is now based.

Barclay No. 2226 of 1946 went new to ICI Dyestuffs in Huddersfield, where it operated trip workings through its extensive network of sidings. One of the last steam locomotives to work there, it was donated by ICI Huddersfield to the KWVR in early 1968.

It doubled-headed with 1999 on one round trip during the timetable trails on April 21,1968, but as public demand for seats boomed and trains became longer, and bigger engines were available, it saw limited use.

Its boiler ticket having expired, it became an exhibit in Oxenhope Museum until it was sold by the KWVR and spent many years as a focal point for the picnic

Manchester Ship Canal No. 31 at Haworth shed on August 27, 1967. Behind it are No. 69023 *Joem* and No. 1247. IAN HOLT

area at Brookside Garden Centre at Poynton near Stockport.

In 2015, it was sold again, this time to Rob Alcock, a volunteer at the Churnet Valley Railway's Cheddleton motive power depot. Once restored, it is planned to use it as the Cheddleton station pilot.

The KWVR also took delivery of two Hudswell Clarke 0-6-0Ts built for the Manchester Ship canal's extensive railway network, the largest privately owned system in Britain, with more than 200 track miles and 70 steam engines on its books on 1959.

No. 31 is a version with short side tanks built in 1903 and arrived on the Worth Valley June 17, 1967, having been purchased by Richard Greenwood. It was fitted with vacuum brake equipment to allow it to work passenger services along with steam-heating equipment to allow for winter duties. However, owing to the gradients on the branch, the engine was usually limited to two or three coaches and as traffic increased, No. 31 was considered more of an off-peak season locomotive. Eventually the condition of the steel inner firebox dictated its withdrawal and it now resides in the museum at Oxenhope.

The locomotive was originally named *Hamburg*, but the nameplates were removed after dockers in Salford demonstrated against the Germans at the outbreak of the First World War in 1914. The name was reinstated in preservation.

No. 67, one of the Hudswell Clarke 'long tanks' with greater water capacity, was bought by Dr J G Blears. No. 67 arrived on the KWVR in the autumn of 1969 having been stored on the Manchester Ship Canal railway system since withdrawal. It was employed, along with No. 51218 on September 14, 1969 on a rail tour to commemorate the 75th anniversary of the opening of the Manchester Ship Canal. As with No. 31, it saw limited use on the KWVR. In mid-1990s No. 67 was moved to the Middleton Railway where it was restored to working order. It was later donated to the Middleton Railway after being returned to traffic in 2002 following reboring of its cylinders and work on the boiler. It is currently non-operational following the expiration of its boiler ticket on New Year's Day 2012, being displayed in the museum there.

Weighing just 15½ tons, the smallest locomotive on the KWVR is Hudswell Clarke 0-4-0ST No. 403 of 1893 *Lord Mayor*, which was built for Salford contractor Edward Nuttall. The railway projects on which it worked included the building of the GWR's Castle Cary line and the dismantling of the Liverpool Overhead Railway.

Its working life ended with George Cohen at Stanningley near Leeds. The firm donated it to the Lord Mayor Trust and it was restored to working order by enthusiast Ben Wade after it came to Haworth in 1968. It was a static exhibit at Shildon Works during the August 1975 celebrations to mark the 150th anniversary of the Stockton & Darlington Railway. On the KWVR, *Lord Mayor* has been steamed occasionally for special events. It is now owned by the Vintage Carriages Trust and is kept in its museum at Ingrow West.

A typical contractor's locomotive, Hudswell Clarke 0-4-0ST *Lord Mayor* is the sole-surviving engine from the curious standard gauge military Spurn Head Railway, built as part of First World War coastal defences and used until the early 1950s. One of three saddle tanks used to build the line, Lord Mayor, survived into preservation, and is now part of the Vintage Carriages Trust collection at the Museum of Rail Travel at Ingrow.

Chapter 6

THE REINVENTION OF
CHRISTMAS

The Santa Special has long been entrenched as part of the modern British Christmas, with virtually every heritage railway running a festive season timetable to entice families. Indeed, receipts from trains taking happy youngsters to see Father Christmas in his grotto today provide a vital financial lifeline for the upkeep of many lines. Yet where and when did they start….?

The first Santa Special may be deemed to have been run in 1949, two years before the railway preservation movement began with the volunteer-led Talyllyn takeover.

It was then that the Fairbourne Railway began running a Christmas train for the pupils at the village school in Beach Road.

Each year John Wilkins erected a large illuminated Christmas tree at Fairbourne, while the bodyshell of Lister locomotive *Gwril* would be removed

and turned into a reindeer. A moth-eaten stag's head from the Fairbourne Hotel was fixed to the front of the grille, and a bearskin rug used to cover the engine. Father Christmas rode on a flat truck suitably decorated for the occasion.

The last such Christmas special ran on the line in 1967, just before the school closed. However, the Fairbourne Santa train was very much a little local affair, far from the gaze of both the summer holidaymakers who visited the Welsh coast and the rest of Britain.

In terms of standard gauge Santa trains, it was the Keighley & Worth Valley Railway that ran the first, and in doing so pioneered a major slice of the heritage sector's annual business.

On December 18, 1965, Santa Claus made his first visit to the Worth Valley branch.

Leaving his reindeer and sleigh at the North Pole, he made his way to Haworth station in the cab of Lancashire & Yorkshire Railway 'Pug' 0-4-0ST No. 51218.

LEFT: The first Santa train in the pouring rain at Haworth. Lancashire & Yorkshire Railway 'Pug' 0-4-0ST No. 51218 left Haworth yard. The public were not allowed to ride on the trains to travel to see Santa, so he had to come to them!

It was the railway's then chairman, Bob Cryer, who dreamed up the idea, his wife Ann later recalled.

She reminisced: "Bob's mother Gladys Evelyn Cryer, a highly skilled tailoress, made the Father Christmas coat, and thinks that later she made a second one for the two-train operation."

The following year, the Santa special was run on Saturday, December 17, the train consisting of prototype English Electric diesel D0226, two coaches with *Joem* running down the branch, ostensibly looking for track workers. Suddenly, a bearded, white-haired old gentleman, dressed in a long red cloak appeared in one of the open coach windows.

He told the train crew that his name was Santa Claus, said he wanted to get to Oakworth station as quickly as possible, in order to keep some secret appointment there.

Staff sought the advice of Bob Cryer, who had mysteriously vanished from the train between Haworth and Ingrow, Nowhere to be seen, the crew decided to do what the old gentleman wanted.

The train had no sooner left Ingrow and cleared the tunnel, when the brakes were applied: Father Christmas wanted to realise his boyhood dream and ride on the footplate.

While stopping a train in such a manner was a serious matter, and would normally incur a £25 fine, as it was near Christmas and the season of goodwill to all men, he was allowed on to the footplate of *Joem*.

He declined the offer of entering the cab down the chimney, but instead climbed up the cab steps.

The train set off again and proceeded to Oakworth station, where a crowd of children were eagerly waiting to meet Santa Claus, who had entrenched himself in the guard's van, where a selection of gaily coloured packages had mysteriously appeared.

He proceeded to distribute them, with seasonal greetings and goodwill to the citizens of Oakworth. After that stop, the train crew, who had refreshed themselves with tea in the buffet car, set off for the next stop, Haworth.

Approaching Haworth the red-coated gentleman decided he would like to operate the whistle. Crowds were waiting to greet him here too, but one or two youngsters asked if his beard was real or made of plastic.

During an hour's stop, *Joem* was re-watered in the good shed, and the train set off for Oxenhope.

Sadly, the weather on those wild and windy moors took a turn for the worse, and only a handful of people were waiting on the terminus platform.

D0226 was uncoupled and *Joem* ran-round the train and then drew it back to Haworth. When it reached the village station, Father Christmas was found to have vanished. At the same time, Bob Cryer reappeared as if by magic.

The chairman refused to say where he had been all afternoon, and the train crew dispersed to the local watering holes to discuss the day's events.

Santa never forgot his rides on the Worth Valley, and made a point of visiting as many heritage railways as possible in the decades to come.

The value of his annual visits to the sector was rarely more apparent than on December 10, 2017, when heavy snowfalls across much of the country led to Santa trains being cancelled.

The Severn Valley Railway had to hand back around £35,000 in refunds to passengers.

Today, it is impossible to count the many, many millions of pounds that have benefitted thee sector over more than half a century since that first standard gauge 'Santa' courtesy of the 'Pug'.

A simple idea revolutionised the preservation movement by time – and it all started at Haworth – even before the railway began running trains for the general public. A milestone indeed. But much, much more was around the corner!

BR Class J72 0-60T No. 69023 *Joem* heads a Santa train through a snow-clad Worth Valley in December 1967. KEN ROBERTS

Chapter 7

THE DAY THE
TRAINS
CAME BACK

"Oh to be a football fan on FA Cup final day" ran the old saying.
However, on Saturday, June 29, 1968, it was "Oh to be a railway enthusiast
– or a local resident – on the day the Worth Valley branch was reopened."
It may be a short line, but the six years of hard slog to restore services to
the branch was not only an achievement in itself, but the reopening day
marked a seminal moment in the history of UK transport heritage.

A defining moment in the history of railway heritage: Ivatt 2MT 2-6-2T No. 41241 pilots USA 0-6-0T No. 72 across Mytholmes Viaduct with the reopening special on June 29, 1968. JOHN SCAFE

In its bespoke Keighley & Worth Valley Railway maroon livery, Ivatt 2MT 2-6-2T No. 41241 heads the reopening special as crowds pack the platforms at Oxenhope. M CHAPMAN/COLOUR-RAIL

Keighley mayor Alderman James Waterworth cutting the ribbon before the departure of the reopening special from the town's station to Oxenhope. KWVR

At the end of the aforementioned visit of Col J R H Robertson on June 8, 1968, during which he carried out detailed inspections of the track, locomotives and rolling stock, he told delighted KWVR Preservation Society officials that he was prepared to recommend that the railway be given the green light to open for passenger traffic.

However, he stipulated that a number of conditions must be met first, the most important of which was the production of the public liability policy, which he was shown only in draft form.

He also insisted on the placing of a padlock on Oxenhope platform gate and the erection of a notice at the station warning goods trains to pin down brakes.

The date was quickly set for reopening, on June 29, and for the volunteers who had toiled for this moment for so long, one last big push was needed in the three weeks that lay ahead.

The opening day was barely a month after the British Railways Board (Keighley and Worth Valley) Light Railway (Transfer) Order 1968 had come into force on May 27, and the volunteers were raring to go.

Already, a draft timetable, which had taken months to prepare, had undergone trial runs, on April 21, when the proposed Saturday service was run.

The timings allowed 25 minutes for each journey with turn-round times at Oxenhope of around 15 minutes and at Keighley of 25 minutes.

For those early-spring trials, diesel railbus M79964M was used on the 8.30am from Oxenhope trip, while the 10.05am was worked by the prototype

English Electric diesel electric D0226 and four coaches that formed the rest of the trains for the day.

Ivatt 2-62T No. 41241 worked the next two trips and showed its outstanding capabilities to work the line. Then came the 3.20pm trip with the same four coaches, hauled by Barclay No. 2226 and Peckett No. 1999. However, both locomotives sustained overheated bearings and had to be driven more easily meaning that Oxenhope was reached a little late.

No. 41241 took over again for what was to be the last trip of the day where a 10-min late departure from Oxenhope was turned into a punctual arrival back.

Society officials had toyed with the idea of having a major personality to reopen the line.

And who better (or maybe worse, depending on your standpoint) to ask than the axeman himself, British Railways chairman Dr Richard Beeching, who had closed so much of Britain's railway network.

An approach was made to Dr Beeching to perform the ceremony, but he refused. Indeed, his presence may well have driven a wedge between the society and the otherwise potentially supportive mass of railway employees who had cause to resent his actions. However, he was not averse to railway revival schemes, and the following year, Dr Beeching did perform the reopening of the section of the GWR Ashburton branch, which had been restored by the Dart Valley Railway.

Labour's former transport minister Barbara Castle was also asked to perform the opening ceremony, but

A modest handwritten poster on Platform 4 at Keighley announces the reopening of the branch to Oxenhope. KWVR

ALSO MAKING THE NEWS IN JUNE 1968

▶ West Bromwich Albion and Everton played in the FA cup final at Wembley. West Brom won by a single goal, scored by Jeff Astle.

▶ The same day, US author, political activist, and lecturer Helen Keller, the first deaf-blind person to earn a BA degree, died at the age of 87.

▶ The late Sixties were the time of student protests, and in communist Yugoslavia, police intervened in protests in Belgrade, before President Josip Tito conceded some of the protesters' demands.

▶ Artist Andy Warhol survived an assassination attempt on June 3 when feminist campaigner Valerie Solanas burst into his studio and fired a gun, slightly wounding him and art critic Mario Amaya. She then turned herself into police and served a three-year sentence.

▶ On June 5, US politician and presidential candidate Robert F Kennedy, 42, was shot three times by Jordanian activist Sirhan Sirhan. Kennedy died in hospital the following day.

▶ On June 6, English journalist and politician Randolph Churchill, son of Sir Winston Churchill, died from a heart attack.

▶ Female sewing machinists at the Ford assembly plant in Dagenham went on strike on June 7 demanding equal pay with men. The strike set in motion a chain of events that led to the Equal Pay Act 1970.

▶ On June 8, James Earl Ray, 41, was arrested using a false Canadian passport at Heathrow Airport for the murder of black civil rights leader Martin Luther King Jr.

▶ Italy beat Yugoslavia 2-0 in the replay on the European championship final on June 10.

▶ The controversial film Rosemary's Baby, starring Mia Farrow and directed by Roman Polasnki, was premiered on June 12.

▶ The same day, the merger of the Chicago & North Western Railway with the Chicago Great Western Railroad was approved.

▶ June 17 saw Tom Stoppard's play, The Real Inspector Hound starring Richard Briers and Ronnie Barker opens at the Criterion Theatre in London's West End.

▶ On June 23, a stampede at a football match between Boca Juniors and Club Atlético River Plate in Buenos Aires, Argentina, results in 74 deaths.

▶ The next day, Giorgio Rosa declared the independence of the Republic of Rose Island, an artificial island constructed to his own design off Rimini, Italy, consisting of a 4300sq ft platform supported by nine pylons, equipped with a restaurant, bar, nightclub, shop and post office. Italian police quickly took possession.

▶ On June 25, comedian Tony Hancock, 44, killed himself in his Australian flat.

▶ The Bonin Islands, also known as the Ogasawara Islands, were on June 26 returned to Japan after 23 years of occupation by the United States Navy, and Japanese citizens were allowed to return.

▶ On the same day that the KWVR was opening to the public, the Midsummer High Weekend rock concert was held in Hyde Park, London; featuring Pink Floyd, T-Rex, Jethro Tull and Roy Harper. It was the first large free concert ever held in the UK.

the society was told that she would not be available. TV celebrities were also considered, but eventually the revivalists took a traditional approach, and invited the local mayor to do the honours, and Alderman James Waterworth, the mayor of Keighley, readily agreed.

A whirlwind of pre-publicity led society officials quite rightly to expect a bumper crowd for the opening train, and it was decided that six coaches would be needed, with the train double-headed.

Ivatt 2-6-2T No. 41241, resplendent in a LMS maroon livery with the letters KWVR on the tank sides, colours that it would never have carried in pre-preservation days highlighted the legacy of the branch nonetheless it ran with the by-now golden-brown-liveried USA 0-6-0T No. 72. Nowadays, enthusiasts will judge a locomotive and its operator on how historically and authentically it is turned out, whether it is carrying the 'correct' livery and number. However, at the Worth Valley of the late Sixties, there was a touch of 'back to the pre-Grouping era', when Britain's multitude of independent lines had their own distinctive corporate colours.

PREPARING FOR THE BIG DAY

The neck for the run-round loop at Oxenhope was barely adequate for a small tender engine and tests were carried out to ascertain whether Nos. 41241 and 72 could fit in. They did not.

History was made yet again: the branch had to be extended for the first time ever.

Volunteer navvies lifted out the old bufferstops at the end of the line and then quickly laid 4ft of track on the soil beneath. The short extension ensured that with No. 41241 leading, the two locomotives would clear the points to gain access to the run-round loop.

Invitations were despatched to VIP guests and tickets were printed. A special ticket was printed to commemorate the first train.

Several TIM ticket issuing machines were obtained, for once the official opening train had run, service trains would operate every Saturday and Sunday afterwards.

In the week leading up to the big day, society members cleaned coaches inside and out, and made sure that the chosen locomotives were in faultless condition both externally and mechanically.

All of the stations were cleaned and tidied, while old pallets were used to build a small rostrum for the opening speeches at Keighley, with the tape tied to posts at either side.

A PA system was hired, but in the end the lead proved to be too short to reach the front of the train, so those giving speeches had to raise their voices to be heard.

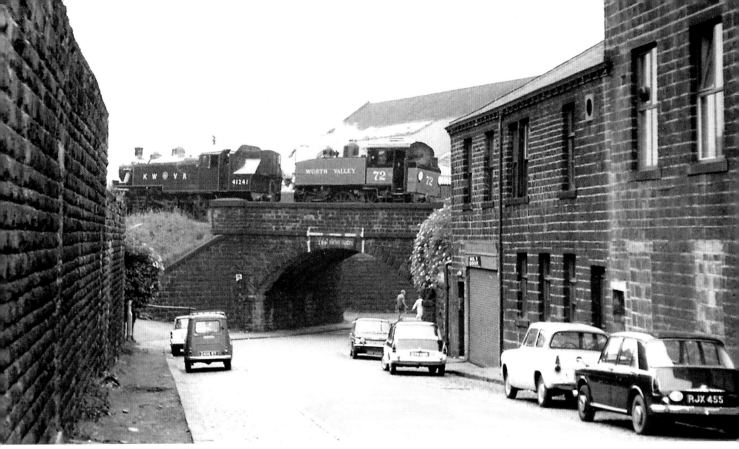

Nos. 41241 and No. 72 dropping back at Keighley on the opening day. IAN HOLT

Meanwhile, out on the main line, British Rail had reached an impasse during a disagreement with trade unions who responded with a work to rule. By the time June 29 came round, British Rail was at a standstill – but no matter – a train was still running at Keighley station!

RIGHT: The stock movement for the opening special passes through Ingrow West, with USA 0-6-0T No. 72 leading. DAVID SMITH

Ivatt 2MT 2-6-2T No. 41241 and USA 0-6-0T No. 72 being prepared for the reopening special in Haworth yard. BERNARD LUMB

THE HERITAGE TRAIN AWAITS!

Both ITV and BBC News turned up for the opening ceremony, which gained extensive coverage in the local and national press.

The rain of the preceding week had let up, flags and bunting fluttered, ladies wore their bright summer outfits and crowds were everywhere. Smoke, steam, loudspeakers, a multitude of cameras, tape recorders, policemen, civic dignitaries and leading society officers, unrecognisable in their suits, white shirts, ties and polished shoes completed the scene.

The train was to run just six weeks before the legendary 'Fifteen Guinea Special' brought the curtain down on British Rail standard gauge steam haulage on August 11. By then, steam had become a rarity in a world dominated by diesels and electrics, and while it brought nostalgia flooding back for many, for the very young in attendance it was an exciting novelty.

The star of the show could not be anything but the train, headed by the two locomotives resplendent in their new 'private owner' liveries.

The six-coach rake included former Southern Railway brake end No. S3554S, the last-surviving example of the South Eastern & Chatham Railway-designed 'matchboards'. Built by the Metropolitan Carriage, Wagon & Finance Company at its Saltley Works in Birmingham in 1924, used on the 'Continental' boat trains between London, Dover and Folkestone, and withdrawn in 1962, it became No. 1 in the KWVR fleet.

Sightseers gather at Low Mill Lane to watch the departure from Keighley of the reopening special. Dignitaries stand on the front of Ivatt 2-6-2T No. 41241 before its departure. ROGER DERWENT

This vehicle had been given a second chance to feature in a reopening train, having been acquired by a group aiming to revive Kent's Westerham Valley branch, which at 4½ miles was slightly shorter than the Worth Valley line.

In 1962, the Westerham Valley Railway Association, the result of a merger between the Westerham Branch Railway Passengers' Association and the Westerham Valley Railway Society, made plans to reopen the branch, which had closed on October 28, 1961.

The plan was to use volunteers to run it as a commuter line on weekdays and as a heritage railway at weekends between April and October. British

Railways offered the ownership of that line for £30,000 on the basis that a commuter service would be provided.

However, the scheme eventually failed in November 1964 when the association could not find the money to pay for a new bridge over the line to carry the Sevenoaks bypass.

In autumn 1965, the Westerham association merged with the Kent & East Sussex Railway Preservation Society, and much of the stock it had amassed was sold elsewhere. By March 1967 the track had been lifted and Westerham station demolished. Part of the M25 was built over the trackbed between 1976-79. Also in that historic KWVR first train

Health and safety officials would have kittens at a scene like this today. Crowds surround the opening train as it awaits departure at Keighley. IAN HOLT

The reopening special at busy Oakworth station. ARTHUR R WILSON

were two of three Metropolitan Railway 'Dreadnought' coaches also acquired from the failed Westerham scheme, which had become KWVR Nos. 2-4. These high-capacity suburban coaches were used by commuters from Aylesbury and north-west London suburbs until they were withdrawn in the mid-Sixties. Originally numbered 465, 509 and 427 respectively, they were built by the Metropolitan Carriage, Wagon & Finance Company, in 1919, 1923 and 1910.

The same firm also constructed one of the two Pullmans used on the special, first-class parlour car *Zena*, a veteran of the GWR 'Torquay Pullman Limited' express in 1923. The other, *Lorna*, was a third-class Pullman car built by the Birmingham Railway Carriage & Wagon Company Ltd in Smethwick in 1930. Ron Ainsworth negotiated with British Railways for the railway to acquire 45212 after a dozen members made generous interest-free loans. The real Pullman *Lorna* had been built for the Brighton Line electrification project and in 1932 and was later scrapped.

The sixth vehicle in the special was LMS third-class nine-compartment No. M12066M, which became KWVR No.6. Built at Wolverton Carriage Works in 1938, and withdrawn three decades later, it was bought as a result of a successful appeal to society members in 1968. With the train loaded to capacity, it created the illusion that this was a rush-hour commuter service at the height of the steam age.

THE UK SINGLES CHART
ON JUNE 29, 1968

1	Gary Puckett and the Union Gap	Young Girl
2	Bobby Goldsboro	Honey
3	Engelbert Humperdinck	A Man Without Love
4	Louis Armstrong	What A Wonderful World/Cabaret
5	The Small Faces	Lazy Sunday
6	The Herd	I Don't Want Our Loving To Die
7	The Love Affair	Rainbow Valley
8	Scott Walker	Joanna
9	Dionne Warwick	Do You Know The Way to San Jose
10	Julie Driscoll, Brian Auger & The Trinity	This Wheel's On Fire
11	The 1910 Fruitgum Company	Simon Says
12	Herman's Hermits	Sleepy Joe
13	Andy Williams	Can't Take My Eyes Off You
14	Jackie	White Horses
15	The Tremeloes	Helule Helule
16	Elvis Presley	US Male
17	John Rowles	If I Only Had Time
18	The Rolling Stones	Jumpin' Jack Flash
19	Tom Jones	Delilah
20	The Equals	Baby Come Back
21	Solomon King	When We Were Young
22	Des O'Connor	I Pretend
23	Showstoppers	Ain't Nothin' But A Houseparty
24	Cliff Richard	Congratulations
25	The Beach Boys	Friends
26	The Association	Time For Livin'
27	Aretha Franklin	Think
28	Otis Redding	The Happy Song (Dum Dum)
29	The Hollies	Jennifer Eccles
30	The Easybeats	Hello, How Are You

Ivatt Class 2MT 2-6-2T 41241 pilots USA tank No. 72 round the curve and out of Keighley with the reopening special. IAN BENTLEY

VICTORY!

At Keighley, speeches were made, the tape cut, two whistles blew, and just before 2.35pm, the two regulators were carefully opened.

Carving history on every inch of the way, with every turn of the wheels, the train proceeded around the curve and tackled the gradient out of Keighley on its non-stop run to Oxenhope.

Crowds were seen to be gathering on every vantage point out of the town.

Belching exhaust, the train passed Great Northern Junction and then accelerated. The platforms at Ingrow were packed with well-wishers waving, exuberant that while the final curtain was ready to fall on the steam era, here was indeed a jubilant encore.

The special entered the tunnel, emerging at the far end to run past the mills and over the river and allotments into more open country. The small station at Damems was passed in a flash.

Standing room only wasn't the word as the first train pulled into Oxenhope.
DAVID SMITH

The first train arriving at Oxenhope on June 29, 1968. IAN HOLT

Rounding the curve into Oakworth, the whistle was sounded to alert the crowds that had amassed on the platform.

The train proceeded over the crossing, past the mill pond, through the woods and over the viaduct.

The high ground surrounding Mytholmes Tunnel was also covered to capacity with onlookers. The train whizzed through the tunnel and into the outskirts of Haworth. It thundered through the station like an express train, past the workshops, the yard, beneath the overbridge and back out. Beyond the packhorse bridge, the train slowed for a gentle entry into similarly crowded Oxenhope station, where Whitworth Vale and Healey Prize Band struck up with Cliff Richards' hit Congratulations.

The first public heritage-era train had arrived. The mayor and lady mayoress were on the footplate as a sea of cameras clicked.

The locomotives then ran round their train and took on water before starting the return trip, a stopping train that departed at 3.20pm.

At Haworth, the guests took tea and inspected the society's headquarters. Beyond there, the train called at Oakworth and Damems, again to be greeted by huge crowds, with many people clamouring to sample this new breed of old train service, before returning to Keighley.

On June 29, 1968, it was evident to all that the miracle had been achieved, one that almost certainly would have inspired the Bronte sisters had they been alive at the time.

BELOW: In a view from the top of Station Drive at Oxenhope, cars were blocking everyone in, as sightseers waited for the arrival of the reopening train. BERNARD LUMB

The last of the steam-era schoolboy trainspotters – or the first of a new generation of preservationists? The reopening special climbs Keighley bank and passes the derelict Great Northern Railway yard and shed. ROBIN LUSH

Keighley mayor Alderman James Waterworth, the railway's Ron Ainsworth – who a few weeks later bought 'Black Five' No. 45212 from British Rail for the line – and their wives on the footplate of No. 41241 during the reopening special. WH FOSTER

Ivatt 2MT 2-6-2T No. 41241 pilots USA 0-6-0T No. 72 with the railway's second train on the reopening day. It is seen passing Haworth shed for Oxenhope. JOHN SCAFE

A UNIQUE SUCCESS

While the volunteer-led railway revival movement was still very much at an embryonic stage, the pioneers of the KWVR had moved mountains to get to the stage where public services could be run again. It was only the third standard gauge heritage railway in Britain to run public services, after the Middleton and Bluebell railways.

The KWVR was followed closely by the Dart Valley Railway in 1969 and the Severn Valley Railway in 1970, but undoubtedly provided a dazzling source of inspiration for more revival schemes in the decades that lay ahead. The KWVR remains the only heritage railway to own the complete length of its original line, from the main

line connection at Keighley to the terminus at Oxenhope (leasing Keighley station and track through the location) and so can accept incoming and outgoing main line charter trains. The headshunt at Oxenhope was lengthened by a further 60ft a couple of years later so that two Black Fives could run round together. The Swanage Railway began running public diesel-hauled services over the full length of the original Isle of Purbeck branch in 2017, but the trackbed is leased. Similarly, the West Somerset Railway may have control over the entire GWR Minehead branch, but again, the trackbed is leased from the local district council.

The Ecclesbourne Valley Railway, the Wirksworth branch in Derbyshire, has

been reopened throughout, but lacks a main line connection at Duffield.

The Paignton to Kingswear Dartmouth Steam Railway, run by Dart Valley Railway plc since being bought from British Rail as an operational line in 1972, is only part of the longer route from Newton Abbot to Kingswear, and may be deemed incomplete because the Churston to Brixham branch has long since gone.

In negotiating the purchase of the branch from British Rail, the KWVR overcame a series of seemingly insurmountable legal hurdles, which blazed a trail for other revival schemes to follow. The KWVR paid the final instalment of its purchase to British Rail in 1992.

Having run round their train, the locomotive pair, prepares to depart from Oxenhope. BERNARD LUMB

No. 41241 stands at a crowded Oxenhope station after arriving with the reopening special. KWVR

LMS 'Black Five' No. 45212 heads towards Oakworth with a demonstration breakdown train. BRIAN SHARPE

MORE POWERFUL
STEAM ARRIVES

Interest in the newly reborn and reinvigorated Worth Valley branch by no means subsided after the opening day and the headlines it generated became last week's news. During July, August and the beginning of September that year, around 2000 tickets were sold every weekend representing about 4000 passenger journeys.

On certain occasions four coaches were insufficient to meet the demand. Even on a cold showery weekend more than 1500 people visited the railway.

However, traffic loadings showed that a more powerful locomotive was needed for the heavier passenger trains on the steeply graded branch

It was now or never to buy one in working order. Using some of the receipts from the opening months of services, the KWVR bought LMS Stanier mixed-traffic 'Black Five' No. 45212 from British Rail.

The locomotive, LMS No. 5212, was built by Armstrong Whitworth at its Newcastle works in 1935 and became No. 45212 after Nationalisation.

It was withdrawn from Lostock Hall (Preston) shed in 1968 after heading the final steam-hauled revenue-earning service for British Railways on August 4, 1968.

It was bought by the KWVR straight out of service and arrived on the KWVR in October 1968.

No. 45212 had been at Low Moor shed in Bradford from new for about 10 years. Decades later it was hired out to Peter Best who overhauled it and operated it on the North Yorkshire Moors Railway.

More recently it has been hired out to Riley and Son (Electromec) Limited of Heywood who have overhauled it to a Network Rail mainline standard. Currently is is often used on the Fort William to Mallaig line and on other

mainline charters.

It is also one of the locomotives used by Carnforth-based Train Operating Company West Coast Railways on its hugely successful 'Jacobite' services over the West Highland Extension between Fort William and Mallaig in the summer months. There was one other factor that played a major part in the launch of the KWVR as a heritage line, and that was publicity on BBC TV.

Before the volunteers reopened the branch, it, along with its locomotives and stock, had been used for the location filming of an early-evening dramatisation of author Edith A Nesbit's turn-of-the century classic The Railway Children for BBC TV.

Early episodes were screened before the line was reopened, and no doubt contributed to the size of crowds that attended on June 29, 1968, to see the first of the new breed of steam trains run through the Worth Valley. Indeed, both the railway and its locality would never be the same again.

BRITAIN'S RAILWAYS IN 1968

▶ August 11 sees British Rail run its last standard gauge steam-hauled passenger train, the 'Fifteen Guinea' special, the day before a mainline steam ban.
▶ Transport Act establishes the National Railway Museum.
▶ Two steam locomotives defied the steam ban imposed after July. 'Black Five' No. 5025 ran light from Hunslet Engine Company to Keighley and a Standard 5MT No. 73050 ran light engine from Newton Heath shed to Peterborough.
▶ Great Western Society runs steam rides over the Cholsey-Wallingford branch.
▶ Birmingham Railway Museum holds its first open day at Tyseley.
▶ Dinting Railway Centre at Glossop opens.
▶ Bill Morris starts Bromyard & Linton Light Railway collection
▶ Leighton Buzzard Narrow Gauge Railway opens.
▶ West Lancashire Light Railway formed.
▶ Embsay & Grassington Railway Preservation Society formed: becomes Embsay & Bolton Abbey Steam Railway
▶ LSWR Siemens A-0 electric shunter No. 75s withdrawn by BR and preserved
▶ Isle of Man Railway's lines from Dougles to Peel and Ramsey closed
▶ Middleton Railway sees Middleton Broom Colliery close
▶ Brush prototype No. HS4000 Kestrel emerges from Brush works.
▶ HM The Queen opens rebuilt Euston station.
▶ Formation of Passenger Transport Authorities
▶ Carnforth closes as BR depot, and becomes Steamtown Railway Museum: now the base of the West Coast Railway Company and not open to the public
▶ Hunslet's South African subsidiary builds last 2ft gauge Beyer Garratt articulated locomotives, SAR Class N9/916 Nos. NG149-156
▶ Class 16 and Class 28 diesels withdrawn
▶ Bluebell Railway buys freehold of line from BR
▶ Britannia Pacific No. 70013 Oliver Cromwell was saved as part of the National Collection and was loaned to Bressingham
▶ Festiniog Railway reopened from Porthmadog as far as Ddualt.

Chapter 8

THE RAILWAY
CHILDREN
AND BEYOND

Rarely, if anywhere, is a railway so closely identified with a major movie success. EMI's big-screen version of The Railway Children was not only a box-office success but springboarded the Keighley & Worth Valley to stardom at a crucial moment in the history of the heritage line.

Railways and drama at first glance may seem strange bedfellows, but some historians claim that they have the same point of origin.

The very basic concept of the railway – deliberate guidance of the wheels of a vehicle – was known to the ancient Greeks, if not invented by them, and was utilised in theatrical performances. The theatre in Sparta, rebuilt around 30BC, had a mobile building that could be rolled on and off the stage as required. The structure, measuring around 114ft long and 26ft wide, was built on a set of wheels, which ran in three widely spaced rows of channelled stone rails. A similar arrangement is evident in the ruins of the theatre in Megalopolis, dating from the third-century BC.

It is also said that the railway concept was used in plays themselves; a scene which, for example, might involve a body being carried on to the stage on a trolley running on stone channel rails, as found at the theatre at Eretria.

This guidance rails principle was also utilised for the cross-country transference of goods over a substantial distance.

The Diolkos or 'railed way' was built across the 3.7-mile-wide Isthmus of Corinth for the conveyance of commodities between the Corinthian and Saronic gulfs, avoiding the dangerous journey by sea around the Peloponnese.

Fast-forward to the 20th century, and a reunion between railways and drama might be said to have been an explosive combination, at least in the world of heritage railways, and one line in particular, the Keighley & Worth Valley Railway.

This particular story begins in Victorian times, with the pen of novelist, poet and political activist Edith A Nesbit, later Edith Bland (August 15, 1858-May 4, 1924). Born in Kennington, Surrey, the daughter of an agricultural chemist and schoolteacher, the death of her father when she was four and the continuing ill health of her sister meant that Edith had a transitory childhood, her family moving across Europe in search of healthy climates only to return to England for financial reasons. She therefore spent her childhood gaining an education from whatever sources were available, local grammar schools, the occasional boarding school but mainly through reading. At 17 her family finally settled in London.

She became a co-founder of the socialist organisation the Fabian Society, a socialist organisation and an important influence on the Labour party, which grew from it.

She also wrote or collaborated with more than 60 children's books. According to her biographer, Julia Briggs, Nesbit was, "the first modern

Class 465 DMU No. 465 165 passes beneath Warren Road bridge as it enters Chelsfield station in March 2006. The station in the London borough of Bromley has been said to have inspired The Railway Children.
ROGER W HAWORTH*

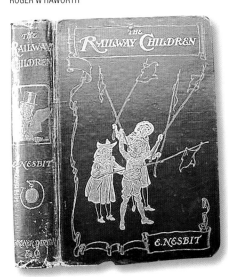

A copy of the first edition of The Railway Children.

Edith A Nesbit, author of The Railway Children.

writer for children" whom she also credited with inventing the children's adventure story.

The most famous of her stories was The Railway Children, which she dedicated to her son Paul Bland (1880-1940). The Railway Children was originally serialised in The London Magazine during 1905 and first published in book form in 1906.

The Oxford Dictionary of National Biography credits London journalist Oswald Barron, who had a deep affection for Edith, with having suggested the plot.

The setting is thought to be inspired by Edith's walks to Chelsfield railway station close to where she lived, and her seeing the building of the railway cutting and tunnel between Chelsfield and Knockholt. The station is on the South Eastern Main Line.

However, in 2011, Nesbit was posthumously accused of lifting the plot from The House by the Railway by Ada J Graves, a book first published in 1896 and serialised in a popular magazine in 1904, a year before The Railway Children first appeared. The children's adventures in both books bear remarkable similarities. While Nesbit's characters use red petticoats to stop the train at the end, Graves has them using a red jacket.

A FAMILY IN CRISIS ARRIVES AT OAKWORTH

The story of The Railway Children and its distinctive characters is now part of literature legend, familiar to many generations of children and adults alike, but for completeness, it runs as follows.

A family comprising mother, daughters Bobbie and Phyllis and son

J72 0-6-0T *Joem* runs past North Ives Bottom Crossing with a three-coach train during filming for the BBC's fourth production of The Railway Children, on March 23, 1968. WH FOSTER

Peter moves by train from London to The Three Chimneys, a house near a railway, which may be in the north of England – perhaps Yorkshire as Edith visited her sister on the North Yorkshire Moors, staying at a house also called Three Chimneys nearby – or maybe in or around London and the Home Counties, where Edith grew up. Nobody knows for certain.

The father, who works at the Foreign Office, disappears in mysterious circumstances and a few days later the family moves to a poorer home in the country. In reality he is imprisoned after being falsely accused of spying. At their new home, the children become friendly with Perks, the station porter, and delight in watching the trains go by.

They become acquainted with an Old Gentleman who regularly takes the 9.15am train near their home. He is able to help prove their father's innocence, and the family is reunited. In the meantime, the family has several adventures. They take care of a Russian

exile, Mr Szczepansky, who came to England looking for his family, and Jim, the grandson of the Old Gentleman, who suffers a broken leg in a tunnel. The story appears to be set in 1905, and there are references to the contemporary Russo-Japanese War and to attitudes taken by British people to the conflict.

The novel was popular for nearly half a century before BBC TV – which had a monopoly on Britain's one-channel television service – adapted it for a TV series in 1951, produced by Dorothea Brooking, with eight episodes each half an hour long.

A second TV version was then produced using some of the footage from the first but with a few cast changes and new material. It had four episodes each an hour long.

BBC TV produced another version in 1957, again produced by Dorothea Brooking, with an eight-episode series. Location filming was carried out at Baynards station in Surrey on the old Guildford to Horsham line. It even made

the front cover of Radio Times! In 1968 the story was revisited again. Little was it realised at the time, but thanks to this production, screened on black-and-white TV in seven 25-minute episodes, The Railway Children was on track to become an international box-office blockbuster.

In February 1968, the Keighley & Worth Valley Railway Preservation Society received an enquiry from BBC TV about the possibility of using the line for location filming. It had all the necessary ingredients – period builds, no regular trains or passengers to get in the way and most importantly, steam locomotives.

The director, Julia Smith, who had been busy working on Dr Who and Sixties soap The Newcomers, and her assistant Nicolas Johns arranged to visit the line and, with the agreement of British Rail, a works train consisting of a diesel railbus was provided.

On Saturday, February 17, the railbus was waiting in Keighley's Platform 4

"Daddy my Daddy!" Jenny Agutter in the closing scene from the BBC 1968 production of The Railway Children. BBC

Three children on the Keighley & Worth Valley Railway for the filming of the BBC 1968 production. BBC

and gave an excellent view of the line. Julia Smith, who had also worked on Dr Finlay's Casebook – and later went on to co-create EastEnders – and her assistant were impressed with all that they saw along the branch, but that did not stop them visiting another railway to compare suitability.

However, the Worth Valley branch won, and on Monday, March 25, the unit arrived and set up headquarters at Oakworth station.

Before then, volunteers had pulled out all the stops to have the closed branch ready. A North Eastern Railway signal was erected at the curve before Oxenhope – it featured in title sequences. It was pulled to the off position by means of a wire fed through the boundary wall.

The shots of the train stopping, the signal releasing and the train starting were more complicated than the audience ever realised. Three men, including two BBC prop men, crouched low out of camera range heaving and tugging on the thin strand of wire emerging from the wall until the signal moved, knees and feet squelching in the familiar products of a farmyard.

Oakworth station had its eight broken windows replaced and was repainted for the occasion. The majority of the fence was given a coat of white paint and the gas lamps, long since smashed, were given new glass globes, the platform edge was adorned with the traditional white stripe and the whole area was cleaned and weeded.

The BBC provided contemporary notice boards, and station signs. Oakworth became 'Meadow Vale', bushes were also planted, on wooden bases, to give the whole station an authentically neat, tidy and well-groomed appearance. Coal in the nearby yard was cleared by the local coal merchant, Norman Feather, to permit a long shot free from pylons.

Three days were allocated for the use of steam engines, and *Sir Berkeley*, *Joem* and No. 31 were rostered. On the first morning, Manning Wardle

Sir Berkeley provided a few anxious moments when the right-hand injector refused to function and the left-hand one seemed sulky and would only work in a half-hearted fashion. However a quick dash to Oxenhope water tank solved the problem and also ended its brief TV career.

During filming at Mytholmes tunnel, two small boys were seen to throw stones at the train. They were not to know that the driver that day was an off-duty policeman. They were quickly apprehended and warned as to their future conduct and that they were never to throw stones at trains again.

The cast featured Joseph O'Conor as the Old Gentleman, Ann Castle as the Mother, Gordon Gostelow as Perks the Porter, Brian Hayes as the Stationmaster, John Ringham as the Doctor, Mary Healey as Ruth the Parlourmaid, Stefan Gryff as the Foreigner, Frederick Treves as the Father, Gillian Bailey as Phyllis, Christopher Witty as Jim, Neil

McDermott as Peter… and Jenny Agutter as Roberta (Bobbie).

The first episode was screened at 5.25pm on Sunday, May 12, 1968, in the BBC's slot for serialisations of classic novels of the day.

The BBC'S 1968 adaptation was placed 96th in the BFI's 100 Greatest British Television Programmes poll of 2000. Of the four BBC TV versions of the Nesbit novel, this is the only one known to survive and was decades later made available on DVD.

Not only that, but its nationwide screening brought swathes of publicity for the branch, and when it reopened on June 29, 1968, no doubt played a significant part in drawing the crowds.

Also watching was English character actor and screenwriter Lionel Jeffries, who was so impressed with the BBC series that his daughter persuaded him to buy the film rights and make his debut as a director. Both the Worth Valley and the world of railway preservation would never be the same again.

DADDY MY DADDY

Taking a BBC drama and adapting it for the big screen was by no means new.

In 1963, the BBC launched Dr Who, a new series about adventures in time and space. The original brief to producer Verity Lambert was a series that would encourage youngsters to take an interest in history, by having contemporary characters, including two schoolteachers and one of their pupils, taken back in time to see key events unfolding for themselves.

The first story involved a trip to the Stone Age where the doctor taught a tribe how to make fire for the first time. However, it was the second story that turned the programme into an overnight sensation, and it had little to do with history. The blue police box made a journey to a distant planet, Skaro, where the time travellers came face to face with the most evil

creatures in the universe – the Daleks! A year later, the BBC brought the Daleks back for a second story, in which they invaded Earth in the future. That clinched it – in school playgrounds all across Britain, you would hear youngsters imitating Daleks or wanting to be the Doctor.

Both stories ended up as big-screen films, but with a different cast, the Doctor being played in both by Peter Cushing. However, the second was not a great box-office success, and over the half century that followed, diehard Doctor Who fans have habitually disregarded both movies in favour of the original TV stories, both of which survive. However, while the BBC's latest production of The Railway Children followed a similar path from small screen to big screen, its impact would be colossal.

In one of the most famous scenes of the EMI film, the three children wave red petticoats to try to stop the train from approaching the landslip. CANAL + IMAGE UK

THE PANNIER OUT OF TIME!

The Great Western Railway's 57XX pannier tank is without doubt one of the most successful British locomotive designs of all time, with 863 of them being built. This figure is second only in number, in Britain, to the London &

North Western Railway's DX class 0-6-0 freight engines, of which 943 were built between 1858-72, including 86 for the Lancashire & Yorkshire Railway.

Designed primarily as a mixed-traffic and shunting locomotive, the 57XXs pannier tank was never going to be the most glamorous Great Western locomotive, paling in comparison with the express passenger flagship Stars, Castles and Kings, but as representatives of the Swindon empire, it is no less iconic.

However, it may be considered the most distinctive and immediately recognisable, with its two square water carriers hung either side of the boiler, just like panniers on a donkey, hence the name of the type.

It is difficult for anyone young or old with even a smattering of knowledge about steam railways to mistake a 57XX pannier. The youngest will recognise it as Duck in the Thomas the Tank Engine stories, while older movie goers will recall the ochre-liveried locomotive in the big-screen version of The Railway Children.

Yet the story was set in a period more than two decades before this particular locomotive type came off the drawing board! There again, on a line of imagination in a land of romance, anything goes provided that it entices and inspires. If you do not quibble as to whether Heathcliff's lodger Lockwood really saw Cathy's ghost at the window of Wuthering Heights, a locomotive appearing a quarter of a century before it left the Swindon drawing board will not make that much of a difference.

Sixteen 57XX pannier tanks exist in the heritage sector today, although

BIG SCREEN, BIG TIME, BIG REWARDS

Lionel Jeffries wrote the script for the movie version of The Railway Children and submitted it to Elstree Studios. At the same time, one of Lionel's former associates, Bryan Forbes, became chief executive at the studios.

Forbes liked the script but rejected the idea of turning the story into a musical and duly allocated a £350,000 budget.

In the autumn of 1969, Lionel and producer Bob Lynn came to Bronte country to inspect the line.

Again, it was chosen because at that time it was the only heritage railway that could offer a sizeable collection of locomotives and rolling stock. Not only that, there was a large number that fitted the Victorian and Edwardian period needed for the story.

Lionel was persuaded to let Oakworth station retain its true identity rather than become Meadow Vale again. That itself was to give the KWVR

a huge publicity boost, for filmgoers would remember the name and then set out to visit the station in real life, giving a huge boost to passenger numbers.

Filming began on April 6, 1970 and lasted until June 12. There were 15 days of filming at Elstree and 39 on location, most of which were in the Worth Valley.

There were three types of train, each with different roles. The local train of four- and six-wheeled wooden-bodied coaches was hauled by Manchester Ship Canal No. 67.

For the 'Scotch Express', there was No. 4744 and No. 957 – which became The Green Dragon – and four bogie coaches.

For the local service, which had the Old Gentleman's Saloon attached to the rear, GWR 57XX pannier tank No. 5775 was used painted in the ochre of the fictitious livery of the Great Northern & Southern Railway.

GWR pannier tank No. 5775 in its correct or typical Brunswick green livery on static display in Oxenhope exhibition shed in 2012. A cut-out of the three children emphasises its starring role in the EMI film.
ROBIN JONES

Great Western 57XX pannier No. 5775 in fictitious Great Northern & Southern Railway livery during location filming. The GN&SR lettering also appeared on the side of the locomotives in the BBC's 1968 production.
HOWARD MALHAM

by no means all of them are running or have at one time. The most famous of all of the survivors must surely be the KWVR's No. 5775. Built at Swindon in September 1929, it hails from the dawn of the 57XX class. First allocated to Neath shed, it was later transferred to Glyn Neath, Neath & Brecon, Danygraig and Carmarthen. Its last Western Region allocation was Pontypool Road, where it arrived in March 1956.

On August 8, 1963, it became the latest of several sold to London Transport for use on Underground works trains. It was repainted in maroon livery and numbered L89. The vacuum and steam heat pipes were removed or blanked off, the smokebox numberplate replaced by indicator brackets for train reporting numbers, while sleet brush fitting brackets were installed.

With the demise of the panniers on London Underground fast approaching, it was sold straight out of service to the KWVR in January 1970. One of its earliest duties in traffic was to take part in the filming of The Railway Children.

Overhauled in 1989, No. 5775 was given the boiler from sister No. 4612, which had been bought for spare parts, and returned to the fictitious GN&SR

livery, it resteamed in time for the 20th anniversary of the film.

Repainted Brunswick green, it spent several years on static display in Oxenhope exhibition shed.

However, in 2014 it was refurbished at Shildon's Locomotion museum back

5775

into the famous fictitious film livery.

When York Theatre Royal was undergoing a major refurbishment in 2015, a temporary theatre was erected in the South Yard on the National Railway Museum. And one of the productions staged there was Mike

Kenny's adaptation of The Railway Children by York Theatre Royal artistic director Damien Cruden. Not only that, but it featured one of the big stars from the movie in No. 5775!

The 'Old Gentleman's Saloon' used in the movie was North Eastern Railway saloon No. 21661, said to be the oldest operational standard gauge passenger coach in the world. It was built in 1871 by the Stockton & Darlington Railway as a six-wheel third class saloon.

In 1876 the S&DR became the North Eastern Railway, which converted it in 1884 to an inspection saloon, No. 1661, for its Locomotive Superintendent Edward Fletcher.

In 1904 it was rebuilt to a 40ft bogie vehicle. It became LNER No. 21661 and BR No. E902179E and was not withdrawn until 1969, only two years short of its 100th birthday! It seats just 14 people.

The cast of The Railway Children with the brass band that appeared in one of the final scenes of the movie. CANAL + IMAGE UK

The children await the arrival of the branch train headed by pannier No. 5775. CANAL + IMAGE UK

The three children exchange pleasantries with the driver of Manchester Ship Canal 0-6-0T No. 67.
CANAL + IMAGE UK

LANDSLIDE!

A major part of the story was the landslide on the bank in the cutting below Mytholmes Tunnel.

To create the illusion of a landslip, three long steel channels were placed in the hillside with three short vertical tubes in each. They were drawn up the hillside by cables and released to slide down as required. The centre tube carried a glass-fibre tree made by the Elstree art department.

When filming took place, the hinged base of the tree caused it to fall over, while 40 tons of Fuller's earth and gravel piled up behind sleepers at the bottom of the cutting were exploded, causing the slippage to slide across the track.

Apart from the railway, other locations around the line were used for location filming. The family's house Three Chimneys is to be found to the north of Oxenhope station. Doctor Forrest's surgery was set inside the Bronte Parsonage in Haworth. Mytholmes Tunnel featured extensively in the film, including being the location for the paper chase scene, as well as the famous one in which the children wave red petticoats to warn the train about a landslide. The fields of long grass where the children waved to the trains are situated on the Haworth side of Mytholmes tunnel.

The scenes of the children sitting on a bridge were filmed outside the valley, at Wycoller near Colne.

THE CAST

Jenny Agutter reprised her role as Roberta (Bobbie) from the 1968 BBC production, and remains the most famous cast member.

Born in Taunton on December 20, 1952, she began her career as a child actress in 1964, appearing in East of Sudan, Star! She also appeared in the critically acclaimed film Walkabout and the TV film The Snow Goose (both 1971), for which she won an Emmy Award for Outstanding Supporting Actress in a Drama.

She relocated to the USA in 1974 to pursue a Hollywood career and appeared in Logan's Run (1976), Amy (1981), An American Werewolf in London (1981) and Child's Play 2 (1990).

Meanwhile, she also continued to appear in high-profile British films such as The Eagle Has Landed (1976), Equus (1977) – for which she won a BAFTA Award for Best Actress in a Supporting Role – and The Riddle of the Sands (1979).

In 1981 she also co-starred in The Survivor, an Australian adaptation of the James Herbert novel, and was nominated for an AACTA Award for Best Actress in a Leading Role.

After returning to Britain in the early 1990s to pursue family life, Agutter shifted her focus to television, and in 2000 she appeared in a new TV adaptation of The Railway Children, filmed on the Bluebell Railway, but this time taking on the role of the Mother! Since 2012 she has starred in the BBC's primetime ratings hit Call the Midwife.

Jenny Agutter, Sally Thomsett and Gary Warren pose with fellow star Bernard Cribbins in front of Lord Mayor for the cover of a vinyl record of The Railway Children narrated by producer Lionel Jeffries.
CANAL + IMAGE UK

She also made a return to Hollywood film-making in 2012, appearing in Marvel's The Avengers, and reprised her role in Captain America: The Winter Soldier (2014).

Agutter is married with one grown-up son. She supports several charitable causes, mostly in relation to cystic fibrosis, a condition her niece suffers

Filming of the closing scene of the movie at Ebor Lane, Haworth, on June 5, 1970.

from, and was awarded an OBE in the 2012 Queen's Birthday Honours for charitable services.

In the 1970 movie, her mother was played by Dinah Sheridan, best known for the 1953 film Genevieve. Bobbie's younger sister Phylis was played by 20-year-old Sally Thomsett – who took the part of an 11-year-old despite being two years older than Jenny Agutter.

As part of her contract, Sally was not allowed to reveal her true age during the making of the film, and neither was she allowed to be seen smoking, drinking,

driving her car, or in the company of her boyfriend during the filming. She received a nomination for the BAFTA Film Award for Newcomer to Leading Film Roles.

The remainder of the cast comprised Bernard Cribbins (Perks); Iain Cuthbertson (Father); William Mervyn (the Old Gentleman); Gary Warren (Peter) Peter Bromilow (the Doctor); Ann Lancaster (Ruth); Gordon Whiting (the Russian); Beatrix Mackey (Aunt Emma); Deddie Davies (Mrs Perks); David Lodge (the bandmaster);

Christopher Witty (Jim); Brenda Cowling (Viney); Paddy Ward (the Cart Man); Eric Chitty (the Photographer); Sally James (the Maid) and Dominic Allen (the CID man).

The full story of the film is available in a booklet The Making Of The Railway Children. Compiled by former volunteer stationmaster of Oakworth Jim Shipley, it is published by the Keighley & Worth Valley Preservation Society, priced £5.95, available from the Haworth station shop. To order telephone 01535 640464 or email shop@kwvr.co.uk

Among the cast for the EMI film was KWVR volunteer Graham Mitchell, who played a train guard. Here he is seen awaiting the 'right away' at Oakworth while passing the time of day with the Old Gentleman, played by William Mervyn. Graham went on to serve for many years as a popular chairman of the heritage line.

CANAL + IMAGE UK

At the end of the movie, the cast broke the 'fourth wall' of drama to wave directly at the audience, with No. 5775 suitably decorated, and Jenny Agutter holding up a sign saying 'The End'. CANAL + IMAGE UK

NOT 'THE END' BY ANY MEANS!

In 1999, the British Film Institute placed The Railway Children 66th its list of the Top 100 British films of all time, while in 2004, the film magazine Total Film named it the 46th greatest British film of the 20th century.

In 2005 the British Film Institute included it in a list of the 50 films you should see by the age of 14. In 2008, the film was in 30th place on Channel 4's list of the 100 Greatest Family Films.

As stated above, a new TV adaptation of the novel, also featuring Jenny

Agutter, was made on the Bluebell Railway in October 1999. It starred Jemima Rooper, Jack Blumenau, J J Feild and North British Railway C class 0-6-0 *Maude* from the Bo'ness & Kinneil Railway. Critical response was good, but while the Bluebell Railway may be

THE RESOUNDING IMPACT

The movie was released by EMI to British audiences on December 21, 1970, with a premiere in London.

Soon afterwards, it was screened at the former Ritz cinema in Keighley.

The railway was quick to cash in on the film's soar-away success. It printed leaflets to be given to cinemagoers, outlining all of the locations in the film.

Steam ended on British Rail in August 1968, but steam locomotives clearly had not lost any of their charm. The movie was the ninth most popular film at the British box office in 1971, and recouped its cost in that country alone.

Highly positive critical acclaim was widespread and remains so to this day. The film received three nominations for awards at the 24th British Academy Film Awards ceremony. Bernard Cribbins was nominated in the category of Best Supporting Actor. Sally Thomsett received a nomination for Best Newcomer in a Leading Role and

Johnny Douglas was also nominated for the Anthony Asquith Award for Film Music.

The movie effectively 'made' the Keighley & Worth Valley Railway. Visitors flocked to the valley to see the places in the film for themselves, and to lose themselves in its magic. Even today, the movie, which is regularly repeated on TV, is held to account for a significant portion of the line's annual visitor numbers.

However, the impact of the film was felt hundreds of miles from Bronte Country. As we saw in Chapter 4, the 1953 Ealing comedy, The Titfield Thunderbolt, opened the minds of the public at large to the concept of ordinary people saving a branch line closed by those in the uppermost corridors of power.

In 1970, the setting for The Railway Children gave unprecedented national publicity to the nascent but buoyant

railway preservation scene.

All over the country, there were enthusiasts and local people alike who saw the huge success of the Worth Valley revivalists on the big screen and were wondering if their closed branch line could be revived. It is impossible to calculate how much inspiration was drawn from the pioneering KWVR through the awesome popularity of the film. Indeed, its release was a landmark moment in the history of Britain's railway heritage: had the film never have been made, the sector would definitely have been so much the poorer for it.

Wuthering Heights, Jane Eyre and The Tenant of Wildfell Hall inspired the imagination like few novels had done before, but The Railway Children and the KWVR presented a no less romantic but possibly more tangible world into which those enchanted by the story could immerse themselves, if only for a day.

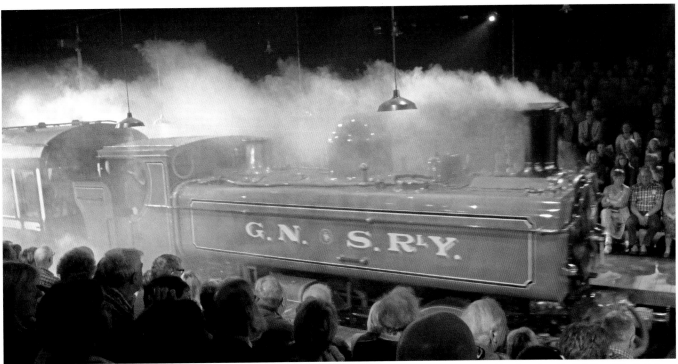

Repainted at the Locomotion museum into its fictional Great Northern & Southern Railway livery, GWR pannier tank No. 5775 on loan from the Keighley & Worth Valley Railway reprises its role as it makes a dramatic entry in the 2015 latest version of the York Theatre Royal's Olivier Award-winning stage production at the National Railway Museum on York the VIP night, August 6, 2015. While the city's theatre was undergoing a major refurbishment, a temporary auditorium known as the Signal Box Theatre was erected in the museum yard. ROBIN JONES

nearer the places where Edith Nesbit grew up and inspired her, it did nothing to take away from the fact that the KWVR had immortalised the story on celluloid and would not be giving it up that easily!

In 2005, The Railway Children was performed for the first time as a stage musical at Sevenoaks Playhouse in Kent, UK, with a cast including Are You Being Served star Nicholas Smith as the Old Gentleman, Paul Henry from Crossroads as Perks and West End star Susannah Fellows as Mother. On March 2, 2010, the Bradford International Film Festival

"Daddy, my daddy" – one of the most famous lines in children's literature. Rob Angell as Father emerges from the smoke of the train bringing him home from a sentence of wrongful imprisonment, in York Theatre Royal's 2015 production, as No. 5775 looks on! ANTHONY ROBLING

concluded with a new restoration of The Railway Children film with the 40th anniversary digital premiere. A 40th anniversary Blu-ray and DVD was accordingly released in May that year with a new digitally remastered print. It included new interviews with Sally Thomsett, Jenny Agutter and Bernard Cribbins. Sadly, the planned commentary by director Lionel Jeffries was not completed as he died in February 2010. A new stage adaptation written by Mike Kenny and directed by York Theatre Royal artistic director's Damian Cruden was staged in 2008 and 2009 at the National Railway Museum in York and featured a real locomotive in the form of the National Collection's Great Northern Railway Stirling single 4-2-2 No. 1.

The production was followed by two seasons at two of the disused international platforms at Waterloo International (winning an Olivier Award for best Entertainment in 2011) and a Toronto production the same year, selling to packed auditoriums, and using London & South Western Railway T3 4-4-0 No. 563, borrowed from the NRM and shipped abroad.

From June 21 to July 2 Denmark's oldest heritage railway Museumsbanen Maribo-Bandholm on Lolland, held a live stage performance at the station in Bandholm, using the line's oldest operational steam locomotive, 1879-built ØSJS 2 Kjøge from 1879, and a rake of their coaches.

The stage adaptation, produced by the National Railway Museum and York Theatre Royal, reopened in December 2014 in a new temporary theatre behind King's Cross station.

It is highly unlikely that the film will ever lose its popularity, and will continue to inspire people not only to bring their families to the KWVR but also to other heritage railways.

"All the world's a stage" is the phrase that begins a monologue from William Shakespeare's As You Like It, spoken by the melancholy Jaques in Act II Scene VII. That may be true, but is not every heritage railway is a stage in itself, providing live theatre every time a locomotive runs? Untold films for both TV and the big screen have been shot on Britain's preserved railways, which can be quickly be adapted to authentically recreate the past, and in so many ways, it was the trailblazing KWVR that led the way early on.

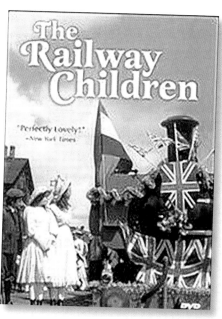

The 2010 DVD release of The Railway Children.

One of my favourite railway pictures of all time! LMS 'Black Five' 4-6-0 No. 45212 stands in Haworth loop covered in wallpaper for a 1970s Solvite advertisement. EDWARD HILL

THE CAMERAS ROLL – AGAIN AND AGAIN AND AGAIN

Following the resounding success of The Railway Children, the KWVR has become a perennial favourite with film producers.

In 1976, Haworth railway station appeared in the premier episode of a Granada TV 1940s-set sitcom called Yanks Go Home in which a group of US Army Air Force pilots arrive by train and alight at the station in a small northern town in Lancashire, north-west of England, during the Second World War.

The same year, the railway was also used for the Disney film Escape From The Dark about three children who save three pit ponies from a Yorkshire coal mine when they are about to be slaughtered. In 1979, an episode of the long-running UK TV sitcom Last of the Summer Wine was filmed partly along the Worth Valley route. The three main characters Compo, Foggy and Clegg attempt to stop a runaway steam train having pulled the brake on purpose

Actor David Suchet examines driver Robin Higgins' Minox camera during a break in the filming of an episode of Poirot. BILL ASHCROFT

Troops returning from the Western Front in 1917 at Platform 4, Keighley, with Metropolitan Railway coaches in the background. This was a scene from the 1997 movie Fairy Tale: A True Story, about the Cottingley Fairies hoax. GRAHAM MITCHELL

(and then only to drive upwards and downwards). The locomotive used was pannier No. 5775 in its London Transport guise as No. L89.

Feature films include Yanks (1979, Universal); Jude (1996, BBC Films): Fairy Tale: A True Story (1997, Icon Entertainment); Brideshead Revisited (2007, Ecosse Films), Selfish Giant (2013, IFC); Testament Of Youth, (2015, BBC Films), Swallows and Amazons (2016, Harbour Pictures) and Lies We Tell (2017, Bradford International Film Associates).

In 1981 a scene from Alan Parker's film, Pink Floyd – Another Brick In The Wall was filmed at the entrance to Mytholmes tunnel.

The railway was used in the filming of Peaky Blinders, a 2013 BBC TV drama about Birmingham criminals set just after the First World War.

Other TV programmes using scenes filmed on the line include The Great Train Robbery: A Copper's Tale, (2013 BBC); Spanish Flu – The Forgotten Fallen (2009, Hardy Pictures); The League of Gentlemen (BBC); Gardener's Word (BBC); Housewife 49 (2006, Granada Television); Poirot (LWT, Granada), A Touch of Frost (ITV Productions); The Royal (Yorkshire TV); Some Mothers Do 'Ave 'Em (BBC); Born & Bred (BBC), Songs of Praise (BBC) and period dramas including, The Way We Live Now (2001); Sons & Lovers (2003); and North & South (2004).

The KWVR has also been in demand for the filming of TV commercials for brands including Budweiser (for the US market), Hovis biscuits, Symbol Crackers – filmed with Ronnie Corbett in Ingrow tunnel; Tetley bitter; Head and Shoulders shampoo – with BR Standard 4MT 2-6-4T No. 80002 at Keighley; as well as the famous Solvite advert when LMS 'Black Five' No. 5212 was 'wallpapered' in Haworth yard.

The National Railway Museum's working replica of Stephenson's *Rocket* and its two replica Liverpool & Manchester Railway coaches stand at Oxenhope station during the filming of a Tetley bitter TV advertisement, Leaves on the Line, in September 1994. FW SMITH

Chairman Graham Mitchell (right) and driver Robin Higgins meet Cliff Richard during the making of an episode of BBC TV's Holiday Programme in 1996. CJ OGILVIE

Last of the Summer Wine: Bill Owen and Peter Sallis who played Compo and Clegg respectively, look out from the footplate of pannier No. L89 (5775) while Brian Wilde who played Foggy is inside. RICHARD GREENWOOD

Camera and lighting crews at work as Ronnie Corbett rehearses a scene for The Frost Report in the Sixties.

Chapter 9

FIRST OUT OF
BARRY

Following the reopening of the branch by volunteers half a century ago,
the Keighley & Worth Valley Railway achieved a major milestone in the
history of preservation. Fiona Kennaugh tells the story of how her father,
Alexander Macdonald, saved the first of 213 steam locomotives
for preservation purposes from the legendary Barry scrapyard.

As the impact of British Railways' Modernisation Plan, published in December 1954, gathered pace and diesel and electric traction replaced steam, there remained one final journey for the 16,000 redundant locomotives to make, and that was to the nearest scrapyard.

Often within days of withdrawal, steam locomotives still with potentially many years of service left in them before their next overhaul fell victim to the cutter's torch and were reduced to piles of scrap. Furthermore, the Modernisation Plan, and BR chairman Dr Richard Beeching's 1963 report also led to the reduction of the wagon fleet from 125,000,000 to 600,000.

The amount of storage needed and scrapping capabilities meant that the BR workshops were stretched to the limit. Therefore it was decided to out-source via tender the job of scrapping of many of the steam locomotives.

David Lloyd Victor Woodham (aka Dai) ran the Woodham Brothers' scrapyard on Barry Island in South Wales. He negotiated a contract to scrap engines mainly from the Western Region plus rolling stock. The more complex locomotives continued to be handled by Swindon Works.

Woodham Brothers won the tender and in 1959 Dai went to Swindon Works to learn how to scrap steam locomotives. In 1964 further contracts were won for the Southern Region and his total purchases by 1968 comprised 297 locomotives.

Further engines arrived from the London Midland Region during 1968.

The preservation movement was then very much in its embryonic stage, and enthusiasts could only watch with sadness as many a historic locomotive class was rendered extinct.

However, Dai made a business decision with huge ramifications for the future of British transport heritage. He found that the scrapping of redundant wagons brought bigger immediate profits than cutting up steam engines. So he parked the condemned locomotives in long sidings in his scrapyard, saving them 'for a rainy day', when the supply of wagons had run out.

There, the great behemoths of steam stood for two decades or more in long lines, rusting away in the salty air of the Bristol Channel.

The first BR steam engines acquired for preservation had been bought out of service, most notably LNER A3 Pacific No. 4472 *Flying Scotsman*, which in 1963 was saved from the scrapman by the late Ffestiniog Railway saviour Alan Pegler.

LEFT: Midland 4F 0-6-0 No. 43924, the first locomotive to be bought from Barry scrapyard for preservation, departs Keighley with the 3.30pm service to Oxenhope on November 5, 2017. MATT EVANS

GWR 4-6-0 No. 7812 *Erlestoke Manor* stands in the foreground of this view of the legendary rows of rusting scrap steam locomotives at the Woodham Brothers yard in Barry, in October 1968. This locomotive was saved for an illustrious life on the Severn Valley Railway, which opened to the public nearly two years after the Keighley & Worth Valley Railway. HUGH LLEWELYN*

BR ran its last main line steam passenger train on August 11, 1968, in the form of the 'Fifteen Guinea Special'. At the same time, the growing army of preservationists needed steam locomotives to get their revival schemes off the ground. Soon, there would be just one place to go in the UK, and that was Barry scrapyard.

The first to leave for a new life in preservation was No. 43924, the only Midland 4F in the yard, which brings to the story my father, Alexander Macdonald.

My father's involvement in railways and steam started early. Known as Alec or Alex at the age of 16, he started his long career with BR at Bank Hall shed on Merseyside as a fitter.

He worked in cramped filthy smokeboxes and lost the ends of two of his fingers on a lathe. He was offered a job for life or a cash pay-out in compensation. He did believe steam would last his career out but it was replaced much earlier than he imagined.

Until 1956 Alec worked at Bank Hall and then moved on to become a chargehand fitter at Walton on the Hill, then back to Bank Hall, before moving on to be shedmaster at Rhyl in 1959. He deputised at Bangor, then Lees – on to Brunswick and ended up as the last shedmaster at Southport for the last six years of steam from 1960-66.

I used to visit my father at Mollington Street in Birkenhead – he was a train crews' inspector, a job that included attending inquests on behalf of BR, and he also worked at Lime Street, Liverpool as well as providing relief/ temporary cover at Speke Junction, Carnforth, and Wigan.

For Alec, steam and engines were his passion and in his life he made many friends in the world of steam because of his knowledge and expertise.

This is what led to Alec being introduced to the then newly formed Midland 4F Preservation Society. Chaired by its founder Ian Johnson, the other members were his brother Alan Johnson, Alan Fleetwood, John Atherton (who exited in 1971), John Collingwood, George Sarsen, Mark Leather and William Cashen.

WHY SAVE A 4F?
In the mid-1960s this group of steam locomotive enthusiasts got together and formed a society with a view to restoring a Midland 4F 0-6-0. For many years this had been the flagship design of the old Midland Railway, so successful in goods and passenger hauling that the LMS continued to build them after the 1923 Grouping. The members of the society felt that such a gem deserved to be saved for posterity.

The Fowler 4F 0-6-0 is a class of locomotive designed by Henry Fowler, Chief Mechanical Engineer of the Midland Railway. They were nicknamed 'Duck Sixes' because of their wheel arrangement.

The Midland Railway built 197 4Fs at Derby before the Grouping in 1923 but the LMS continued to build them, turning out another 575 between 1924-41. All 772 survived to enter BR ownership at Nationalisation on January 1, 1948, However, by 1965 there were only three genuine Midland 4Fs working for BR: No. 43953 at Workington, No. 43967 at Buxton and No. 43924 at Bristol Barrow Road.

No. 43924 heads a local freight working near Gloucester in June 1962. COLOUR-RAIL.COM/W POTTER BRM366

The group began negotiations with BR with the help of Ernest Lawton, who worked for BR at Lime Street Liverpool. Lawton was most valuable to the new society and he made requests to BR for quotes for the three MR 4Fs. He even researched premises with rail access should the locomotive they hoped to procure need to be stored.

BR moved slowly and by the time the society's request was dealt with, all three 4Fs had been sold. All BR offered were Nos. 44377 and 44525, two LMS-built locomotives from Crewe. The deal

was £2000 each and it was a seven-day offer only. The 4F Society could not raise that amount of money in that time.

After further talks with Lawton it transpired that Nos. 43953 and 43967 had been cut up and the only remaining Midland 4F, No. 43924, had also been sold for scrap but was still at Woodham Bros' yard at Barry. By this point Ernest had introduced the society to my father, who could offer many years of expertise on steam engines, and mechanical engineering. I am certain that he did not need to be asked twice and with the

knowledge he brought, it was decided to apply to Dai Woodham for permission to inspect the locomotive with a view to possible preservation. Steam enthusiasts and preservation groups including the Midland 4F society made pilgrimages to Barry and holidaymakers were all fascinated by the rows of sad, forlorn – but not forgotten locomotives.

No. 3924 was built at Derby Works in October 1920, for a cost of £5094 for the engine and £1454 for the tender. Its planned running life was to be a standard 45 years.

Its first shed was Wellingborough, from where it hauled ironstone and coal trains along the Midland Main Line. In March 1930, it was transferred to Saltley shed in Birmingham, and in July 1937 it was switched to Gloucester Barnwood where it stayed for another 25 years.

From there, it handled freight workings to Bristol, Bath, Evesham, Worcester and Birmingham, via the notorious Lickey Incline. It also managed to fit in the occasional passenger turn, and helped out with summer Saturday excursion traffic.

No. 3924 was renumbered 43924 by BR on February 5, 1949.

Its next allocation was to Bristol Barrow Road in August 1962. Its last day's service was at St Phillips Marsh yard on May 15, 1965, and it was withdrawn in June of that year and sold to Woodham Brothers on July 26, 1965. It duly arrived at Barry in October 1965.

No. 43924 doubleheading with LMS 4F 0-6-0 No. 44422 on the West Somerset Railway in 2017. FOTOPHILE 69

CUTTING THROUGH RED TAPE

Alec Macdonald picked No. 43924 and said: "It's a good robust locomotive with a good set of tyres."

Alec had many contacts and could secure any needed parts and what he could not secure he could acquire from other locomotives about to be scrapped. An agreement was made with Dai to put a deposit on the engine, although he could not sell it outright as BR had stipulated there were to be no resales of any of the stock.

The late Cpt Peter Manisty MBE, DSN, RN was one of the most influential men in the British railway preservation movement. A leading light in the founding of the Bluebell Railway, he helped set up the Association of Railway Preservation Societies (now the Heritage Railway Association) of which he was chairman for many years. He was also instrumental in overturning this BR stipulation regarding resales.

On December 5, 1967, BR notified the North Eastern Locomotive Preservation Group (NELPG) that NER Q6 0-8-0 No. 63395, which had been retained in store at Tyne Dock for purchase by the group, had been disposed of for scrap and was no longer available. Urgent enquiries established the locomotive had not moved to the scrapyard, but

although willing, the company concerned was unable to resell to NELPG because of the clause in the BR contract banning resale.

NELPG approached Peter Manisty at the ARPS to try to get this clause in the contract changed. He felt it was better that a representative of all interested preservation societies made an approach to the British Railways Board rather than the individual group itself. He therefore arranged a meeting with BRB in mid-December 1967, which resulted in an agreement to a change to the standard terms and conditions of the BRB sales contract to allow resales – not just of the Q6, but across the board, which effectively cleared the way for the purchase by preservationists of the locomotives at Dai Woodham's yard.

Previously the 4F Society had approached Mr Cheetham, a BR scrap controller as he could sanction the sale, but he had declined. Cheetham told Ian: "BR policy was not to sell these scrapped engines."

Woodham Brothers was not allowed to sell on any engines and BR did not want to set a precedent of so doing. The clause stipulated that the scrap dealer could only sell the locomotives on in pieces – this is where

No. 43924 with LMS Fowler tender without coal rails at Dai Woodham's scrapyard in Barry in July 1968, three months before it made transport heritage history with its move to the newly opened Keighley & worth Valley Railway. HUGH LLEWELYN*

the prospective owners put money down in parts to secure the engine for future purchase. However, Dai was very understanding and this aided other societies to secure their engines for preservation and raise the cash slowly.

The 4F Society had affiliations with the ARPS and had previously engaged its assistance as well as similar requests from many other groups. This helped in tackling the decision of the BR scrap sales controller but it was Cpt Manisty, working with NELPG, who was persuasive with overturning the decision.

GWR mogul No. 5322 was the first rescue appeal for a Woodham's locomotive but MR No. 43924 was the first to be bought and moved out.

After the sale of No. 43924 for £2000 the society was looking to move

it out of the Welsh scrapyard in September 1968, as it took time and a lot of work to ready the rusting, stripped-down locomotive for its journey and get paperwork to be signed by BR to allow movement on the main line. After No. 43924 went north, two more engines left Barry scrapyard in early 1969. SR Maunsell U class 2-6-0 No. 31618 moved in January of that year to a site in Kent, and eventually to the Bluebell Railway. GWR 2-6-0 No. 5322 left in March 1969 for Caerphilly, and later the Great Western Society's Didcot Railway Centre.

Many others followed these to heritage railway sites all over the country. The total number of engines that left Woodham's yard for preservation purposes is 213, a large proportion of which have been returned to steam.

Without the assistance of men like Cpt Manisty, and Dai Woodham, and enthusiasts' preservation groups and societies such as the NELPG (Q6, J72 ,K1, J27) and the 4F Society (43924), who never gave up and thought outside the box, would we have heritage railways today?

Cpt Manisty's ground-breaking achievement in December 1967 meant that for the first time, steam locomotives could be resold to preservation groups, making him a real contender for the man that saved steam – for us all to enjoy today, from small children entranced by the sounds and smoke to the elder generation with steam-filled memories, and photographers perched waiting for the smoke plume.

No. 43924 exits Myholmes Tunnel on October 7, 2014. NEIL SCOTT*

INVOICE

Telephone: **BLYTH 3666**
Telegram: "Battleship Blyth"

BATTLESHIP WHARF,

No. X. 2301

M: Major W.B. Greenfield, M.B.E.
North Eastern Locomotive Preservation Group,
104 Dryden Road,
GATESHEAD, on TYNE 9,
Co. Durham.

BLYTH, 30th January, 19 68

Dr. to **HUGHES BOLCKOW LIMITED.**
(MEMBER OF THE METAL INDUSTRIES GROUP OF COMPANIES)

Your Order No. ....   Issue Instruction No. ....

Description	Unit Price	Total
to B.R. Locomotive No. 63395, class Q6.		£2,300. -.
		CHEQUE FOR £1,200. ALREADY RECEIVED.

1170   Date 1 FEB 68.   The sum of £ s. d. 1186 1200

Received the sum of One thousand Two Hundred Pounds only
From N.E. Loco Preservation Group
per pro. HUGHES BOLCKOW LIMITED
Accountant

TERMS - STRICTLY NET   **Monthly Accounts**

Please make out cheques payable to the order of Hughes Bolckow Limited.

Packing must not be deducted from Account unless actually returned to above address Carriage Paid within 2 months from date of Invoice, and Credit Note received for same.
If goods are not delivered in 10 days from this date we should be advised immediately as British Railways will not accept liability for loss unless notified within 14 days from date of despatch. Claims for goods damaged in transit cannot be acknowledged unless signed for as "damaged" or "quantity and condition unknown" and Notification sent to British Railways within three days of delivery.

BRITISH RAILWAYS BOARD

B.R. 22008

Telephone No.: 21021   Extn. 2412
Telegraphic Address:

Divisional Manager's Office,
Marland House,
Central Square,
CARDIFF.
CF1 1NN.

Please quote this reference when replying EF/SR3/34741   Your reference:- -

14th August, 1968.

Dear Sir(s),
recent enquiry
In reply to your enquiry of .... I have pleasure in quoting hereunder rates for carriage by Merchandise Train. They are subject to (a) the Board's Conditions of Carriage applicable to the traffic named below, (b) where appropriate, the Board's Conditions of Carriage by Water and (c) the Board's Charging Regulations for traffic by Merchandise Trains, copies of which are available on application.

From:	Description of Traffic	Rate and Conditions
Sidings on Dock Lines at Barry	One Steam Locomotive 43924 "Dead on Own Wheels"	Lump Sum £500. 0s. 0d.
To: Keighley	Inclusive of Examination and Provision of Caretaker.	
	Subject to locomotive being prepared for movement to the Divisional Maintenance Engineer's satisfaction.	
	Will you kindly advise me if the rate is acceptable, together with the date traffic is likely to pass.	
	If I do not hear from you within a period of six months, the quotation will be considered withdrawn.	

British Railways Board reserves the right, at its discretion, to withdraw or modify these rates.

I shall be glad to furnish any further information desired.

Yours faithfully,

PETER C. HILTON

Chairman,
To Midland 4F. Preservation Society,
C/o. "Plas-y-Coed,"
52, St. Michael's Road,
Blundellsands, Liverpool 23.

Notes: "C" denotes Collection and "D" Delivery within usual limits. "S" denotes Station: P.S." Private Siding: "O.R." Owner's Risk. Rates quoted with the condition "O.R." or "Owner's Risk" are given on the terms that the Consignor shall sign a request that the traffic is to be forwarded at Owner's Risk.

British Rail's quotation for moving No. 49324 from Barry Island to Keighley (left) and the receipt from Hughes Bolckow Ltd for payment by NELPG for NER Q6 0-8-0 No. 63395, the first BR steam locomotive resold by a scrap merchant for preservation, effectively paving the way for 213 locomotives to eventually be rescued from Barry scrapyard.

A NEW HOME IN BRONTE COUNTRY

It has been said that when saving a locomotive from Barry scrapyard, buying it was the easiest part. It was after then that the real work started.

BR initially allowed the locomotives to be towed behind a diesel 'dead on its own wheels' with a brake van at the rear, but after a few instances of overheated axleboxes owing to lack of lubrication, by 1976 BR had banned all rail movement for these saved locomotives and they went by road via the M4.

The new home selected for No. 43924 was Haworth on the Keighley & Worth Valley Railway, which in June 1968 had reopened as the second operating standard gauge preserved steam railway.

No. 43924 had to be prepared for the trip up to Haworth, which is where Alec called the shots.

He went to Barry with Ian and John Collingwood in John's minivan. They stayed three days in a local guesthouse working all day with No. 43924, jacking it up on each axle and lubricating and using packing, otherwise it would run hot and seize.

Cardiff Canton diesel locomotive traction maintenance depot (shedcode 86A) contacted them to ask if they needed jacks. John replied: "yes please, three jacks and a couple of fitters."

John went to collect them in his van and with the jacks and fitters, the minivan was a faster ride down Wenvoe Hill (between Barry and Cardiff) because of the extra weight, leading them to joke about, "getting your boots out if you want to stop at the bottom."

The journey began on September 10, 1968; a meticulous job was done preparing No. 43924 as BR stated that if it seized on the main line, it would be cut up there and then.

Alec came up with the compromise of a 15mph speed limit to reduce the probability of running hot while being towed along the main lines by a diesel overnight, changing the lead diesel at each BR boundary.

John remembers being told of a driver at one changeover saying: "I'm late and want to get back". Fortunately Alec had done a very good job preparing No. 43924 and it did not overheat.

The route from Barry was via Cardiff, Newport, Hereford, Shrewsbury, Crewe, Stockport, Edgeley, Stalybridge, Huddersfield and Shipley.

No. 43924 arrived on Platform 3 at Keighley facing the wrong way at 5.25am on September 11, 1968. It was turned on the Shipley triangle before making its way behind Hudswell Clarke 0-6-0T No. 31 to the yard at Haworth. John recalls a bitterly cold snowy first winter working on the locomotive outside, as the sheds were full at that time.

The locomotive steamed again in its

The Midland 4F 0-6-0 in its guise as LMS No. 3924 at Haworth in September 1974. HUGH LLEWELYN*

second life in 1970 and it was obviously a proud moment never to be forgotten.

In LMS black livery, No. 43924 ran on the Keighley & Worth Valley Railway for many years and became a solid workhorse and a popular sight.

In 1979 the Barry Steam Locomotive Action Group was formed with the aim of combining potential preservation groups, Woodhams, funders, and financial contributors to 'grease the wheels'.

As the number of locomotives remaining at Barry dropped near to 100 it was apparent that Woodhams would begin once again scrapping the engines but fortunately only two were dealt with and BR Standard 9F 2-10-0 No. 92085 and GWR 2-6-2T No. 4156 were the last to be broken up at Barry.

However, it was the 4F Society that had paved the way for the floodgates to open meaning we now can enjoy visits to preserved railways all over the country, with trains often being handled by locomotives rescued from Barry.

FAME AND FORTUNE

In 1987 it became apparent that the engine needed a complete overhaul; not just routine repair; something that the 4F Society could not afford to do.

Sets of tubes and superheater flues are not in the same league as a new boiler but it would cost £85,000 or more to get it back in steam.

As a result the society decided to sell No. 43924 to the KWVR as it was beyond its resources to continue to maintain the engine. I know my father did not want to let it go but in the best interests of the locomotive the members all agreed and a sum of £33,000 for the sale was reached, each society member receiving a cheque for £4125.

On January 3, 1990 there was a written agreement made between the KWVR and the society outlining that there a plaque would be fitted on the cab to mark the preservation society's achievements and the best bit; the members of the society were allowed to use the locomotive for a day or two each year.

I personally called it Train Day and loved it. I got to see my dad at his happiest, clipboard in hand organising footplate riders.

Sadly we did not see No. 43924

British Railways Western Region

Marland House
Central Square
Cardiff   CF1 1NN
Cardiff 21021 Ext: 2412

R. C. Hilton, Divisional Manager, Cardiff

J. Johnson Esq.,
Chairman,
Midland 4F Preservation Society,
"Plas-y-Coed',
52 St. Michael's Road,
Blundellsands,
Liverpool 23.

y/r
o/r   EF/SR3/34741   Date   28th June, 1968.

Dear Sir,

Locomotive 43924

This locomotive has been examined at Barry and the following defects have been noted:-

(1)   Part of the inside motion has been left in position.

(2)   The tender hand brake is rusted solidly in the off position.

(3)   Trailing drag link missing.

In view of the length of time this locomotive has been standing without attention it would be necessary for the following work to be carried out:-

(a)   Engine to be lifted and all axle boxes to receive attention

(b)   Rusted inside motion to be removed

(c)   Tender hand brake to be freed and put in working order

(d)   Trailing drag link to be replaced

(e)   Corks to be fitted to side rods

(f)   Engine to be oiled throughout

Please let me know whether you would be prepared to have this work carried out to my Engineer's satisfaction otherwise it would be necessary to consider movement of the locomotive other than on its own wheels.

Yours faithfully,

For R. C. HILTON

A. DOWLING
CHARGES OFFICER

BR 2001/13

British Rail's list of requirements for the movement of No. 43924 from Barry.

running again until 2011, after it spent 25 years in many pieces in sheds while its boiler was sent to Crewe for overhaul.

Money was the main delay but then when it was the 4F's turn, the stricken BR Standard 4MT 2-6-4T No. 80002 jumped the queue. The end result was that the overhaul eventually cost about £250,000, substantially more than the £50,000 originally quoted on the donation box.

A complex machine well made and looked after; No. 43924 has lasted double its proposed life and this is where I applaud the hard work and care of the shed crew at Haworth. Their knowledge and love of this engine is apparent.

It has now clocked up more than 1.5 million miles and is 98 years old. This is thanks to the people who saved it from scrap and those who have kept it going at Haworth. No. 43924 has many hits on YouTube and more magazine covers than a top model. TV star Lisa Riley chose Haworth as her Holiday of My Lifetime with Len Goodman and, of course, No. 43924 was featured.

In the 2014 film Testament of Youth, the 4F has a starring role on the platform, and two years later was in the opening sequence of Swallows and Amazons. There have also been events such as Bristol Barrow Road 82E shed-men's day out. The locomotive

spent most of its working life around the Midlands and the Gloucester area, mainly pulling coal.

There was also a visit to Bombardier Transportation on May 12, 2014 for the 175th anniversary celebration of train building at Crewe and another road trip to the Severn Valley Railway for the autumn gala in 2014.

More recently the engine made a road trip to the West Somerset Railway in spring 2017, where No. 43924 joined LMS 4F No. 44422 as well as S&D 7F 2-8-0 No. 53808, both ex-Barry scrapyard, with some doubleheading during the event.

But Train Day 2011 was a great celebration. It was fantastic. My dad was 81 by then and he was very happy and proud of the great achievement and his part of saving the locomotive.

The five surviving members were

In 2014 Ian Johnson organised a memorial train day with No. 43924 as a tribute to Alexander Macdonald.

In 2011, No. 43924 was given its first run out in 25 years. At the time the surviving members of the Midland 4F Preservation Society were Mark Leather, Alan Johnson, Ian Johnson, John Collingwood and Alec Macdonald.
FIONA KENNAUGH

Midland 4F No. 43924 climbs the 1-in-58 gradient away from Keighley. BRIAN SHARPE

The author and her father Alexander Macdonald on the footplate of No. 43924 in 2011. P WALKER

No. 43924 works hard as it climbs from Oakworth to Haworth on a line that is a continuous climb from Keighley to Oxenhope, averaging out at 1-in-90.
ANDREW*

No. 43924 climbs towards Oakworth on November 5, 27. KEN WOOLLEY

there; Ian, Alan, John, Mark and Alec.

However, my father started to decline in 2012. He had a series of strokes and these stripped away the vital man he used to be. He died in July the following year, aged 82, having had vascular dementia in the latter stages of his life.

In 2014 Ian Johnson, who was a good kind friend to my father, organized a memorial train day, which was another wonderful day to remember at the KWVR. My father's ashes went into the firebox as per his request – into the locomotive he loved and helped to save.

My father was proud of what he did with the society and I am proud of him, and thank him for the early introduction to Haworth and steam engines.

I would not say it is easy being female and enjoying being around steam and diesel locomotives – I have come across the 'old boys network' and lost a few times, but I have also met some wonderful chaps who are delighted to see a female and her camera at various steam events.

September 2018 brings the 50th anniversary of No. 43924's escape from Barry, and 2020 will see No. 43924's centenary. No. 43924 has much more to offer and so do many other fabulous engines on preserved heritage railways around the UK.

*Additional reporting by Robin Jones.

No. 43924 and crew at Minehead station on the West Somerset Railway, with Alan Dorrington in denim. ALAN DORRINGTON

The BBC Holiday Of My Lifetime programme featuring Lisa Riley with Len Goodman was filmed in August 2015 when the 4F was the service locomotive that day. ROGER FRANCE

Testament of Youth is the First World War memoir of Vera Brittain. The film was made by Heyday Films, and directed by James Kent. The railway sequences were filmed at Keighley station on March 25- 27, 2014. The 4F was used alongside LNWR Coal Tank 0-6-2T No. 1054 and carriages from Vintage Carriages Trust and the Lancashire & Yorkshire Trust. The 4F was largely used for general 'set dressing' and only really appeared in a sequence meant to be Charing Cross station. ROGER FRANCE

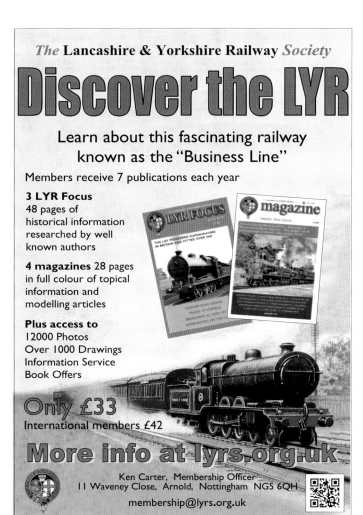

The Lancashire & Yorkshire Railway Society

Discover the LYR

Learn about this fascinating railway known as the "Business Line"

Members receive 7 publications each year

3 LYR Focus
48 pages of historical information researched by well known authors

4 magazines 28 pages in full colour of topical information and modelling articles

Plus access to
12000 Photos
Over 1000 Drawings
Information Service
Book Offers

Only £33
International members £42

More info at lyrs.org.uk

Ken Carter, Membership Officer
11 Waveney Close, Arnold, Nottingham NG5 6QH
membership@lyrs.org.uk

HERITAGE RAILWAY
THE BRIGHTER STEAM NEWS MAGAZINE

SPECIAL OFFER!

3 issues for £5

followed by £20 every six months

Offer expires: 31/12/18

- Steam era preservation
- Rare archive material ● Get your copy early!

CALL – 01507 529529 and Quote: HR160
VISIT – www.classicmagazines.co.uk/hr160

SUBSCRIBE TODAY!

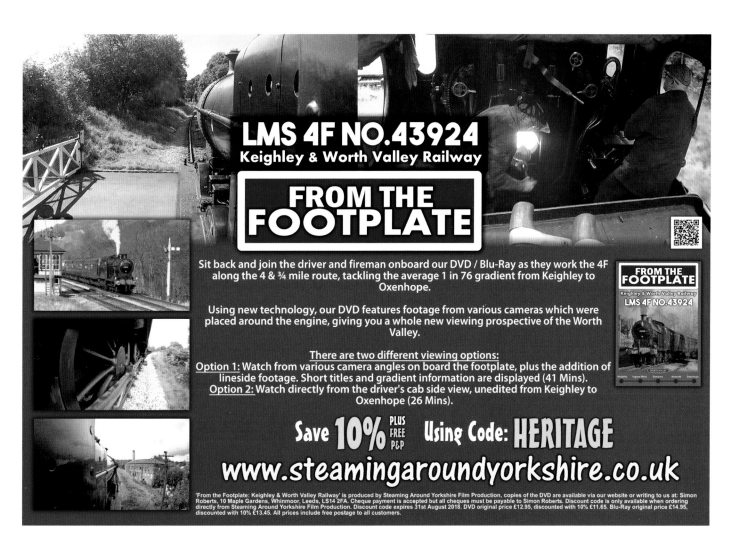

LMS 4F NO.43924
Keighley & Worth Valley Railway

FROM THE FOOTPLATE

Sit back and join the driver and fireman onboard our DVD / Blu-Ray as they work the 4F along the 4 & ¾ mile route, tackling the average 1 in 76 gradient from Keighley to Oxenhope.

Using new technology, our DVD features footage from various cameras which were placed around the engine, giving you a whole new viewing prospective of the Worth Valley.

There are two different viewing options:
Option 1: Watch from various camera angles on board the footplate, plus the addition of lineside footage. Short titles and gradient information are displayed (41 Mins).
Option 2: Watch directly from the driver's cab side view, unedited from Keighley to Oxenhope (26 Mins).

FROM THE FOOTPLATE
Keighley & Worth Valley Railway
LMS 4F NO.43924

Save **10%** PLUS FREE P&P **Using Code: HERITAGE**

www.steamingaroundyorkshire.co.uk

'From the Footplate: Keighley & Worth Valley Railway' is produced by Steaming Around Yorkshire Film Production, copies of the DVD are available via our website or writing to us at: Simon Roberts, 10 Maple Gardens, Whinmoor, Leeds, LS14 2FA. Cheque payment is accepted but all cheques must be payable to Simon Roberts. Discount code is only available when ordering directly from Steaming Around Yorkshire Film Production. Discount code expires 31st August 2018. DVD original price £12.95, discounted with 10% £11.65. Blu-Ray original price £14.95, discounted with 10% £13.45. All prices include free postage to all customers.

Chapter 10

THE FABULOUS
STEAM FLEET!

As the newly opened Keighley & Worth Valley Railway soared in popularity and grew from strength to strength, more and bigger locomotives were needed to pull longer trains. At 4 ¾ miles it may be one of the UK's shortest standard gauge heritage lines, but it boasts one of the best steam fleets in the business!

THE *BAHAMAS* AND DINTING STORY

LMS Stanier Jubilee 4-6-0 No. 45596 *Bahamas* has many a tale to tell. Not only was it the last engine used by BR for experimental purposes for improved draughting arrangements, but it has the unique honour of having two venues set up specially to accommodate it and its supporting society.

Bahamas was built by the North British Locomotive Company and entered service in January 1935 numbered 5596, initially allocated to Crewe before moving on to various sheds around the England and finally, as No.45596, to Stockport Edgeley in 1962.

What makes *Bahamas* historically significant is its double blastpipe and chimney. Although used on other classes of steam locomotives, the double chimney exhaust arrangement fitted to *Bahamas* is regarded as the last experiment by British Railways to improve the performance of its fleet of steam locomotives.

It had not been the only Jubilee to be fitted with a double chimney. No. 5684 was so fitted between May 1937 and October 1938. No. 5553 was also fitted with a double chimney and blast pipe in 1940 but they were removed quite soon afterwards. No. 5742 had a double chimney from February 1940 to October 1955. Nos. 5735 and 5736 were rebuilt in 1942 with a double chimney each. Whereas those on Nos. 5553 and 5742 were a simple exhaust arrangement, that on No. 5684 was of the Kylchap type.

Although the concept and design of the latest double chimney arrangement for the 'Jubilees' had evolved at the Rugby Testing Station during 1956-57, it was not until May 1961 that *Bahamas* was fitted with the equipment during overhaul at Crewe Works.

Bahamas remained at Stockport Edgeley for four years and after hauling a number of enthusiasts' specials was withdrawn from traffic.

It had been a popular engine in the locality and as it was the last 'named' locomotive on the shed roster, enthusiasts tried to buy it under the banner of Manchester Jubilee Locomotive Preservation Society. However, after much wrangling this plan came to nothing, and British Rail agreed to sell *Bahamas* to Drapers, the Hull scrap dealer.

On its way to Birmingham on November 26, 2013 for its overhaul to begin, *Bahamas* made a detour to publisher Mortons Ltd's headquarters in Horncastle, Lincolnshire, where it was displayed to townsfolk in the company's Morton Way car park. ROBIN JONES

LEFT: LMS Jubilee 4-6-0 No. 45596 *Bahamas* crosses Mytholmes viaduct on March 24, 1990. BRIAN SHARPE

Jubilee 4-6-0 No.5596 (later BR No. 45596) *Bahamas* – built by North British works No.24154 in 1934 and completed that year before delivery to the LMS for entry into service in January 1935 – with double chimney in LMS crimson lake livery at Dinting Railway Centre in April 1980. HUGH LLEWELYN*

It took the intervention and subsequent discussions between Stockport North MP Arnold Gregory and the chairman of the British Railways Board Sir Stanley Raymond, that led to the cancellation of the sale to Drapers.

However, it was bought by the rebranded Stockport (Bahamas) Locomotive Society in summer 1967, and was then moved to the Hunslet Engine Company in Leeds for overhaul, being restored to service in LMS crimson lake livery.

On March 1968, at a formal ceremony at Hunslet, *Bahamas* was handed to its new owners, together with an invoice for £6500, before the engine departed for Stockport.

On November 15, 1968, *Bahamas* was moved to the old steam shed at Dinting near Glossop in Derbyshire, which the society was developing as the Dinting Railway Centre, volunteers turning a weed-choked site into a significant tourist attraction.

Dinting held its first public steam weekend over four days during Easter 1969.

Hudswell Clarke 0-6-0T *Nunlow* had arrived from G&T Earle's Hope cement works in early April, and within two weeks entered traffic to work alongside *Bahamas* providing footplate rides for the deluge of visitors during that four-day Easter event.

LMS Royal Scot 4-6-0 No. 46115 Scots Guardsman arrived the following month (see below) from the Keighley & Worth Valley Railway and, almost immediately, the cosmetic restoration to its former LMS livery was started. Its completion within six months provided an opportunity for a renaming ceremony to be held in October, with the local Scots Guards Association in attendance which brought the colourful sight and sounds of this Scottish military regiment to the Derbyshire hillside.

By 1973, the society had completed a new exhibition hall capable of handling up to nine large locomotives.

Following the expiry of its boiler certificate, that year proved to be last steaming for *Bahamas* until extensive boiler repairs could be undertaken. Fundraising began in order to have the work undertaken and make the engine operational once more – an event that would not take place until 15 years later.

At its peak the museum featured visits by famous engines including *Flying Scotsman*, *Bittern*, *Blue Peter*, *Sir Nigel Gresley*, *Clan Line* and *Green Arrow*. However, in 1990, the centre closed when the landlord wanted the site back after the lease ran out. The site was leased from one of the society's members – but the group later failed to renegotiate favourable terms with him, as a result the society had to move within six months.

A small group of society committee members was tasked with exploring options for new premises. The East Lancashire Railway was first considered, and then under the microscope several acres of disused sidings next to the West Coast Main Line at Weaverham near Northwich, including a disused branch line into the ICI works in the town. Vale Royal Council offered £70,000 towards relocation costs. Sadly, ICI was not ready to release any land. Peak Rail at Buxton was also considered.

The KWVR approached the Bahamas group initially on an informal basis, knowing it needed a base from which to operate *Bahamas* on the main line. During the winter of 1989-90 there were two 'secret' meetings with KWVR officials, one at a supermarket cafe in north-east Lancashire, and another a

In late 2016, the new tender tank for *Bahamas* is lifted by the Bahamas Locomotive Society's own steam crane at Ingrow following delivery. BLS

The boiler of *Bahamas* passes its steam test at Tyseley Locomotive Works on December 21, 2017, its overhaul being carried out as part of a £776,000 Heritage Lottery Fund grant. The boiler had not been steamed since December 1997. Its first 'warm through' firing was on December 12. BLS

Actor Patrick Mower, who plays Rodney Blackstock in the TV soap Emmerdale, turned up at the Mortons offices in Horncastle to inspect *Bahamas*, and is pictured meeting the publisher's marketing staff.
ROBIN JONES

visit to Ingrow itself on a wet winters day, followed by a visit to another cafe in Keighley town centre. The Bahamas members were offered the Midland Railway goods warehouse adjacent to Ingrow West station, and were made welcome by KWVR officials. The offer on the site was accepted.

Restored to its British Railways condition, *Bahamas* successfully operated 37 railtours on the main line between 1989 and 1994, over and above the previous four since the society owned the locomotive. These were followed by visits to various heritage railways until the expiry of its boiler certificate in 1997 resulted in its withdrawal from operation.

The engine then went on public display in the museum of the Keighley & Worth Valley Railway at Oxenhope, where it stayed until 2012 when it was invited to attend the Railfest 2012 event at the National Railway Museum in York. Its stay at York was extended until the following year, when it returned to Ingrow West.

In March 2013, the Heritage Lottery Fund awarded £776,000 to the society, not just for the overhaul to main line standard of *Bahamas*, but for the creation of a unique learning coach, as featured in Chapter 14. So *Bahamas* went off to Tyseley Locomotive Works for its first heavy overhaul since 1961. On the back of a low loader, en route *Bahamas* paid a visit to *The Railway Magazine* and *Heritage Railway* publisher Mortons' Horncastle offices on November 26 that year, and among the crowds that turned up to see it was Emmerdale star Patrick Mower (Rodney Blackstock). By December of that year work had commenced on the boiler, wheels and frames, and following a successful hydraulic test the first fire was lit in the firebox of the completed boiler on December 12, 2017 as a 'warming fire' only, the first lit in Bahamas since December 1997. The boiler test was passed on December 21, and the message was loud and clear – Bahamas was on its way back, maybe for 2018!

THE NATIONAL TRUST'S LNWR CLASSIC

Designed by LNWR Locomotive Superintendent Francis Webb, the so-called 'King of Crewe', the first of the Coal class 0-6-0 tender locomotives appeared in 1873. As the name suggests, were designed for hauling slow heavy coal trains.

The 0-6-2Ts were a later version which came out in 1881, with the same cheaply produced cast iron wheels and H-section spokes as the tender engines. A trailing radial truck supporting the bunker was added also with two similar cast-iron wheels.

A total of 300 coal tanks was built between 1881-97. Altogether, 292 survived at the Grouping of 1923 and passed to the LMS, and 64 passed into BR ownership in 1948.

No. 1054 was built at Crewe in September 1888 and during its working life, it was based at Aston, Edge Hill, Abergavenny, Bangor, Shrewsbury, Patricroft, Warrington, Plodder Lane, Bletchley, Craven Arms and Abercynon sheds. It also briefly worked on NCB lines.

In October 1949 it received its British Railway number 58926 and found use at Bletchley, and again at Shrewsbury, before going on loan to the National Coal Board in 1954. As the last surviving member of the class, No. 1054 was store at Abergavenny, where it was fitted with a snow plough in event of disruptive snowfalls during the winter months. With LNWR 'Super D' 0-8-0 No. 49121, it was brought out of storage to haul the last train on the Abergavenny-Merthyr line plus the Ebbw Vale and Rhymney branches with a Stephenson Locomotive Society railtour on January 5, 1958.

Immediately after this trip, No. 58926 moved to Pontypool Road where it was briefly used as a stationary boiler. It was finally withdrawn during November 1958

and moved to Crewe for scrapping. An attempt to raise funds to buy it and save it from the cutter's torch was spearheaded by J M Dunn, the former shedmaster at Bangor. He organised the Webb Coal Tank Engine Preservation Fund, and within six months had raised the purchase price of £500, and so No. 1054 was the first locomotive to be saved for preservation as a result of a public appeal. For £150 it was repainted into LNWR livery at Crewe works.

In 1961, the coal tank was taken to Hednesford in the care of the Railway Preservation Society' Midland's Area Group. During 1963, No.1054 was donated to the National Trust and moved to Penrhyn Castle in North Wales.

Although now on display to the public, the accommodation prevented any long-term conservation work and so arrangements were made for the engine to be cared for by the Bahamas Locomotive Society.

As a consequence, it moved to the Dinting Railway Centre in 1973 where it was restored to operational condition in time for it to take part in the 150th anniversary celebration, during 1980, of the opening of the Liverpool & Manchester Railway.

The engine was regularly operated at Dinting, worked a series of trains for the Wilsons brewery from Manchester during 1984 and, significantly, during 1986, worked a special train from Shrewsbury to Stockport organised by the Stephenson Locomotive Society to celebrate the 80th birthday of William Arthur Camwell, the man who had organised the aforementioned special in 1958. When the centre closed, like No. 45596 *Bahamas*, No. 1054 came to the KWVR in 1990.

The engine has recently undergone its third overhaul by volunteers at the Bahamas Locomotive Society's Ingrow base, and returned to steam in late 2011.

No. 1054, the sole-surviving LNWR coal tank, heads up the gradient out of Keighley on February 2, 2011.
BRIAN SHARPE

It made its first appearance in traffic at the Keighley & Worth Valley Railway gala in February 2012, and during that year took on its former identities as British Railways No. 58926 and LMS Railway No. 7799. For 2013 the engine reverted to its LNWR identity as No.1054, visiting the Great Central Railway in April, and the Pontypool & Blaenavon Railway and the Locomotion museum at Shildon during September.

In October 2013, No. 1054 celebrated its 125th birthday during the 'Coal Tank 125' event on the KWVR, in October, during which it was presented with the Institution of Mechanical Engineers' Engineering Heritage Award by past president Professor Isobel Pollock.

LNWR Webb Coal Tank 0-6-2T No. 1054 approaches Oxenhope with a winter special, the green secondary headboard acknowledging its ownership by the National Trust. BRIAN SHARPE

OVERSEXED, OVERPAID, OVERSIZED AND STEAMING OVER HERE!

During the Second World War, a steam locomotive type, the outline of which nobody in Britain had seen the like of before, was steaming over our network, and in the service of the Big Four companies.

When the USA entered the war against Hitler, the United States Army Transportation Corps saw the urgent need for a cheap and efficient locomotive type that could be employed on the wrecked railways of Europe, hauling both military hardware and civilian freight.

Major JW Marsh of the US Army Corps of Engineers looked at two earlier designs, one an update of a Baldwin Locomotive Works' First World War design in contingency for war transportation, which became the S159 class. The other was the S200 2-8-2 class, which was introduced in 1941 and Lend-Leased to the UK for use in the Middle East, and fitted into the British loading gauge.

The major produced a blueprint for the S160 Consolidation class of 2-8-0s, again on austerity principles and with an emphasis on efficient and fast construction speed rather than longevity, and so compromises in design were made.

With cast frames and cast wheels, the front two driving axles were sprung independently from the rear two driving axles to allow for running on poor-quality track. The larger eight-wheel tender layout was derived from the similar design for the British WD Austerity 2-8-0, (which itself was based upon a First World War design for the US Army for use in Europe) with the coal bunker inset above the water tank to improve visibility when running backwards.

Features that were uncommon in Britain at that time, included a large enclosed cab area, an air gap for maintenance purposes between the wheels and the boiler, a sand

USATC 'Big Jim' 2-8-0 No, 5820 as 28201 in Keighley Great Northern goods yard surrounded by extras in US Army uniform and period military truck in 1978, during the making of the movie Yanks. ROBIN HIGGINS

container on top of the boiler in order that the heat would keep the sand dry, a Westinghouse brake pump by the smokebox door, and, less obvious, the use of bar frames, instead of frames made from solid sheets of steel.

A total of 800 S160s were built in 13 batches in 1942-43 by ALCO, Baldwin and Lima Locomotive Works, and also supplied on a Lend-Lease basis. Incidentally, although S160 has been popularly adopted as the class identification for this type,it has never been verified as an official designation. The Baldwin designation for the design, 2-8-0-19S, is found on some drawings, and is stamped on to major locomotive components on examples built by the firm.

The S160s were shipped to South Wales and despatched from the GWR shed at Newport, Ebbw Junction. No. 1604 attended a handover ceremony at Paddington station on December 11, 1942, when it entered service in Britain. Attached to the smokebox were the flags of the USA and Britain. During the ceremony Lord Leathers, Minister of War Transport, formally accepted the locomotive from Col N A Ryan, chief of transportation of the US Army.

The first 43 locomotives were

transferred to the LNER's works at Doncaster for completion and running in over the East Coast Main Line. Each of the Big Four companies eventually deployed a total of 400 S160s for 'running-in' purposes while they awaited shipping to the continent for D-Day. In reality, rather than being tested, they were replacing damaged stock and increasing the capacity of the British network to facilitate the movement of military equipment and troops.

No. 5820 was built in 1945 by Lima of Ohio for the US Army to aid the war effort in Europe, being shipped directly to Poland. After the war the locomotive was taken into stock by Poland State Railways and renumbered TR203-474, while allocated to Katowice shed. The engine remained in Poland until withdrawal for preservation by the Polish Railway Museum in Warsaw.

In the mid-1970s, a number of Worth Valley members made several visits to Poland and enabled No. 5820 to be purchased for use in the Worth Valley.

It arrived at Haworth in November 1977, entering service in the following year still carrying Polish livery and became known as 'Big Jim'. (No. 30072 was known as 'Little Jim' at Guildford) During this time the engine was re-liveried to USATC grey and chosen to appear in the feature film Yanks, filmed on location in Keighley.

Following withdrawal in the early 1990s because of the condition of the driving axleboxes, the locomotive was laid aside until a lengthy restoration was undertaken. After a thorough overall the engine returned to service in February 2014, temporarily painted in British Railways unlined black, fictitiously numbered No. 95820. For the Easter holiday No. 5820 regained its number and authentic USATC grey livery and is regularly seen working trains along the branch.

Its boiler ticket expires in 2023.

THE 'THIRD' BAHAMAS LOCOMOTIVE

Hudswell Clarke 0-6-0T No. 1704 of 1938 Nunlow was supplied new to G&T Earle Cement Manufacturers for use on its industrial railway connecting its works at Hope in Derbyshire, with the Midland Sheffield to Manchester line.

It continued to work for Earles until 1964 when it was put into store after being replaced by diesels.

In 1969 it was purchased by the Bahamas Locomotive Society for £500 and arrived at Dinting Railway Centre in time for the society's first Easter Steam Weekend. No. 1704 entered into service, giving footplate rides every Sunday throughout the season.

On closure of Dinting, No. 1704 moved permanently to Ingrow West in 2003 when the society took over the old Midland goods shed.

After overhaul the locomotive returned to steam in 2008 and can occasionally be seen at work on KWVR trains, especially on gala weekends. Its boiler ticket expires in April 2018.

Hudswell Clarke 0-6-0T No. 1704 of 1938 *Nunlow* makes a spirited departure from Keighley on June 4, 2008. BRIAN SHARPE

TAFF VALE SURVIVOR

Taff Vale Railway Class 02 0-6-2T No. 85 was built in 1899 by Neilson Reid, and was taken over by the GWR in 1922 and given the number 426. The whole class soon became surplus to requirements in the face of the Swindon empire's policy of standardisation and was withdrawn in 1927. While the majority of the class were scrapped at Swindon, 85 was sold in 1929 to the Lambton, Hetton & Joicey Colliery Company, which had its own extensive system in County Durham. The loco was used to haul coal trains between the inland collieries and the coast. When the coal industry was nationalised in 1947 it became NCB No. 52 and remained in service there until 1968. Following withdrawal, it arrived on the KWVR in December 1970, where it was steamed once before being stored in the Oxenhope exhibition shed.

It was rebuilt to its original outline by a group of Worth Valley volunteers in the 1990s and gave good service until withdrawal in 2010.

Seen as an ideal locomotive for the branch, No. 85 entered the workshops at Haworth and re-entered service at the 2016 winter steam gala in its original fully lined out Taff Vale Railway livery.

The other Taff Vale Railway locomotive to be preserved is O class No. 28, owned by the National Railway Museum. It requires a major overhaul if it is to be steamed again.

West Yorkshire weather is no problem for Valleys veteran Taff Vale Railway 02 0-6-2T No. 85, seen in action on a snowbound January 21, 2018. POINT AND SHOOT PHOTOGRAPHY

LEFT: Lancashire & Yorkshire Railway freight 0-6-0 No. 957 is backed by Taff Vale Railway 02 0-6-2T No. 85 on this departure from Keighley on February 19, 2016. The Keighley & Worth Valley Railway runs on many days in winter when other heritage lines are closed. BRIAN SHARPE

BRITISH HERITAGE RETURNED FROM SWEDEN

With the outbreak of the Second World War, it became clear the Britain would need a new instant but cheaply built generation of locomotives, not only to supplement traffic on the national network, which was now being run by the government again, but for use overseas when the Axis-occupied territories were freed.

Robert Riddles, the director of transportation equipment at the Ministry of Supply (and from 1948 onwards, member of the Railway Executive for mechanical and electrical engineering, the top man in charge of British Railways' locomotive policy) based his Austerity 2-8-0 design on the Stanier 8F, which had already been chosen by the government as the standard War Department freight locomotive design for the Second World War.

Riddles tweaked and modified the design to apply 'no frills' austerity principles – as with the USATC S160s, a cheaper build but a shorter life expectancy.

His economies included a boiler of simpler construction, which was parallel rather than tapered and a round-topped firebox rather than a Belpaire one, and one that was made of steel rather than the more expensive copper. The WD 2-8-0 was faster to build with a simple construction using fabricated components instead of heavy expensive castings and cast iron in place of steel for items such as wheel centres.

A total of 935 Austerity 2-8-0s was built between 1943-45, 545 of them by the North British Locomotive Company of Glasgow and 390 by Vulcan Foundry of Newton-le-Willows. Indeed, the first batch of 80 were ordered as LMS 8Fs. Within a few months, they became one of the biggest classes of British steam locomotive of all time.

All but three were employed by the Army on the continent after D-Day. The conflict over, the War Department disposed of 930 locomotives, 200 being sold to the LNER where they became Class O7 533 more bought by the British Transport Commission, which set up British Railways in 1948.

In 1946, 12 were exported to Hong Kong, while 184 stayed in service on the continent, most working in The Netherlands for national operator Nederlandse Spoorwegen.

The 733 WD 2-8-0s inherited by British Railways were eventually withdrawn and scrapped, rendering the class extinct. However, one is still running in Britain today, on the KWVR!

Built in January 1945 by Vulcan Foundry works No. 5200, it became WD No. 79257, and was shipped to the continent on completion. After the war, it was among those sold to the Nederlandse Spoorwegen where it became 4300 class No. 4464.

In 1953 it, along with a sister locomotive, were sold on to Statens Järnvägar, the Swedish State Railways, extensively modified and given the classification G11. At Örebro works it had a new fully enclosed cab and electric lighting and its tender was shortened to enable it to fit Swedish turntables. The chimney, the original of which had been replaced with a taller one by the Dutch, was cut down, even though it was still taller than the original.

Re-emerging from the works in a decidedly Swedish outline and renumbered 1931, it entered service in 1954.

Statens Järnvägar had bought the pair on the cheap, effectively as war surplus, to evaluate if they could replace locomotives obtained through the nationalisation of the private railways during the 1940s. However, the trials were less than satisfactory and with dieslisation looming, no more were bought.

The pair were withdrawn after a few years and became stored undercover in an isolated forest clearing at Mellansjo in northern Sweden as part of a strategic reserve, after some minor restoration work had been carried out.

KWVR members heard about the survival of the two WD 2-8-0s, albeit continental outline, and a visit Sweden to inspect both locomotives was soon arranged. They decided that No. 1931 was in a slightly better condition than its sister No. 1930 and in September 1972, it was bought by three working members of the KWVR. Unfortunately, No.1930 was later scrapped in error.

Once purchased, No. 1931 was hauled the 500 miles or more to the port of Goteborg where the locomotive and tender were hoisted aboard trailers for the sea and road journey to Ingrow.

No. 1931 arrived back at Hull Docks on January 12, 1973 and was carefully driven off the Svea Line vessel *Sverus*. No. 1931 was offloaded at Ingrow the following afternoon.

On account of the locomotive's excessive size, the chimney extension, safety valves and whistle had to be removed before No. 1931 on its trailer would fit on the ship, for the trip to Haworth it was also necessary to remove the cab and tender steps. The locomotive had clearly been well looked after and needed only a minimal amount of work mechanically but a fair amount of work to return it to a British loading gauge, before it could enter traffic on the heritage line, running in its Swedish outline on the classic West Yorkshire line for a couple of years.

It was withdrawn in 1976 because of the condition of the tyres and a number of broken stays and was sidelined until 1993 when a heavy overhaul commenced with the aim of back-converting it to its as-built British guise.

The frames and wheels of an original and historically appropriate eight-wheel tender were located in a steel works in the Netherlands and were purchased

Heavy freight 2-8-0 No. 90733 heads a goods train at Oakworth in 2011. BRIAN SHARPE

Repatriated and re-Anglicised: WD 2-8-0 No. 90733 calls at Oakworth on September 18, 2007. BRIAN SHARPE

by members of the group leading the overhaul as a start on replacing the Swedish six-wheel tender. The frames were given a complete overhaul using the best components from the two tenders. A new tender tank was fabricated and fitted to the frames by British Steel at Scunthorpe.

It was decided to continue the series of numbers for repatriated engines on British Railways, and so it became No. 90733, one higher than the last BR WD Austerity 2-8-0, No. 90732 *Vulcan*. Incidentally, WD Stanier 8F No. 48773 was incorrectly given that number when it was taken in BR stock in 1957, after being mistaken for an Austerity 2-8-0.

The majority of the overhaul was undertaken by volunteers at Haworth, but the necessary boiler was found to be beyond the capabilities of the volunteers and it was necessary for the boiler work to be contracted out. The KWVR Trust, which by now was the owner of the locomotive, applied to the Heritage Lottery Fund for a grant to go towards the costs of the boiler overhaul.

The trust was awarded a grant to cover about 75% of the cost of the boiler work, with the owners having to fund the remainder themselves. As part of the boiler overhaul contract, the locomotive, less tender, was transported to the contractor's works for the fitting of the boiler and final assembly. A final steam test was carried at the contractor's works where the locomotive was run up and down the yard without the tender.

No. 90733 returned to Haworth on April 16, 2007 for the attaching of the tender and a period of testing and running-in.

It officially re-entered traffic on Monday July 23, 2007, and in doing so effectively resurrected a lost class of BR locomotive, plugging a gap in the UK steam fleet, thereby making a signification contribution to the UK heritage sector,

A 'new build' locomotive at a war surplus price?

October 16, 2005, saw GWR 4-4-0 No. 3440 *City of Truro*, which unofficially became the first locomotive to break the 100mph barrier in 1904, is backed by BR Standard 4MT 2-6-4T No. 80002 at Haworth on October 16 2005.

EVOLVING AN LMS DESIGN

As Mechanical Engineer with the newly-formed Railway Executive, Robert Riddles was in no doubt that the long-term future of Britain's railways would be electric traction.

However, in the dark days of post-war austerity, Riddles took a more pragmatic view and openly argued the case for steam, claiming that it was cheaper than the alternatives then on offer.

Coming off the drawing board in the wake of the Locomotive Exchanges of 1948, his BR Standards, as they came to be known, officially incorporated the best practices of all of the Big Four railway companies. However, five of the 12 classes were visibly based on LMS design and practice, including the Standard 4MT 2-6-0 and 2-6-4T.

At nationalisation, the London Midland Region inherited a number of LMS tank engines and the Western Region had many GWR large prairie 2-6-2T types.

These locomotives were particularly suited to commuter and secondary services.

However, in certain are particularly in Scotland and the Southern Region, the situation was not so good with large numbers of pre-Grouping types soldiering on.

Designed at Brighton, the Riddles 2-6-4T was a tank version of the BR Standard 4MT 4-6-0. A total of 155 were built between 1951-56, mostly in Brighton with small batches in Derby and Doncaster.

They were in many respects an updated version of the LMS Fairburn 4P 2-6-4Ts but with higher boiler pressure and smaller cylinders to fit within the BR loading gauge. They were shared between the Southern Region, LMR and Scottish Region, with a few on the North Eastern Region.

After nationalisation, the Southern Region built 41 LMS Fairburn 2-6-4Ts

LEFT: BR Standard 4MT 2-6-4T No. 80002 in August 2012. ROBIN JONES

at Brighton Works for its own use, replacing much older tank engines. However, once the new Standard 2-6-4Ts came on stream, the LMS-designed ones on the SR moved to the LM region in exchange for a similar number of standard tanks.

They became particularly associated with the London, Tilbury & Southend line, until it was electrified in 1962, and with Glasgow's suburban services.

The Standard 4MT tanks were more handsome in appearance than their LMS predecessors, and were well liked by their crews for their comfortable cabs, free running, good steaming and economical operation.

They performed their duties well but were very quickly replaced by more modern traction on the kind of duties they were designed for. An order for further engines was cancelled as it was becoming clear they would not be needed because of dieselisation and electrification. Built in October 1952 at Derby, No. 80002 was sent straight to Scotland and remained north of the border throughout its BR career, including use as a banking engine on the famous climb up to Beattock summit. The engine was withdrawn from service in November 1967 but retained as a carriage-heating boiler at Cowlairs (Glasgow).

The engine was purchased for preservation by the KWVR in 1969 and was towed to Keighley on May 20 that year. Once overhauled from near scrap yard condition, No. 80002 worked for many years, while needing major work to enable it to keep running. This work has included the fitting of a new inner firebox made of steel rather than the originally designed copper.

Although the engine's relatively large driving wheels can result in wheel-slip when departing Keighley on a wet rail, it has proved more than capable of handling the KWVR's heaviest trains.

No. 80002 was finally withdrawn in 2013 and is now on static display in the Oxenhope exhibition shed.

ANOTHER STANDARD WITH LMS ANCESTRY

The British Railways Standard 2MT 2-6-0 is a direct development of the LMS-designed Ivatt Class 2MT 2-6-0 and was built at the former LNER workshops at Darlington. By the end of production there were 65 Standard examples in traffic working alongside 128 engines of the LMS design.

No. 78022 was delivered new from Darlington on February 28, 1954 to Millhouses Depot in Sheffield with a final allocation at Lostock Hall (Preston) from where the engine was withdrawn from traffic September 1966 and found its way to Barry scrapyard, where it arrived in February 1967, the first of its class to arrive there.

Having successfully purchased No. 75078 with restoration well in hand, the Standard Four Locomotive Preservation Society turned its attentions to purchasing a second locomotive from Barry. After some debate, the society decided to purchase Standard 2MT 2-6-0 No. 78022. While it was not the best example of the remaining locomotives of its class, it was the only one still attached to its own tender.

In 1975, two years before No. 75078 was to turn a wheel in anger, the society purchased No. 78022. The engine arrived

BR Standard 2MT 2-6-0 No.78022 in BR lined black livery with 1956 totem at Haworth shed in April 1993. HUGH LLEWELYN*

on the KWVR on June 11, 1975, but was stored at the back of Oakworth yard for about three years before restoration could commence. The locomotive was first steamed on October 4, 1992, but it was spring 1993 before it formally entered traffic, proving a very popular among Worth Valley footplate crews and was more than capable of handling five-coach services on off peak turns of duty.

When the locomotive's boiler certificate expired on New Year's Eve

2000, No. 78022 was retired to static display at Oxenhope and remained there while the overhaul of No. 75078 proceeded.

However with completion of No. 75078 getting nearer, No. 78022 was moved out of Oxenhope to take up residence at Haworth shed. A thorough assessment of the engine has been made to gain the level of work required to return this popular locomotive to active duty and restoration is now proceeding.

NO. 75078 – AN IDEAL SIZE FOR THE BRANCH

Completed in 1956, Standard 4MT 4-6-0 No. 75078 is one of a class of 80 engines that came from a batch of 15 supplied to the Southern Region of British Railways

As this region did not have any water troughs, No. 75078 was attached to a tender with larger water capacity, than others of its class.

Furthermore, it was fitted with a double blast pipe and chimney during its only general overhaul in October 1961 with the aim of increasing the amount of steam that the boiler could produce with more economic returns in coal and water consumption.

The locomotive went new to Exmouth Junction in January 1956 before being transferred to Basingstoke in May of the same year, eventually being withdrawn from Eastleigh shed in July 1966 and sold for scrap to Woodhams.

The Standard 4 Preservation Society was formed in 1969 with the intention of purchasing BR Standard 4 2-6-0 No. 76077 from Woodhams in Barry. It was later decided, however, that the remaining examples of this particular class were not in the best of condition and that a member of the 75XXX class would be a better choice for preservation.

The original society was reformed becoming The Standard Four Locomotive Preservation Society with

Standard 4MT 4-6-0 No. 75078 double-heading with Midland 4F No. 43924 at Ingrow. BRIAN SHARPE

the aim of purchasing No. 75078 and in 1972, the purchase of No. 75078 was concluded and it was moved to the KWVR that June where it was stored in Oakworth yard for a short time till space became available at Haworth

The restoration to running order took five years and in February 1977 the locomotive was steamed for the first time and soon entered service on the branch and has proved popular with locomotive crews ever since.

It is considered ideal-size locomotive for the KWVR, handling six-coach summer services with ease.

No. 75078 found fame in 1978 when it

appeared as LMS No. 5078, along with No. 5820, in the feature film Yanks which starred a young Richard Gere.

Both these locomotives made light engine moves for turning on the triangle at Shipley to face north for the filming and then again to face south for normal use.

The locomotive had a further overhaul that was commenced in 1986 but was withdrawn from traffic in December 1998 upon expiry of its boiler ticket and a long-term overhaul commenced.

No. 75078 returned to traffic in February 2015 and is once again in action along the branch.

A 'JINTY' FOR GOOD MEASURE

The LMS 3F 'Jinty' 0-6-0Ts tanks are a direct development of former Midland Railway 0-6-0 designs built primarily for shunting duties. A total of 422 of this class was built between 1924-31. They became a typical of both LMS main lines and branches. No. 47279 was produced by the Vulcan Foundry at Newton-le-Willows in Lancashire in 1924 and was originally numbered 7119. It spent its early years shunting the vast marshalling yards at Toton in Nottinghamshire before being transferred to Nottingham Depot in 1934 when it was renumbered 7279 by the LMS. It was later shedded at Wellingborough, Bedford and Workington.

By now carrying the BR number 47279, the 'Jinty' was withdrawn from Sutton Oak near St Helens in December 1966 and sold to the Woodham brothers.

After languishing at Barry for 12 years, the engine was purchased by The South Yorkshire 3F Fund for use on the KWVR,

LMS 3F 'Jinty' 0-6-0T No. 47279 heads a rake of suburban coaches over Mytholmes viaduct on June 9, 2006. BRIAN SHARPE

becoming the 101st to be bought from Barry for preservation purposes, arriving on the railway in August 1979, bereft, after so many years, of many parts. The engine was painstakingly restored and first steamed in preservation in 1987.

Upon returning to traffic it was used for a wide variety of duties on the branch, from passenger workings to use on works trains for the civil maintenance department. However, its first 10-year

boiler certificate expired on New Year's Eve 1997. A full overhaul followed and No. 47279 re-entered traffic in 2001. However, 2011 saw the expiry of that 10-year boiler certificate and No. 47279 now rests in the exhibition shed at Oxenhope awaiting its turn in the restoration queue. No. 47279 was purchased by the railway from the South Yorkshire 3F Fund just before the expiry of its first 10-year boiler certificate.

A LMS STANIER 8F BUILT AT GWR SWINDON

The LMS 8F class was originally designed by William Stanier to improve availability in heavy freight engines and so the design first appeared in 1935.

The class was initially chosen by the Ministry of Supply during the Second World War as the standard heavy freight design for war work and No. 8431 was built in 1944 by the GWR at Swindon for temporary use in service by that company. It was based at Newton Abbot and Gloucester sheds and hauled heavy ore trains from South Wales to Plymouth.

At Nationalisation in 1948, British Railways numbered it 48431. The locomotive was withdrawn in May 1964, and sold for scrap to Woodhams in Barry.

In 1947, the class was returned to the LMS from being on loan to the GWR and that March, No. 48431 began an eight-year stint at Royston in Yorkshire.

In 1955, all the WD 2-8-0s on the Western Region were exchanged with LM Region for Swindon-built 8Fs. In August 1955 No. 48431 was allocated to Newton Abbot shed but was soon on the move to St Philip's Marsh shed, Bristol in September 1955, and as well as heavy freight duties, headed the occasional passenger service.

At the start of 1960, it moved to Old Oak Common, running down the West of England Main Line as far as Plymouth. It also saw use on trains to Thames Haven Oil Refinery in Tilbury.

In December 1962, it moved to Bristol Barrow Road, and in January 1964 was transferred to Bath Gren Park, from

where it was withdrawn in May that year, and sent to Barry scrapyard.

There it stayed until May 1972, when was it purchased by the KWVR. The 19th locomotive bought from the scrapyard, it arrived by road at Haworth in 1972.

On initial purchase the engine was regarded as a long-term restoration project by the society. After much dedication and hard work, however, the engine had been steam-tested by the end of 1974 and re-entered service on the KWVR in December 1975.

The engine has performed passenger and demonstration freight turns over the years on the KWVR but was finally withdrawn after a second restoration at the end of December 2000. It is now again considered as a long-term restoration project and remains on static display in the Oxenhope exhibition shed.

No. 48431 (in BR unlined black livery and with a Fowler 3500 gallon tender outside Haworth shed in June 1968. HIGH LLEWELYN*

Stanier 8F 2-8-0 No. 48431 resplendent in black in the Oxenhope exhibition shed in September 2016. ROBIN JONES

LANKY TANK AWAITING REASSEMBLY

Lancashire & Yorkshire Railway Class 23 0-6-0ST No. 752 was originally built by Beyer Peacock in 1881 as an 0-6-0 tender engine of exactly the same class as the company's Class 25 0-6-0 No. 957.

However, by the time John Aspinall was appointed as L&Y Chief Mechanical Engineer, the original design was becoming obsolete. He decided to rebuild all but 20 of the class as saddle tanks, with No. 752 being one of them.

At the Grouping in 1923 No. 752 was renumbered by the LMS as No. 11456 and was withdrawn in 1937, being sold on into industrial use at the Blainscough Colliery Co of Coppull, Lancashire.

In 1947, it became the property of the North Western Division of the National Coal Board, reallocated to the Parsonage Colliery at Leigh in Lancashire, where it was finally withdrawn and left lying in open storage for nine years before being made available for preservation in 1967.

The engine was purchased in understandably rundown condition by the Lancashire & Yorkshire Saddle Tanks Fund (now the Lancashire &

Bulleid West Country light Pacific No. 34092 City of Wells and Lancashire & Yorkshire Railway Class 23 0-6-0ST No. 752. BRIAN SHARPE

Yorkshire Railway Trust) and arrived on the KWVR in November 1971.

It was returned to steam in May 1977 and worked several brake van specials for members. In 1979-80 further work was carried out on the locomotive to allow the engine to participate at the 150th celebration of the Liverpool & Manchester Railway at Rainhill.

Although returned to steam, No. 752 was not the fittest of engines and was withdrawn once more until funding became available for the long list of work required to begin.

At the moment the locomotive has now been relocated to the ELR by the L&Y Trust for the remainder of its overhaul.

AN OLD SOLIDER NAMED *BRUSSELS*

At the outbreak of the Second World War, the War Department had initially chosen the LMS 'Jinty' 3F 0-6-0T as its standard shunting locomotive, but was persuaded by the Hunslet Engine Company that a simplified version of its more modern 50550 design would be more suitable.

The first locomotive rolled off its Leeds production line at the start of 1943.

As part of the war effort, the type became the standard British shunting locomotive during the conflict, and production continued until 1964 at various locomotive manufacturers.

In all, a total of 485 of them were turned out. No. 118 *Brussels* was built by Hudswell Clarke in 1945 and spent all of its working life in military service, being based at the Longmoor Military Railway, which was the Army's training railway. Indeed, many military railway personnel were 'passed out' for firing and driving on *Brussels*. In 1956 *Brussels* returned to Leeds to be rebuilt as an oil burner and remained as such for the rest of its military career.

In 1970, the Ministry of Defence announced its intention to discontinue railway operational training and thus the Longmoor site was to close.

Earmarked for a possible preservation centre on the military railway, a local supporter of the project purchased No. 118 but once this scheme failed to materialise, *Brussels* was purchased

by the KWVR and arrived at Haworth in September 1971.

When first steamed in 1972, it was found that it would not steam in comparison to a sister locomotive on the railway at the time. However, with a number of modifications to the firebox and front end, the engine at last became efficient for the steeply graded KWVR line and it found useful service on the railway.

The locomotive is now on static display at Oxenhope with no plans to return it to steam.

Hudswell Clarke Austerity 0-6-0ST No. 118 *Brussels* on display in the Oxenhope exhibition shed on September 29, 2016. ROBIN JONES

Brussels' nameplate reiterates its military past. Before it closed, the Longmoor Military Railway in Hampshire was briefly used as a base for preservationists who had bought steam locomotives. ROBIN JONES

Bulleid West Country light Pacific No. 34092 City of Wells outside Haworth shed, with USA 0-6-0T No. 30072 to the left, in December 1989. POLYRUS

A BULLEID IN BRONTE COUNTRY!

Built to OVS Bulleid's West Country light Pacific design, No. 34092 was built in March 1949 after nationalisation. It was one of the final batch of 20 West Countries ordered, and was first based at Stewarts Lane. It was originally named *Wells* but was renamed *City of Wells* a year later.

When completed, it went directly to the London being regularly used on such prestigious duties as the 'Golden Arrow' boat train between London and Dover.

The locomotive also had the honour on April 18, 1956 of hauling the train carrying Soviet politician Bulganin and president Kruschev from Portsmouth to London Victoria and later the same year hauled the Royal Train carrying King Feisal II of Iraq from Dover to Victoria.

No. 34092 was withdrawn from Salisbury in November 1964 and sold to Barry scrapyard, with 502,864 miles on the clock.

It remained there until it was purchased by a group of individuals in 1971 who brought it to the KWVR that November. It was the 17th locomotive to leave Woodham Brothers' scrapyard for preservation.

It was returned to service in 1979 with a rededication/naming ceremony at Keighley station being carried out by the then Mayor of Wells, Ernest Wright on April 1, 1980.

In November 1985, it worked a special from Marylebone and therefore became

the first Southern Pacific to depart from a London terminus since 1967.

In May 1986, it was equipped with a Giesl ejector to improve combustion, similar to that fitted in 1962 to sister No. 34064 Fighter Command on the grounds that a desired spark arrestor would 'suffocate' an ordinary blastpipe, Following some adjustment, the ejector improved No. 34064's smoke deflection and fuel consumption, allowing it to steam well with low-grade coal.

City of Wells worked all over the country on special charters, earning it the nickname 'the volcano' owing to its volcanic chimney 'eruptions' and dramatic smoke displays when working hard over the Settle and Carlisle route in the Eighties. The locomotive was withdrawn in 1989 to begin, what turned out to be, a 25-year restoration back to running order.

The heavy general overhaul, much of it carried out by volunteers to reduce costs, saw it equipped with a new high-capacity tender tank built to the original drawings by foundry engineers Acetarc at its premises in Dalton Lane, Keighley. Several of the old components including the doors for compartments used by the fireman and driver were retained, while much of the air-smoothed streamlined casing was also renewed.

The rebuilding of the engine, including a return to as-built appearance, was finally completed in August 2014, the Bulleid triumphantly returning to traffic on the August 16.

The locomotive is currently named *Wells*, as first named when entering traffic, it has since had a second rededication ceremony and is now called *City of Wells*.

In 2015, the locomotive visited the East Lancashire Railway for the summer season. Two years later, owners Richard Greenwood, Graham Bentley and John Adams decided to sell it to that heritage line, and an appeal was duly launched to raise £340,920 towards the purchase price by the end of 2018.

FAMOUS FRIENDS FROM THE PAST...

In its early years, the KWVR had the pleasure of medium-term loan visits from several famous locomotives.

Great Northern Railway No. 990 *Henry Oakley*, part of the National collection, was on loan to the nascent heritage line during 1977-78. Built at Doncaster in 1898, it was the first 4-4-2 in Britain and the only locomotive on the GNR to carry a name – that of the general manager of the company – until 1922 when the first of Gresley's Pacifics appeared.

Withdrawn from Lincoln shed in October 1937, it was placed in the LNER's York museum and restored to steaming condition 1953 to take part in a series of specials to mark the Doncaster Works centenary, and again in 1975 for the Stockton & Darlington 150th anniversary celebrations, before entering the National Railway Museum

THE OLDEST-SURVIVING 'BLACK FIVE'

The KWVR was for five years home to the oldest surviving Stanier 'Black Five', No. 45025, which was built at Vulcan Foundry in August 1934 and was withdrawn by British Rail in August 1968.

A veteran of the Highland Line, it was bought by Scottish railway heritage pioneer Ted Watkinson for use the proposed preserved railway between Aviemore and Grantown-on-Spey, which became the Strathspey Railway.

However, that railway was not ready to receive it, so Ted looked around for another heritage line on which it could be used in the meantime.

In June 1969, it joined aforementioned sister No. 45212 on the KWVR, and ran in service there until 1974.

As No. 5025, its LMS number, the locomotive went back north of the border the following year, first for an overhaul at the Andrew Barclay works in May that year, and then on to the Strathspey, where it hauled its first train on August 27, 1975.

Ted felt that another preserved railway should have use of the engine until the Strathspey Railway was ready to receive it, so it ran on the Keighley and Worth Valley Railway from June 1969 until 1974. No. 5025 then came north for an overhaul at Andrew Barclay's works in Kilmarnock in May 1975. Its running between Aviemore and Boat of Garten started on August 27, 1975.

LMS 'Black Five' No. 5025 at Haworth station on October 29, 1974. MJ RICHARDSON*

Sadly, Ted died in Boat of Garten in 1981 after one of his many days on the Strathspey, which he was instrumental in setting up.

No. 5025 ran on that line until 1994, and also hauled specials on the main line.

That year, it was withdrawn from traffic for major repair and restoration work. Major items of necessary work related to the boiler, wheels, bearings and tender water tank.

The locomotive passed into the ownership of the WEC Watkinson Trust, a charitable body set up in 1999 in line with Ted's wishes.

The trust has been working hard to raise the £354,000 to cover its restoration, and was boosted in 2011 by a Heritage Lottery Fund grant of £50,000.

As the time of writing, there were hopes that No. 5025 could be back in Strathspey service in 2018.

in 1975 as a part of the National Collection.

It was loaned to the KWVR during 1977-78 to haul passenger trains, but was taken out of service after boiler problems. Nowadays it is on static display at Bressingham Steam Museum at Diss in Norfolk.

Another National Collection engine that appeared on the KWVR is early days was LMS 'Crab' 2-6-0 No. 2700.

Back in the Sixties, with the demise of steam, it became obvious that there was no chance of British Railways housing the entire National Collection, and at the time, there was no National Railway Museum. The solution was to loan locomotives to heritage lines.

No. 2700 was built at Horwich in 1926 and was one of the last Hughes 2-6-0 to remain in service. As No. 42700 was withdrawn from service in March 1966 and stored at Hellifield, but two years later it was towed to Keighley in a mixed goods train.

Only a small amount of work was needed to get it steaming again in late 1968 and it ran on the KWVR for a short time.

While on loan to the East Lancashire Railway in the Nineties, a study showed that it was worn out and another

The last word in steam: BR Standard 9F 2-10-0 No. 92220 *Evening Star* in BR Brunswick Green livery and GWR-style copper-capped double chimney and BR1G tender in action in the Worth Valley. DAVE COOPER

return to steam would be prohibitively expensive.

At the Locomotion museum in Shildon in 2010, it was repainted into LMS crimson with its original number 13000. It is now on static display inside Station Hall at the National Railway Museum in York.

From June 1973 until August 1975, the last steam locomotive built for British Railways – BR Standard 9F 2-10-0 No. 92220 *Evening Star* – was on loan to the KWVR and hauled passenger services.

Outshopped from Swindon Works on March 18, 1960, *Evening Star* was withdrawn in 1965, after a working

Great Northern Railway 4-42 No. 990 Henry Oakley double-heads a KWVR passenger service, backed by Robert Stephenson & Hawthorns 0-6-0ST No. 57 Samson in Worth Valley livery. *Samson* was one of three 0-6-0 saddle tanks bought by KWVR members from Stewarts & Lloyd's iron and steel planet at Corby in Northamptonshire, which arrived in 1969. The second, No. 63 was named *Corby* on the KWVR, and is now based at Ruddington on the Great Central Railway (Nottingham) while the third, No. 62, was in 1982 sold to a member of the East Lancashire Railway Preservation Society. A star of the EMI movie The Railway Children that took the three children and their mother from London to Oakworth and brought in the train that had the children's father on board. No. 57 is now at the Spa Valley Railway in Kent. Members of this type were nicknamed 'Uglies' because of their appearance. COLOUR RAIL

life of only five years. Placed into storage and earmarked for the National Collection, in late 1966 it was towed to Crewe via Shrewsbury for overhaul and restoration.

It has now been many years since No. 92220 steamed, and it is on static display in the National Railway Museum at York, with no current plans to restore it to running order.

A fourth locomotive that appeared on the KWVR in earlier times but which is also no longer resident there was Midland Railway 'half cab' 0-6-0T No. 41708 (LMS 1708).

Built in 1880, it was first allocated to Burton-on-Trent that year.

In 1947 it was transferred to Staveley (Barrow Hill) shed for shunting duties at Staveley Ironworks, where it worked until it was replaced by diesels in 1965. Placed in storage at Canklow, near Rotherham, it was withdrawn in 1966, and bought by the Midland Railway Locomotive Fund, which became the 1708 Locomotive Trust Ltd.

The group chose the KWVR as the

National Collection LMS 'Crab' No. 42700 sits between BR Standard 4MT 4-6-0 No. 75078 and LMS 'Black Five' No. 45212 at Haworth. KWVR

base for the locomotive and it steamed there again in April 1971. It briefly hauled passenger trains before it was taken out of traffic with defective boiler tubes in early 1972. It stayed at Haworth out of service, until 1974 when it moved to the Midland Railway Centre at Butterley, where its restoration was

completed. No. 41708 then ran on other heritage lines including the Swanage Railway where it hauled the inaugural train in March 1989. In 1997, it made a return visit to the KWVR.

In 2005, it returned to Barrow Hill, where it is now on static display in the multi-award-winning roundhouse.

One-time Worth Valley resident No. 13000 (BR 42700) on display in the National Railway Museum's Station Hall at York. ROBIN JONES

Midland 1F 'half cab' 0-6-0T No. 41708 at Oxenhope on September 21, 1997. COLOUR-RAIL

A SCOT TOO POWERFUL

One of two surviving members of the LMS Royal Scot class of 4-6-0s spent the latter half of the Sixties at the Keighley & Worth Valley Railway.

Built by North British in Glasgow in 1927, No. 6115 was named *Scots Guardsman* the following year., after the Scots Guards. After receiving smoke deflectors, it starred in the 1936 film Night Mail.

The last member of the class in British Railways service, No. 46115 – as it was numbered after nationalisation – was condemned in December 1965 and was bought for preservation by the late Mr RA Bill. It arrived at Haworth on August 11, 1966, and indeed, was one of the first locomotives on the heritage line.

However, *Scots Guardsman* was never steamed at Haworth. Its sheer size placed it well down in the list of restoration priorities.

Furthermore, its axle loading would have precluded any regular use on the branch.

So in 1969 it left the KWVR for a succession of preservation sites. It went to Dinting Railway Centre and was restored to working order by the Bahamas Locomotive Society.

From there it ran three main line livery in LMS black as No. 6115, the first being a single test run from Guide Bridge to Sheffield on September 21,

Deemed too heavy for the Keighley & Worth Valley Railway, rebuilt Stanier 6P Royal Scot 4-6-0 No. 6115 *Scots Guardsman* returned to steam at Dinting Railway Centre, where it is seen in 1946 LMS lined black livery in April 1980. Since its rebuilding by West Coast Railways, Scots Guardsman has become a popular member of the modern-day main line steam scene. HUGH LLEWELYN*

1978 which, having been successful, was followed by trips to York and back on October 14 and November 11 that year.

However, *Scots Guardsman* did not run again on the national network and had only very limited use until it was bought for David Smith's West Coast Railways stable at Carnforth. Restored to main line standard, its first test run was from Carnforth to Hellifield on

June 20, 2008. Its first railtour was 'The Settle-Carlisle Venturer' from Hellifield to Carlisle and back on August 16, 2008.

Its surviving sister locomotive, No. 6100 Royal Scot, will go where *Scots Guardsman* has never been before, and run on the KWVR as part of the line's 50th anniversary celebrations. It was booked to run on the heritage line between June 25-27, 2018.

THE ONE THAT GOT AWAY

When Banbury boatyard owner Ray Treadwell cast his eyes on a pile of unwanted rusting scrap locomotive parts at Haworth station yard in 1987, it was just what he – and obviously he alone – wanted.

For many years he had dreamed of owning a GWR tank locomotive, but by that time, there were none left at Barry in reasonably sound condition. The only other option was to buy one that had already been preserved, from a private owner, but to acquire one in running order would be expensive. The components he saw at Haworth comprised the frame, wheels (including one cracked spoke), axleboxes, bunker and the bottom halves of the cab sides from GWR pannier tank No. 4612, plus the discarded boiler from sister engine No. 5775, one of the stars of The Railway Children.

What made No. 4612 different from most steam locomotives bought from Dai Woodham's scrapyard at Barry was the fact that it had been bought not for restoration – but for dismantling and use as spare parts to keep another pannier tank going.

Such an action would today be all but unthinkable, in view of the fact that any steam locomotive is now considered priceless even if only in terms of being an irreplaceable historical artefact. However, back then it was then a case of 'as needs must'.

Built at Swindon in 1942, it was withdrawn in 1965, sent to Barry scrapyard, and bought by the KWVR in 1981 for spares.

Six years later, Ray and his wife Elaine were delighted to pay the KWVR £5000 for what remained of No. 4612, and they subsequently spent around £250,000 on rebuilding it to as near as new condition at Bill Parker's Flour Mill workshop at Bream in the Forest of Dean.

As its long restoration drew towards a conclusion in 2001, inquiries were received from prospective hirers of the locomotive, including the Bodmin & Wenford Railway.

Bill suggested to the Treadwells that they might like to consider selling No. 4612 to the Cornish line, and that is indeed what happened. It made its debut in passenger traffic at Bodmin on July 24, 2001.

The one that got away! GWR pannier No. 4612 was bought as a source of spares for sister The Railway Children star No. 5775, but ended up being sold to a private buyer who resold it. Now owned by the Bodmin & Wenford Railway Trust, it is seen in steam outside Bodmin General shed on August 8, 2008. Ironically it is in service while No. 5775 has spent many years on static display waiting for its turn in the KWVR overhaul queue comes round again. TONY HISGETT*

Chapter 11

DAYS FOR DIESELS

While many of Britain's heritage lines set out with steam as the primary, if not sole, focus the Keighley & Worth Valley Railway found a niche for diesel heritage as long ago as 1966, and has never looked back.

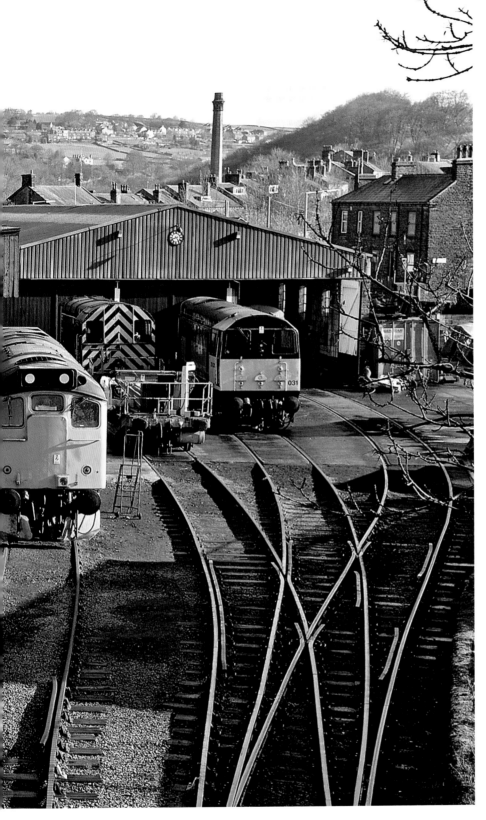

ABOVE: D0226 in crimson lake livery at Haworth in 1997.

LEFT: All set and raring to go: home-fleet engines and visitors line up in Haworth yard for the April 20, 2013 diesel gala. FRED KERR

Somerset and Bluebell railways. Not so long ago it would have been considered sacrilege to talk about running a diesel train to Sheffield Park, but now the Bluebell holds its own specialist diesel events. The line recognises that diesels too have their place in preservation, and offer another string to the preservation bow.

As outlined in Chapter 3, diesel multiple units were a late newcomer to the Worth Valley branch, making their debut 18 months after they had been introduced on local services in Airedale and Wharfedale. Any saving they made was not sufficient for BR to keep the line open. Nevertheless, diesels are part and parcel of the line's heritage.

Indeed, it was early on that the revivalists took possession of a diesel that is now unique, and represents the start of the big changeover from steam to modern traction on British railways.

Following the publication of the Modernisation Plan, locomotive builders embarked on a 'goldrush' to produce prototype diesels which, if they pleased bosses on the nationalised rail network, might well result in lucrative orders.

English Electric made several prototypes for British Railways to test and evaluate and several designs went into production for everyday service, not least of all which was the famous Class 55 Deltics for the East Coast Main Line.

D0226 and D0227 were two prototype diesel shunters built in 1956 by English Electric at its Vulcan Foundry in Newton-le-Willows as demonstration locomotives. They had been designed for shunting and transfer work between yards and stations.

They originally carried numbers D226 and D227, their Vulcan Foundry works numbers, but these were amended in August 1959 to avoid clashing with the numbers of the new Class 40 locomotives.

They were both 0-6-0s fitted with English Electric 6RKT engines of 500hp, and were painted black with an orange stripe along the middle of the bodyside, which turned into a 'V' at the nose end. The major difference between the two locomotives was that D0226 had diesel-electric transmission and D0227 had

Many of today's heritage railways came into existence through the burning desire of enthusiasts to find bastions where steam could be kept alive. Others, such as the Keighley & Worth Valley Railway, had their foundations in the wishes of local people to keep their local branch line open, with the traction operating it very much a secondary concern.

Steam remains the predominant image of the heritage sector, and for decades the armies of hardcore enthusiasts would not countenance the 'D-word' – diesels.

However, classic modern traction eventually developed its own sizeable following, and many preserved lines realised that there was a place for diesels on them. Not only could they carry out mundane day-to-day chores such as shunting and stock movements without the time and expense of lighting a fire in a steam locomotive's boiler, but they were become part and parcel of heritage for the generations that followed the end of British Rail steam haulage on August 11, 1968.

Indeed, as we saw earlier, the first trains on the revived Ffestiniog Railway and the heritage-era Middleton Railway were hauled by traction other than steam.

The last two strictly steam-only heritage lines in the UK were the East

The line's Class 101 DMU and Midland 4F No. 43924 stand at Keighley during a night shoot on October 6, 2014. NEIL SCOTT*

diesel-hydraulic transmission. BR tested both locomotives at its Stratford depot in East London so that comparisons could be made between them. D0226 saw service at Liverpool, Doncaster, Sheffield, Stratford Bristol and Swindon, and results showed that diesel-electric transmission was more powerful than diesel-hydraulic. D0227 was subsequently scrapped.

During its three-year loan to BR, D0226 travelled 38,000 miles.

However, it was declared to be too powerful for usual shunting duties and not versatile enough for any other useful work.

So it was placed in storage at Vulcan Foundry for six years.

In March 1966, however, D0226 was sent by English Electric to Haworth on permanent loan.

As the Worth Valley branch has a 25mph maximum speed limit, many of the limitations found in BR service did not apply. The 500hp power rating means it can deal with works trains at a speed that does not hamper passenger services working on the opposite path.

The engine is capable of standing in on passenger services in the event of a steam engine failure in traffic. All in all, this engine has found a niche in preservation, something it didn't really have during its working life.

In 1980, it visited Doncaster Works for wheel reprofiling on the ground lathe. It was named *Vulcan* and repainted in 1984 into crimson lake livery. It also reverted to its original number D226, but has since been repainted into BR green as D0226.

In 2014 D0226 had its greatest passenger triumph when it was one of two diesel locomotives used to haul the downhill leg of the intensive two-train operation that brought spectators to the Worth Valley during the Tour de France that July.

How many other heritage lines can boast of having an experimental locomotive in their fleet, and not only that, but one in running order?

April 12, 2015, was a *Vulcan* running day. The experimental locomotive is seen at Keighley. POINT AND SHOOT PHOTOS*

CLASS 20 BO-BO DIESEL ELECTRIC D8031/20031

Outshopped from the Robert Stephenson & Hawthorns works in Darlington in late 1959, this locomotive entered British Railways' service in January 1960 numbered D8031. Initially allocated to Scotland, D8031 was renumbered 20031 in 1974 under the new TOPS classification system.

Withdrawn from Toton Depot in Nottinghamshire on September 14, 1990, it was bought by a private consortium of KWVR members and arrived at Haworth on August 14, 1992, after a visit to MC Metals for asbestos investigation and removal.

It has been used on early-morning passenger services and works train duties for the civil department. It also hauls the occasional demonstration freight for photographic charters or diesel gala weekends.

Class 20 No. 20031 on June 8, 2014. MARSHD200*

Rare visitor: the National Railway Museum's Western Region diesel hydraulic D1023 Western Fusilier departs Oakworth with a 2.15pm Keighley to Oxenhope service on June 6, 2008. FRED KERR

CLASS 25 BO-BO DIESEL ELECTRIC D5209/25059

A classic first-generation main line diesel, its design was developed under the Modernisation Plan.

D5209 was built by BR at Derby in 1963 and was first allocated to Toton depot. After 24 years' service it was withdrawn from Crewe on March 24, 1987.

Stabled at Vic Berry's scrapyard in Leicester, where it was undergoing asbestos removal, No. 25059 was bought directly from BR by a group of private individuals for use on the KWVR. BR would not sell locomotives

that still contained asbestos. This group donated the engine to the Keighley & Worth Valley Railway Preservation Society, and it worked its first trial runs on the line on October 10, 1987.

During the heritage era the locomotive has carried both BR green and blue liveries.

It has worked regular passenger services, works trains, demonstration freight duties and other special events.

It returned to service in 2016 having undergone heavy body repairs.

Class 25 No. 25059 pictured in British Rail blue livery at Oakworth on June 8, 2014, heading the 12.20pm Keighley to Oxenhope service. FRED KERR

Class 37 No. 37075 in Railfreight livery approaches Mytholmes Tunnel with a service from Keighley to Oxenhope on June 9, 2014, during a diesel gala weekend. DAVE THISTLETON IMAGES*

CLASS 37 CO-CO DIESEL-ELECTRIC D6775/37075

Another successful product of the Modernisation Plan, Class 37s were designed for both freight and passenger service, with the first batch of 42 entering service between 1960-62.

D6775 was built by English Electric at its Robert Stephenson & Hawthorns works and was released into traffic on September 24, 1962. It was initially allocated to Thornaby depot.

On New Year's Eve 1973, it was renumbered to 37075 under TOPS.

No. 37075 was based at Stratford in east London for several years. It was during its stay that it was involved in a shunting incident at Dagenham, which is why it has different nose ends.

In 1989 it returned to Thornaby and worked there for two years for Railfreight in its Metal sector before being transferred to Tinsley (Sheffield) in 1991 to work in the Distribution sector. March 1994 saw No. 37075 return yet again to Thornaby depot before it was placed in storage that August. Three years later, it made its

final move to Immingham TMD to await its fate.

In 1999, it was bought from EWS reservation by the Class 37 Locomotives Association, which formed a limited company, Corporate Blue Traction, whose shareholders bought and owned the locomotive.

It moved initially to the Great Central Railway (Nottingham) and later the Great Central Railway at Loughborough in 2000. Two years later, it was bought by the 5C Locomotive Group and moved to the Ecclesbourne Valley Railway, and by 2007 it was on the move again, this time to the Churnet Valley Railway.

It was resold in 2012 to a consortium of KWVR volunteers who moved it to Haworth where it is based today. It sees use on passenger services and, when a larger engine is required, on works trains.

In 2013, it became a star on the small screen, when it masqueraded as Class 40 D326 in the BBC drama The Great Train Robbery.

TWO CLASS 08 SHUNTERS

The line has two Class 08 diesel electric shunters, representing what became the biggest class of locomotives on British Rail, with a total of 996 built.

The design was based on the LMS 12033 series (Class 11), which was built from April 1945 to December 1952. In turn, this type had been based on a near-identical earlier batch built by the LMS between 1934 and 1936.

The first Class 08, No. 13000 (now preserved at Peak Rail) was built in 1952 although it did not enter service until 1953. Production continued until 1962.

As the standard BR general-purpose diesel shunter, the class became a familiar and immediately recognisable sight at major stations and freight yards.

However, since their introduction, rail traffic in Britain changed considerably. Freight trains now mostly comprise fixed rakes of wagons, while passenger trains are mostly diesel or electric multiple units, neither needing a shunting locomotive. Therefore, a large proportion of the class has been withdrawn from mainline use and stored, scrapped, exported (five went to Liberia) or sold to industrial or heritage railways.

Their low-maintenance requirements mean that most of the survivors are still in operational condition. More than 80 ended up on heritage lines.

D3336 was outshopped from Darlington Works as No. 13336 in 1957, and was the last example to be turned out in black.

First allocated to Sheffield Darnall shed, it stayed there for three months and returned in 1958 by which time it had been renumbered D3336. It was renumbered to 08266 under the TOPS system and was eventually withdrawn from Shirebrook in Nottinghamshire.

The KWVR realised the benefits of having a decent cost-effective shunter and after No. 08226 was withdrawn, the line rescued it from the Swindon scrap heap. On the KWVR, its main duties include shunting the steam locomotives around Haworth yard and occasionally undertaking works train duties. On rare occasions such as galas and other special events, it has also hauled passenger services.

The second member of the class on the Worth Valley is D3759/08993.

Built at Crewe Works in October 1959 as D3759, in December 1973 it was renumbered 08592. In 1985 it was withdrawn from traffic and was chosen to be one of five Class 08s to be rebuilt into a Class 08/9, receiving a cut-down cab reducing its height to 11ft 9in, allowing it to be used on the freight-only Burry Port & Gwendraeth Valley line in South Wales. This route was built on the course of an old waterway, the Kymer's Canal, and suffered from a number of low bridges. Therefore,

Class 37 No. 37075 in BR blue livery in August 2012. ROBIN JONES

Class 08 shunter No. 08266 pictured in 2011. TONY HISGETT*

LEFT: In EWS livery, No. 08993 *Ashburnham* stands on the end of No. 9 Road of the Corus Northern Service Centre at Castleton on July 24, 2006. DAVID INGHAM*

locomotives with a lower headroom clearance were needed.

No. 08993 has carried two names in its lifetime, the first one being *Olive*. In 1986 it gained the name *Ashburnham*, which it still carries today.

At Privatisation, No. 08993 entered EWS ownership along with cut-down cab classmates Nos. 08994 and 08995 where they worked in various yards up and down the country on shunting duties. In 2007 the remaining three 08/9s helped with the track re-laying project

on the Manchester Metrolink.

That year, Deutsche Bahn purchased EWS and rebranded it DB Schenker UK and, more recently, DB Cargo UK. Under DB Cargo ownership No. 08993 worked at various yards but mainly at Doncaster Carr depot. It worked there until the depot's closure on April 30, 2014 then spent the rest of its working life for DB in Stoke-on-Trent before being offered for sale in May 2015.

With No. 08266 needing work, the KWVR decided to buy another and so

No. 08993 arrived by road at Haworth in October 2015. This locomotive has the advantage over its stablemate in that it is dual braked, a useful attribute for shunting any air-brake-only vehicles such as cranes. Having worked for 56 years the locomotive was in need of considerable attention and it received an engine overhaul by shed staff in Haworth Works where it was also given a fresh coat of EWS maroon and gold livery.

It returned to service in June 2016.

WITHDRAWN WITH STEAM

By the early Sixties, British Railways had decided which of the first generation of diesels would stand the test of time and which had not made the grade, however, it did not close the door on evaluating further designs.

Hudswell Clarke built a batch of 10 diesel mechanical 0-6-0 shunters, with Gardner 8L3 engines capable of 204hp at 100rpm.

D2511 was one of these and was delivered to BR in 1962, being allocated to Barrow and Workington for use on the dock systems at these ports.

Being non-standard, BR withdrew the entire class by 1968, the same year that steam haulage on the main line ended, and D2511 found a second life with the National Coal Board at Brodsworth Colliery near Doncaster.

Withdrawn following severe collision damage, the engine was bought by KWVR members by Ben Wade and Arthur Stone and it arrived at Haworth in August 1977. Following restoration, it entered service in 1980.

Hudswell Clarke 0-6-0DM D2511 (11150) in BR green livery at Haworth shed in May 1998. HUGH LLEWELYN*

The engine been used for shunting in the yards and works train duties. On occasions, it has been allowed to haul a two-coach passenger train during

special events and can just about manage line speed with this load.

At some point in time, Arthur sold his share to Ben who is now the sole owner.

A WIZARD SAVED!

Hudswell Clarke of Leeds began produce internal-combustion engine designs in the 1920s, and in 151 outshopped 0-6-0DM *Merlin* for the Port of Bristol Authority, where it was used on the dockyard system at Avonmouth alongside steam engines.

Freight being handled in the docks rapidly declined in the Sixties. In early 1971 No. 23 was sold to R O Hodgson Ltd of the English China Clay Group where it was used at its general warehouse at Carnforth, Lancashire as a shunting locomotive.

In 1984 it was sold to KWVR in 1985, initially as a source of spares for No. 32 *Huskisson*, and so was apparently destined for oblivion by dismantling. However, as luck would have it, an alternative source of spares was found, and so No. 23 was returned to traffic on the KWVR, with the missing vacuum-brake system replaced during a thorough rebuild. It has been used for a wide variety of duties from general shunting to hauling occasional passenger trains during special events. However, it is now in poor mechanical condition and stored at Haworth depot until its turn for overhaul arrives.

REMEMBERING THE 'FIRST' RAILWAY DEATH

The dock estates at Liverpool and Birkenhead were for many years controlled by the Mersey Docks & Harbour Board which, over the years, operated a fleet of steam and diesel locomotives for shunting in the sidings and transferring wagons between sites.

In 1944 Hunslet delivered 0-6-0 diesel mechanical shunter No. 32. It was named *Huskisson* in memory of William Huskisson, the Liverpool politician who was killed on September 15, 1830, the opening day of the Liverpool & Manchester Railway, and became the world's first widely reported railway fatality.

By 1970 the amount of freight handled by the docks system had declined to such an extent that the older locomotives in the diesel fleet were sold off. No. 32 was the first to be offered for sale.

It was bought by Ben Wade, a private member of the KWVR Preservation Society, and arrived on the Worth Valley under its own power in January 1971. It saw much useful service on the railway, mainly as a yard shunter in one of the railway's yards and saw occasional use on the main branch line on works trains as well as hauling passenger services during special events.

After 40 years' service, the original Gardner 8L engine was replaced by another in 1989.

A major overhaul was completed in time for No. 32 to take part in the June 2014 diesel gala.

No. 32 *Huskisson* works the 11.15am Ingrow to Keighley service on June 8, 2014. FRED KERR

0-6-0DM *Merlin,* pictured in 2009, was originally bought as a source of spares for No. 32. HELENA*

BELOW: On November 3, 2012, the Keighley & Worth Valley Railway received a rare visit from a Class 125 High Speed Train, headed by Class 43 power car No. 43059 comprising the 'Worth Valley Wanderer 125 Special' railtour, organised by charity The Railway Children, which helps abandoned and destitute children at stations across the world. This tour was run as a fundraising special, for the Samaritans and Weston Park Hospital in Sheffield. It is seen at Oxenhope with the 1.15pm departure to Keighley. FRED KERR

The Keighley & Worth Valley Railway is by no means content to rest on its laurels by using only members of its home fleet for diesel galas, but often hires illustrious guests, and as such proves a big draw for diesel followers. For its gala on June 8, 2014, 1962-built Class 31 A1A-A1A Brush Type 2 D5830 from the Great Central Railway was the special guest. Withdrawn in June 1966 with weak springs and was initially bought from EWSD as spares by the Type One Locomotive Company, it arrived on the GCR, near its Loughborough birthplace, on January 30, 1998. It was found to be in better condition than the sister locomotive for which it was to have been a parts donor, and so was restored in its own right. It was painted in British Railways' early experimental golden ochre livery, uniquely carried by sister D5579, and carried this number for a short while before reverting to D5830. It was initially intended to carry the livery for only a year but it proved far too popular to change. MARSHD200*

NO PROFIT IN *JAMES*

Diesel electric 0-4-0 shunter *James* was built in 1959 by Ruston Hornsby of Lincoln for the steel company Stewarts & Lloyd Ltd of Bilston, West Midlands, where it received its name. It continued in service there until being sold in the mid-1980s for scrap. However, it was bought by a company that specialised in the renovation of diesel engines, with the intention of giving the engine a full overhaul and selling it back into industrial use at a profit. No buyer could be found, and the company offered *James* to the heritage railway sector at a fraction of the cost it took to return it to full working order. It was purchased by member of the Bahamas Locomotive Society and arrived on the KWVR in 1990.

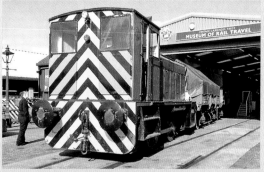

Diesel electric 0-4-0 shunter *James*. KWVR

Waggon und Maschinenbau railbus No. 79964 calls at Oakworth with the 10.50am Keighley to Oxenhope service on January 20, 2013. A popular feature with early-morning visitors is the increased forward visibility afforded by the line's railbuses and DMUs, giving passengers a totally different perspective of the line. FRED KERR

MINIMALIST OPERATIONS WERE NOT ENOUGH

It is often said that many of the Beeching closures could have been prevented if branch lines had been pared down to the bare minimum in terms of staff, and operated by diesel railbuses.

Indeed, looking at the number of people employed at even little-used stations back in the Fifties, it comes as little surprise that many rural lines did not pay their way. In the late Fifties, British Railways indeed began to experiment with railbuses produced by a number of different manufacturers, such as Waggon und Maschinenbau, Park Royal and Wickham, years before Beeching arrived. They were intended for use on lightly patronised branch lines in rural areas.

Five single-car diesel railbuses seating just 56 passengers were ordered from Waggon und Maschinenbau in Donauworth, West Germany. They were numbered by British Railways

E79960-E79964 and amazingly, four out of the original five survived into preservation after the branches they were bought to serve closed. The savings that they made were deemed insufficient to keep the branches on which they ran open. Many of these small lines were closed in 1964 at which point the work for these railbuses ceased.

Delivered new to the Cambridgeshire area, E79964 was transferred to Buxton in Derbyshire, for work on the branch to Millers Dale and was renumbered M79964, denoting that the railbus had been transferred to the Midland Region (M) of British Railways.

When the Millers Dale branch closed, the railbus was sold and arrived on the Keighley & Worth Valley Railway in 1967.

It still has its original Bussing 150hp engine, as has 79960 which is currently at the Ribble Steam Railway.

Unlike E79962, M79964 was re-engined with an AEC 150hp engine in BR ownership. This engine was

subsequently exchanged with a similar engine from a London Transport bus. This ran well for a number of years prior to a major failure. A fully overhauled railway specification AEC engine was then fitted which is still in service and subsequently the vehicle has been in regularly use on KWVR morning services.

Both railbuses were outshopped in the BR green livery of the early 1960s. Regularly seen singularly or paired with M79964, E79962 was a fixed sight on the morning services until time caught up with this aged vehicle and it was retired from active service pending an overhaul. However, with no prospect of being restored in the foreseeable future, E79962 was transferred into the ownership of the Vintage Carriages Trust at Ingrow and was moved into its workshops in 2014. Restoration to as-near-original condition has commenced with a complete strip-down, and the unit is now receiving care and attention.

Waggon und Maschinenbau railbus No. 79964 on August 9, 2012.
ROBIN JONES

Railbus E79962 in the Vintage Carriages Trust workshop at Ingrow in late 2016.
ROBIN JONES

A PAIR OF DIESEL MULTIPLE UNITS

Fifty years ago, first-generation Diesel Multiple Units were to be seen almost everywhere across the UK, apart from most of the electrified Southern Region lines. Despite having long since been superseded by newer DMUs, several of them have found a niche of their own on heritage lines.

They may not be steam traction, but their large windows allow them to double up as observation cars, allowing passengers to see more of the passing countryside.

Introduced during 1954, the original Derby Lightweight units, predecessors of the Class 108s were the first DMUs to be introduced in the West Riding of Yorkshire. All were built by BR's Derby Works and were designed primarily for use on local and branch line work.

When new, cars Nos. M50928 and M51565 were paired together and started their working lives in Leeds. The pair was eventually split, however, and coupled to others, each

The line's Class 101 set, comprising cars Nos. M51565 and 50928, is seen departing Keighley for Oxenhope. WILSON ADAMS*

probably having several partners.

One remains more or less as it was built, as evident from the domed light shades, while the other was given a full refit during its life, with fluorescent lighting throughout. They were preserved in 1992 when Bradford Metropolitan Borough Council based them on the KWVR.

They were quickly repainted into green with half-yellow panel and the original two-character

headcode box was returned to the front end.

Having worked Worth Valley services for more than 20 years, the pair is now stored out of use at Haworth awaiting attention to return them to traffic.

Their early-morning run has been taken over by Metropolitan-Cammell Class 101 cars Nos. M51189 and Sc51803.

The type was introduced in large numbers during the 1950s and 60s and built in Birmingham.

Intended for use on both branch lines and some shorter inter-city routes they could operate at most locations around the country.

In 2007 the railway recognised the need to overhaul the Class 108 in the near future, and so acquired a Class 101 set

The two vehicles, which are paired together on the KWVR, never ran together during their career for British Rail. No. Sc51803 was first allocated to Leith Central working services between Edinburgh and Dundee, and Stirling and Dunblane, while No. M51189 was allocated to Ryecroft depot in Walsall for local services out of Birmingham New Street.

Arriving in a fairly rundown state, the Class 101 DMU has been restored to a high standard, and has proved a reliable unit since restoration was completed in 2013, when the Class 108 set was withdrawn.

In September 2015 overhaul of the Class 108 set was started, with a bogie rebuild being the first job.

The line's Class 101 newly arrived at Oxenhope on September 28, 2016. ROBIN JONES

Chapter 12

YOUR CARRIAGE AWAITS,
MADAM...
YOURS TOO SIR

Having a magnificent and much-varied fleet of pristine locomotives has made the Keighley & Worth Valley a first-choice destination for decades. However, that is only one part of the story, for the line has a stunning collection of classic carriages to match, and not one but two expert groups to look after them.

In 1965, the Vintage Carriages Trust was formed by a group of volunteers whose interest was in wooden-bodied carriages, by then a rapidly disappearing breed.

They identified a need to specialise in the preservation of coaches which were in danger not only from being declared obsolete but also from the ravages of weather. Long redundant on main line railways, those that could be saved could be restored for use on heritage lines.

The trust, a registered charity, at present owns nine carriages, also three small industrial steam locomotives, a railbus, and a collection of railway posters and other railwayana.

It also owns the showpiece Museum of Rail Travel at Ingrow, which has been built in three phases over the past two decades. It is, however, far more than a museum, because it also doubles up at the trust's workshops and headquarters.

Four major grants helped the trust develop this museum, which is seen as a significant attraction in its own right. They came from the Museums & Galleries Commission, the English Tourist Board, the Keighley Single Regeneration Budget and the Heritage Lottery Fund, which came up with £222,800.

However, while justifiably proud of their museum, trust officials stress that their entire organisation is 'museum on the move' and that their vehicles can be seen not only in the Worth Valley but on other lines too. As we saw in Chapter 5, Haydock Foundry well tank *Bellerophon* is on long-term loan to the Foxfield Railway.

While grant aid and subscriptions from the trust's 600 or thereabouts members form a key source of income, filming and other carriage hire, both

LEFT: The Ingrow-based Vintage Carriage's Trust Metropolitan Railway 'Dreadnought' coach No. 465 was reunited with Metropolitan Railway E class 0-4-4T No. 1 during the start of a loan at the Buckinghamshire Railway Centre on February 17, 2013. No. 1 had pulled two 'Dreadnoughts' when it visited the KWVR in April 1994. ROBIN JONES

on the KWVR and at other venues, is a sizeable funding stream. Further grants towards equipment, facilities and restoration work from have come from the Yorkshire Museums Council, and from the Museums & Galleries Commission's PRISM (Preservation and Restoration of Industrial & Scientific Material) Fund.

The museum at Ingrow contains a large railway relics shop and also sells books, magazines and refreshment. Sales profits have been important since the early days of the trust.

The work of trust volunteers in carriage restoration has been rewarded with recognition over the years with the organisation collecting several national awards.

In 1998, the museum building itself and the efforts put into improved access for disabled visitors achieved a national ADAPT (Access for Disabled people to Arts Premises Today) Award in the museum section. They were also were runners-up in the volunteer sector of the Yorkshire Electricity/

This four-wheeler is the flagship of the Vintage Carriages Trust. It was built in Gorton in 1876 by the Manchester, Sheffield & Lincolnshire Railway. It is a "tri-composite", having compartments for all three classes - one First Class, one Second Class and two Third Class compartments, with a central luggage compartment. The MSLR was renamed the Great Central Railway in 1897mand the 34-seater carriage ended its British Railways day as a tool van and was bought in a dilapidated state. Restoration in earnest did not start until 1983, being completed in 1985. It has been restored to early Great Central Railway livery. PAUL HOLROYD

Yorkshire & Humberside Museums Council Access Awards. While the Ingrow museum remains a major source of pride for members, the trust's website www.vintagecarriagestrust.org has for long made a major contribution to the knowledge and understanding of railway carriage and wagon heritage.

Two surveys are available online - the Railway Heritage Register Carriage Survey Project, and the Railway Heritage Register Wagon Survey Project.

Both of these surveys allow users to browse the history of virtually every carriage in preservation and grounded bodies that are not, as well as wagons. For historians, researchers and enthusiasts at all levels, both are an immensely valuable source of information.

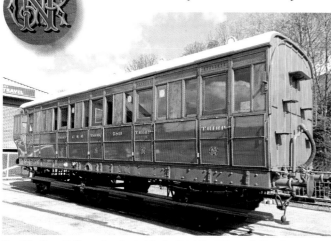

Great Northern Railway six-wheeled Brake Third No. 589 was built at Doncaster in 1888. Doncaster Works was famous for varnished teak exterior panelling. Its interior would have been quite comfortable, compared with other third-class carriages of the same period. The four compartments had buttoned, upholstered seats (not yet restored), lit by gas, and the guard's compartment had "ducketts" by which means he could view down the length of the train. It became a civil engineer's department stores van at some time before 1942 and ended its days in Departmental use as British Railways No. DE940281E. It was withdrawn 1966 with damage to one of the guard's doors and has been preserved by the Vintage Carriage Trust, arriving on the KWVR on May 25, 1966. It can be seen in the workshop area of Museum of Rail Travel at Keighley. It has appeared in numerous films over the past half century. They include Testament of Youth (2014 version); North and South; He Knew He Was Right; Sons and Lovers; The Way We Live Now; Possession; Timewatch; The Woman In White; Jude; The Secret Agent (1995 cinema version); Tomorrow's World; The Feast of July; The Secret Agent (1992 BBCTV version); I've Been here Before; Trains from the Arc; The Adventures of Sherlock Holmes - The Final Problem ; A Testament of Youth; Raffles: The First Step; Country Matters - The Black Dog, and last but not least - The Railway Children (1970 EMI version and the1968 BBCTV version). PAUL HOLROYD

The Worth Valley branch proudly retains its Midland Railway heritage in so many ways, yet this is the only Midland coach on the line! This six-wheeled Composite was built at Derby in 1886 as No. 358 and has a central baggage compartment, two first-class and two third-class compartments. It was typical of carriages that would have run on the Worth Valley branch. It ended its working life under British Railways as a signal and telegraph engineer's stores van at Edge Hill depot, and was bought by the Vintage Carriages Trust in 1968, arriving at the heritage line by rail. One of only three surviving Midland Railway six-wheeled passenger-carrying vehicles still on their original chassis, it is subject to a long-term restoration at Ingrow, where it is pictured in September 2016. ROBIN JONES

COACHES OWNED BY THE VINTAGE CARRIAGES TRUST

Manchester, Sheffield & Lincolnshire Railway four-wheel No. 176: built 1876
Midland Railway six-wheel Composite No. 358: built 1886
Great Northern Railway six-wheel Brake Third No. 589: built 1888
Great Northern Railway Lavatory Brake Composite No. 2856: built 1898
Metropolitan Railway Seven Compartment Brake Third No. 427: built 1910
Metropolitan Railway Nine Compartment Third No. 465 built 1919
Metropolitan Railway Seven Compartment First No. 509 built 1923
Southern Railway Corridor 'Matchboard' Brake Third No. 3554: built 1924
British Railways Bulleid-designed Third Open No. S1469: built 1950

VINTAGE CARRIAGES TRUST: THE A LISTERS!

Locomotives and rolling stock from the Vintage Carriages Trust collection have appeared in more than 80 productions, maintaining the unique bond between the Worth Valley and the fields of dramatic arts and literature.

SEPTEMBER 2016 BBC TV Railways: The Making of a Nation documentary. Historian Liz McIvor explores how Britain's expanding rail network was the spark to a social revolution.

JULY 2015 Swallows and Amazons. Based on the classic Arthur Ransome novel and starring Kelly Macdonald, Andrew Scott, and Rafe Spall.

JUNE 2015 Jericho. ITV eight-part drama about life in the shanty town of Jericho, used to build Ribblehead Viaduct, starring Jessica Raine, Hans Matheson and Clarke Peters.

MARCH 2014 Testament of Youth. Heyday Films Ltd production starring Alicia Vikander, Kit Harington, Dominic West, Emily Watson. Joanna Scanlon, Jonathan Bailey.

DECEMBER 2013 The Woman in Black: Angel of Death, Film starring Phoebe Fox, Jeremy Irvine, Helen McCrory, Oaklee Pendergast.

NOVEMBER 2013 Louis, Documentary made for the 2013 Leeds International Film Festival about Louis Aime Augustin Le Prince, pioneer of moving pictures, who disappeared on September 16, 1890 after boarding a train from Dijon to Paris.

JANUARY 2013 This Week BBC TV political programme presented by Mary Ann Sieghart.

NOVEMBER 2012 Peaky Blinders Six-part Caryn Manderbach/ Tiger Aspect co-production for BBC TV, starring Sam Neill, Helen McCrory, Iddo Goldberg, Paul Anderson, Annabelle Wallis, Sophie Rundle, Andy Nyman, Tommy Flanagan and Cillian Murphy.

SEPTEMBER 2010 South Riding BBC TV drama series starring Anna Maxwell Martin. Featuring Penelope Wilton, Bernard Wrigley and David Morrissey.

JUNE 2009 Cranford II BBC TV period drama. Haydock Foundry well tank Bellerophon filmed at Foxfield Railway.

JUNE 2008 Timeshift: Between The Lines BBC TV documentary presented by Andrew Martin.

AUGUST 2007 The Story of BP A feature-length documentary, by Lone Star Productions, about Britain's largest company at the time of its 100th anniversary in 2008.

JUNE 2007 Brideshead Revisited Film starring Matthew Goode, Hayley Attwell, Ben Whishaw, Emma Thompson, Greta Scacchi

JULY 2006 Housewife, 49 Granada TV drama starring Victoria Wood, Jason Watkins. Also featuring David Threlfall, Lorraine Ashbourne, Sally Bankes.

MAY 2005 Booze Cruise III Yorkshire TV comedy drama starring Mark Benton, Brian Murphy and Neil Pearson.

JULY 2004 North and South BBC TV drama series starring Daniela Denby-Ashe, Richard Armitage, Sinead Cusack, Lesley Manville, Tim Pigott-Smith, Pauline Quirke, Brendan Coyle.

SEPTEMBER 2003 Inside Out BBC TV documentary investigating the mystery of the two unidentified children who died in the crash at Charfield, in October 1928.

AUGUST 2003 He Knew He Was Right. BBC TV drama with Bill Nighy, Oliver Dimsdale, Ron Cook, Laura Fraser, Geoffrey Palmer, Geraldine James, Anna Massey.

OCTOBER 2002 The Forsyte Saga. Granada TV series with Emma Griffiths Malin, Lee Williams.

AUGUST 2002 Calendar. Yorkshire TV news magazine presented by Nicola Crompton.

MAY 2002 Sons and Lovers. Company Productions for ITV. Starring Sarah Lancashire, Georgina Chapman, Keeley Forsyth, Rupert Evans, James Murray, Hugo Speer.

APRIL 2002 Hound of the Baskervilles. Tiger Aspect for BBC TV. Starring Richard Roxburgh, Ian Hart, Matt Day, John Nettles: also featuring Danny Webb.

MARCH 2002 No Man's Land. EsKay Productions with Paul Clerkin, Brian Ingham.

JANUARY 2002 Turner. BBC TV arts documentary presented by Tim Marlow.

OCTOBER 2001 A for Acid. Yorkshire TV drama with Martin Clunes and Keeley Hawes.

JUNE 2001 The Hours. Film with Nicole Kidman, Stephen Dillane, Meryl Streep, Julianne Moore, Ed Harris.

APRIL 2001 The Way We Live Now. Episode 3 of BBC TV series with Shirley Henderson, Lila Baur, Peter Gunn, Paloma Baeza, Cillian Murphy, David Suchet, Matthew Macfadyen, Cheryl Campbell, Allan Corduner.

NOVEMBER 2000 The Cazalets. BBC TV series with Frederick Treves, Hugh Bonneville, Stephen Dillane, Paul Rhys, Anastasia Hille, Lesley Manville, Joanna Page, Anna Chancellor.

SEPTEMBER 2000 Possession. Cinema film with Gwyneth Paltrow, Aaron Eckhardt, Jeremy Northam, Jennifer Ehle.

AUGUST 2000 The League of Gentlemen. BBC TV comedy.

APRIL 2000 The History of the London Underground. Granada TV documentary (archive footage).

MARCH 2000 Secret Agent: the true story of the Special Operations Executive. Documentary - Darlow Smithson Productions for BBC.

JULY 1998 Timewatch. BBC TV children's educational programme.

MAY 1998 Commercial for pensions and financial services.

APRIL 1998 Out and About. BBC2 Travel Programme.

DECEMBER 1997 The Grand. Granada TV period drama with Susan Hampshire.

OCTOBER 1997 The Unknown Soldier. Carlton TV production with Gary Mavers, Juliet Aubrey, Frederick Treves, Pip Torrens and David Westhead.

MAY 1997 The Woman in White. BBC TV/Carlton TV period drama with Tara Fitzgerald, Justine Waddell, Andrew Lincoln, Simon Callow, James Wilby and Ian Richardson.

JUNE 1996 Fairy Tale: A True Story. Film with Paul McGann, Bob Peck, Harvey Keitel and Peter O'Toole.

JUNE 1996 Holiday. BBC TV with Cliff Richard.

FEBRUARY 1996 Commercial for Budweiser beer.

JANUARY 1996 Jude. Film with Christopher Eccleston and Kate Winslet.

NOVEMBER 1995 A History of British Art. BBC TV series.

AUGUST 1995 The Secret Agent. Film with Patricia Arquette, Gerard Depardieu and Bob Hoskins.

JANUARY 1995 Tomorrow's World. BBC TV with Carol Vorderman.

NOVEMBER 1994 Cruel Train. BBC TV drama with David Suchet, Saskia Reeves, Adrian Dunbar, Bryan Pringle, Alec McCowen and Minnie Driver.

AUGUST 1994 The Feast of July. Merchant Ivory Productions. Film with Embeth Davidtz, Tom Bell and Gemma Jones.

JANUARY 1992 The Secret Agent. BBC TV with David Suchet.

1989 I've been here before. Endboard productions

1989 Portrait of a Marriage. Episodes 2 and 3 of BBC TV serial starring Janet McTeer, David Haig and Cathryn Harrison.

APRIL 1987 Sherlock Holmes: The Bruce Partington Plans. Granada TV production with Jeremy Brett and Edward Hardwicke.

APRIL 1987 Sherlock Holmes: Wisteria Lodge. Granada TV with Jeremy Brett and Edward Hardwicke.

1987 The Return of Sherlock Holmes: Silver Blaze. Granada TV with Jeremy Brett and Edward Hardwicke.

NOVEMBER 1987 Without a Clue. Film with Michael Caine, Ben Kingsley, Jeffrey Jones, Lysette Anthony and Peter Cook.

APRIL 1987 Trains from the Arc. Video 125 VHS video presented by John Huntley. Colour sequences filmed at Oakworth to link with archive silent footage of Victorian Steam Railways. Produced by Peter Middleton.

OCTOBER 1985 Sherlock Holmes: The Abbey Grange. Granada TV with Jeremy Brett and Edward Hardwicke.

OCTOBER 1984 Return of the Antelope. Episodes 2 and 3 of Granada TV serial starring Alan Bowyer, Clauda Gambold, Derek Farr, Fiona McArthur.

1984 The Adventures of Sherlock Holmes: The Final Problem. Granada TV with Jeremy Brett and David Burke

1984 Sherlock Holmes: The Copper Beeches. Granada TV with Jeremy Brett and David Burke.

APRIL 1984 A Woman of Substance. TV serial with Jenny Seagrove, Liam Neeson and John Duttine.

JUNE 1984 My Brother Jonathan. BBC TV.

JUNE 1984 How we used to live. Yorkshire TV.

APRIL 1983 Sorrell & Son. Yorkshire TV drama with Richard Pasco, John Shrapnel, Stephanie Beecham, Malcolm Terris, Gwen Watford.

1981 Brideshead Revisited. Granada TV serial with Jeremy Irons, Anthony Andrews and Bill Owen.

MAY 1981 Fanny By Gaslight. BBC TV

APRIL 1981 Fame is the Spur. BBC TV

OCTOBER 1980 My Father's House.

1979 BBC TCV documentary about 1929 Rugby League Cup Final at Wembley.

*Not all of these were filmed on the Keighley & Worth Valley Railway. In addition, VCT vehicles appeared in many of the films and TV series/ programmes and other advertisements that include scenes from the line, as outlined in Chapter 9.

Great Northern Railway six-wheel Brake Third No. 589: built 1888, outside the Museum of Rail Travel at Ingrow. PAUL HOLROYD

Built for the newly formed Southern Railway by the Metropolitan Carriage, Wagon & Finance Company of Birmingham in July 1924, this 'Matchboard' Brake Third is almost identical to vehicles built by the South Eastern & Chatham Railway for boat train traffic to and from the London termini and Dover or Folkestone, and is known on the KWVR as the 'Chatham' coach. Carrying its British Railways' number S 3554S, the 42-seater is seen in the VCT museum at Ingrow. ROBIN JONES

NO. 465

Metropolitan Railway nine-compartment Third No. 465, along with the Vintage Carriages Trust's other two 'Dreadnought' carriages, represents the pinnacle of the Metropolitan Railway's coaching stock. In the late 19th century, the Metropolitan Railway was pushing north-west from London towards Aylesbury and beyond. It eventually met up with the Great Central Railway's London Extension. The beautiful coaches of the GCR shamed the Metropolitan Railway into producing these 'Dreadnought' coaches, of which nearly 100 built between 1910 and 1923. Special features can be found on them are the unusually wide footboards and the curved tops to the doors, reducing the risk of damage if accidentally opened in tunnels.

No. 465 was built by the Metropolitan Carriage, Wagon & Finance Company of Birmingham. This type of carriage survived until electrification reached Amersham in September 1961, allowing replacement of this locomotive-hauled stock by electric tube trains. London Transport then stored six carriages at Upminster until needed in May 1963 for the Underground Centenary celebrations.

The three Metropolitan Railway carriages owned by the trust were all initially purchased privately by Mr David Kitton from London Transport for the then-proposed Westerham Valley Railway preservation project. When this scheme failed, the carriages were loaned to the Worth Valley Railway in July 1965 and Nos. 427 and 465 formed part of this railway's reopening train in 1968. The Vintage Carriages Trust purchased all three carriages from Mr Kitton in 1974.

Although originally all turned out in varnished teak, the three coaches are restored to the different liveries that they carried during their years of service. The nine-compartment carriage is finished in London Transport's final dark brown livery.

These carriages are occasionally used on the KWVR as a vintage train set. In February 2013, No. 465 returned to its 'home territory' when it was placed on extended loan to the Buckinghamshire Railway Centre at Quainton Road, which was once part of the Metropolitan Railway. There, it ran behind restored Metropolitan Railway E class 0-4-4-T No. 1, which has been returned to steam by Bill Parker's Flour Mill workshops at Breaming the Forest of Dean to take part in major celebrations to mark the 150th anniversary of the Metropolitan Railway, the world's first underground line.

The trust has also embarked on a programme of cleaning, checking and making good where necessary the bogies and underframes of all three of the Metropolitan carriages, the others being seven-compartment First No. 509 and seven-compartment Brake Third No. 427 of 1910. The bogie and underframe

overhaul of No. 465 was completed in June 2004.

THESE ARE THE SOLE-SURVIVING 'DREADNOUGHT' CARRIAGES

No. 469 has appeared in This Week; Peaky Blinders; South Riding (BBC TV); Brideshead Revisited (2007 version); The History of the London Underground (archive footage); Commercial for pensions; The Grand; The Unknown Soldier; Fairy Tale - a True Story; Holiday; Jude; The Secret Agent (1992 BBC TV version); Portrait of a Marriage; Sherlock Holmes - the Bruce Partington Plans; Sherlock Holmes - Wisteria Lodge; Without A Clue; Return of the Antelope; A Woman of Substance; My Brother Jonathan; How We Used To Live; Sorrell and Son; BBC TV documentary about 1929 Rugby League Cup Final at Wembley; Yanks; The Seven Per Cent Solution.

Before it was bought by the Vintage Carriages Trust, it appeared in a commercial for Schweppes, The Railway Children (1970 EMI version) and The Private Life of Sherlock Holmes. It is seen shortly after being loaned to the Buckinghamshire Railway Centre in February 2013. ROBIN JONES

THE LANCASHIRE & YORKSHIRE RAILWAY PRESERVATION TRUST

The second group on the KWVR that concerns itself with classic historical carriages as well as locomotives is the Lancashire & Yorkshire Railway Trust, formed in 1988 by the Lancashire & Yorkshire Railway Preservation Society to replace the L&Y Saddletanks Fund, which was founded in 1964.

The group's carriages are usually displayed in the Oxenhope exhibition shed when not in service. As previously stated, the group owns both surviving L&Y 'Pugs' and saddle tank No. 752.

The trust's collection includes No. 47, the Blackpool Club Car built in 1912 at Newton Heath for the exclusive use of businessmen commuting between Blackpool and Manchester. Its underframe was removed when withdrawn by British Railways in 1951, and the body was then used as a cricket pavilion at Borrowash in Derbyshire.

It was bought for £1 from Redrow Homes for £1 in 1993 prior to site redevelopment, and its restoration was completed using an underframe from a BR standard suburban carriage. Indeed, many of the classic wooden bodies coaches you will see in traffic on today's heritage lines have been rescued and rescued after decades of use as private homes, holiday lets, farm outbuildings and chicken coops. The restoration of each is a miracle in itself.

Then there is No. 1474, Hughes taper-end bogie Brake Third built at Newton Heath in 1910, used initially on Leeds, Bradford and Liverpool expresses. By the time Nationalisation came around in 1948, it had already been downgraded into a mess van. No. 1474 was acquired from British Railways Departmental service in 1965, and restoration was completed in 1993.

Six-wheeled five-compartment Third No. 507 was built at Newton Heath in 1882. It was withdrawn by 1910 when its body was sold off and moved to Valley Gardens at Hapton near Burnley.

It was donated to by the late Tom Bell in 1991 and painstakingly restored to working order by 2005 at a cost of £17,000. It uses an underframe from LMS BGZ carriage M32988 built in 1938 and acquired from the Strathspey Railway, where the body had been damaged beyond economical repair by an arson attack. The latest coach in the society's collection to be completed was 1880 First Class six-wheeler No. 279, following a £45,000 restoration project on the KWVR that lasted a decade.

Volunteers and several specialist companies in the locality were involved in the overhaul of the coach, which was built at Newton Heath works.

It was joined on Wednesday, June 21, 2017 by three already restored carriages for a special train making three round trips on the line.

Invited as guest of honour was Marjorie Moran, who was born in the carriage after it was grounded near Burnley in 1910 and used as accommodation for mine workers and their families as new shafts were sunk at Hapton Valley Colliery near Burnley.

The new frame and its adaptation to accept the coach body cost more than £10,000 and a similar amount was needed for the bodywork timber. Outside specialists carried out some of the work.

Local upholsterer Margo Avrill-Lee of Oakworth completed the seat coverings and Metcalfe Castings of Keighley, made several items including door locks and grab handles.

Most of the funding for the initiative was provided by members, but a £1200 grant was received from the Preservation of Industrial and Scientific Materials Fund and a similar amount was raised through hiring out the pre-restored carriage for use in the BBC TV series South Riding.

As with the Vintage Carriage Trust's showpiece collection, the Lancashire & Yorkshire Railway Trust's coaches have an enviable track record of film and TV appearances. Credits include The Golden Age of Steam Railways, BBC Four TV series regularly repeated on BBC and cable TV channels, which features early years of the KWVR and the restoration of 'Pug' No. 51218.

Testament of Youth, a 2015 BBC Films production of the First World One memoir of Vera Brittain, featured all of the trust's carriages while BBC2's Peaky Blinders, a drama series about an early 20th-century Birmingham gang used Nos. 47 and 1474.

BELOW: LNER saloon No. 21661, far better known as the Old Gentleman's Saloon in The Railway Children film, is arguably the oldest operational standard gauge passenger coach in the world and seats just 14 people. It started life in 1871 as Stockton & Darlington Railway six-wheeled third-class saloon. It was bought from British Rail for preservation in 1969 by KWVR Preservation society member John Dawson and is seen inside the Museum of Rail Travel at Ingrow. ROBIN JONES

Lancashire & Yorkshire Railway magnificence restored: First Class six-wheeler No. 279. PAUL HOLROYD

Lancashire & Yorkshire Railway taper-end bogie Brake Third No. 1474 in the exhibition shed at Oxenhope. ROBIN JONES

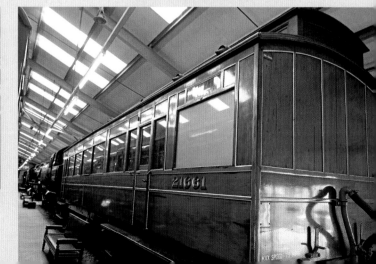

The Snug Cottage and Chapel View Cottage

Mr & Mrs L Usher 07999 820558 Email: enquiries@haworthcottages.co.uk **f** www.facebook.com/haworthcottages

These self-catering holiday cottages are in the heart of Haworth, the nerve centre of the Keighley & Worth Valley Railway, and are just two minutes' walk from the main street and railway station.

THIS heritage village, with its cobbled streets and independent shops, is on the edge of Yorkshire's industrial West Riding, a short drive to Skipton – 'The Gateway to The Yorkshire Dales', a perfect base for exploring the area. The rugged surrounding moorland inspired the talented Brontë family, who wrote their much-loved novels at the parsonage (now a museum) near to the cottages.

Also nearby is Haworth Old Hall, a recommended pub/restaurant dating back to circa 1580 and there are many other character pubs and cafes.

Myriad local walks criss-cross the surrounding landscape. A well-behaved dog will love the open moorland and is welcome to share a holiday at either cottage.

In addition to the Keighley & Worth Valley Railway, there is lots more to interest the rail buff, with the Embsay & Bolton Abbey Steam Railway in neighbouring Wharfedale, in Leeds the historic Middleton Railway, the Kirklees Light Railway and, of course, the National Railway Museum in York. At nearby Bradford, there's free admission to both the National Media Museum and the Bradford Industrial Museum.

The Snug cottage

This comfortable 18th century stone built terrace cottage is ideal for long or short breaks, offering as it does a happy blend of stylish modern features with wooden beams and all the original character.

Set out over three floors, it offers a well equipped kitchen diner and living room with cosy woodburner (starter pack of wood supplied free). There's a very comfortable first floor double bedroom with modern shower, wc and basin. The 2nd floor mezzanine over main bedroom with single bed is a favourite with children on an adventure.

Externally there is a pleasant seating area (not fenced). One well behaved pet is welcome at The Snug by prior arrangement. **Sleeps three based on two sharing plus one.**

Chapel View cottage

This comfortable 19th century stone built terrace cottage is ideal for long or short breaks, offering as it does a happy blend of stylish modern features with wooden beams and all the original character.

Centrally heated, there are three floors, with a well-equipped ground–floor dining kitchen, first floor sitting room with cosy woodburner and above, a delightful double bedroom and modern bathroom. **Sleeps two.**

Chapter 13

FABULOUS FLYING SCOTMAN'S
FLEETING VISIT

Bronte Country saw bumper crowds turn out in early spring 2017 when the world's most famous steam locomotive, A3 Pacific No. 60103 *Flying Scotsman*, set off from Oxenhope with a special train to mark the reopening of the Settle and Carlisle line, and then stayed for nine days on the heritage line. At just 4¾ miles, the Keighley & Worth Valley Railway is tiny in comparison with *Flying Scotsman*'s stomping ground, the 393-mile East Coast Main Line from King's Cross to Edinburgh Waverley, but that did nothing to diminish the A3's magnificence – far from it!

No. 60103 heads the first train of the day away from Keighley on April 8, 2017. ALAN WEAVER

For decades, LNER A3 Pacific No. 4472 *Flying Scotsman* has been hailed as the world's most famous steam locomotive.

And following the completion of its £4.5 million overhaul both by and on behalf of the National Railway Museum in 2016, it also became the world's most expensive one, if you take into account the £2.31 million that the York venue paid to buy it from its previous owner, Flying Scotsman plc, in 2004.

Just as when it snatched the official 100mph steam speed record in 1934, in 2016 *Flying Scotsman* again generated global headlines and deservedly so. Tens of thousands of people turned out to watch its inaugural run from King's Cross to York along its East Coast Main Line home territory on Thursday, February 25, 2016, and they were not disappointed.

It had been more than 10 years since the locomotive had last turned a wheel,

after what became an increasingly complex and often controversial overhaul expertly completed by Ian Riley at his Bury workshops.

Yet such problems quickly evaporated in the bright sunshine that graced the route as *Flying Scotsman* triumphantly headed its comeback train.

The trip marked the start of owner the NRM's Scotsman season, sponsored by ECML operator Virgin Trains, whose chairman Richard Branson had stumped up a significant portion of the £2.31 million needed to buy the A3 12 years earlier.

For its official main line launch, the engine appeared in fully authentic BR Brunswick green livery as No. 60103 – its BR number – still with its double chimney and smoke deflectors.

It has even had its smokebox handrail split and the front numberplate correctly positioned on the top hinge, to make it look exactly as it was when it was

withdrawn by BR in January 1963. At every vantage point along the route, overbridges, fields and embankment tops were lined with countless photographers, videographers and enthusiasts, who, along with locals, simply wanted to see the locomotive thunder past, many of them waving and cheering as it did so. South of Doncaster, one lady was spotted standing on top of a pile of manure to get a better view. Welcome to Yorkshire boss Sir Gary Verity said: "This is part of history. You've only got to look at the crowds. They're on every vantage point, every gantry, every bridge, even up on cherry pickers."

Five helicopters followed the train at various points, two of them belonging to Sky News and BBC News.

Flying Scotsman approaches Ais Gill summit eight minutes late, returning from Carlisle on March 31, 2017.
BRIAN SHARPE

Sadly, spectators decided to stand on the wrong side of the fence in some areas and at points near St Neots and north of Doncaster, the locomotive was forced to come to a sudden stop because of trespassers.

A guard aboard the *Flying Scotsman* train leaned out of a window and shouted to the trespassers "Will you get right off the lineside? You are causing the railway to be shut. Right off the lineside!"

Similar scenes had been witnessed on July 4, 1999, when the locomotive made its previous comeback run along the ECML following a major overhaul under then owner the late pharmaceutical entrepreneur Dr Tony Marchington.

At York in 2016, Platforms 9 and 10 were heaving with spectators for up to two hours before the train finally arrived. Station and museum staff handed out special *Flying Scotsman* flags and sweets.

Its comeback year brought bigger than ever crowds flocking to see No. 60103 wherever it went including the North Yorkshire Moors and Severn Valleys railways, the Locomotion museum in Shildon and the NRM in York, where it became the centrepiece of

A3 Pacific No. 60103 *Flying Scotsman* crosses Batty Moss viaduct at Ribblehead eight minutes early on March 31, 2017. BRIAN SHARPE

a major exhibition lasting several weeks. In 2017, it was the turn of the Keighley & Worth Valley Railway to host the legendary crowd puller… but the A3 had to do one very big job first, before it could steal the show exclusively in Bronte country.

No. 60103 launched its 2017 programme by reopening the Settle and Carlisle line, heading a sell-out excursion across one of Britain's most spectacular rail routes from Oxenhope on the KWVR.

The legendary route had been closed north of Armathwaite since February 9, 2016 following a 500,000-ton landslip at Eden Brows.

Network Rail's engineers and contactors had spent 14 months rebuilding and stabilising the trackbed. Sitting more than 240ft above the River Eden, reinstatement of the subsided section was the subject of a £23-million engineering marathon involving building an enormous concrete and steel structure to sit beneath the railway and driving high-strength piles into the bedrock of the Eden Gorge.

The work had involved clearing the 70m slope of vegetation and excavating four metres below track level before installing the piles.

Around 16,000 tons of spoil had to be removed from site before a concrete guide wall could be installed to assist with piling works using 226 steel-cased piles, followed by the pouring of 1300cu m of concrete.

The line was scheduled to be reopened to regular through traffic on March 31, but the steam special was to run two days before that.

Along with its support coach, *Flying Scotsman* travelled from the York museum to the KWVR on Wednesday, March 29, ready for the excursion to Carlisle, which was run in conjunction with Northern, Network Rail and the Friends of the Settle & Carlisle group.

Departing from Oxenhope at 8.30am, on March 31, with a 10-coach train of maroon Mk.1 stock supplied by Carnforth-based train operator West Coast Railways, *Flying Scotsman* joined the Aire Valley main line at Keighley to head for a water stop at Hellifield.

Following an on-time departure, the special topped the climb to Blea Moor eight minutes early, continuing to Appleby where it was greeted by a piper, and speeches were made to mark the occasion.

After Appleby, the train crossed the newly reinstated section of track at Eden Brows with much whistling, looking on was the large team of engineers that had carried out the work of rebuilding the line.

The engine was turned and serviced at Carlisle before retracing its steps to Keighley, from where a banking engine was required over the 1-in-58 gradients of the Worth Valley branch. All seats on the train at £220 per ticket were sold many weeks in advance and the event made headlines nationally, although the BBC was criticised for using old footage of new-build A1 Peppercorn Pacific No. 60163 *Tornado* on Ribblehead viaduct instead of *Flying Scotsman* on the day!

Heading West Coast Railways' fleet of maroon-liveried BR Mk.1 coaches, Flying Scotsman steams down the Aire Valley between Skipton and Keighley on its way back to Oxenhope from the Settle and Carlisle line on March 31, 2017. IAN GRATTON*

On a cold sunny spring day, April 3, 2017, the first *Flying Scotsman*-hauled train on the KWVR, the 10am departure from Haworth, with cylinder cocks open disturbs debris in the ballast and blasts past Haworth Yard before bursting through the portals of Bridgehouse Lane bridge. PAUL LIVSEY

No appearance of *Flying Scotsman* today would be complete without bagpipes. Members of the welcoming pipe band pose at Ingrow with longstanding member and KWVR Preservation Society director Bill Black. DEBORAH CROSS/KWVR

Flying Scotsman accelerates away from Oakworth on April 8, 2017. ROBERT FALCONER

Two extra trains were run on Wednesday, April 5, 2017, for *Flying Scotsman*'s visit and No. 60103 is seen heading the first of these past a closed Damems Junction signalbox.
ROBIN LUSH

As April 2, 2017 draws to a close, the service train headed by WD 2-8-0 No. 90733 passes on the last service of the day.
ANDREW DENNISON

No. 60103 passing through Oakworth on April 9, 2017.
IAN GRATTON*

Flying Scotsman hauls a KWVR service train into Oakworth during its much-celebrated visit. BSHARPE

TAKING BRONTE COUNTRY BY STORM

Following the high-profile relaunch of the stricken line, *Flying Scotsman* helped draw around 17,000 visitors during its nine-day stint in service on the Keighley & Worth Valley Railway from April 1-9. One family came from as far away as Australia.

As the locomotive passed through the intermediate stations on its arrival around 8.30am the day before, the platforms and overbridges were packed with sightseers holding mobile phones aloft to chart its passage, with a sense of excitement building up as the telltale white plume of smoke was spotted in the distance.

The first two days, April 1-2, saw the

A3 on static display at Ingrow West, where visitors were invited to savour the 'Flying Scotsman Experience', which allowed access to the locomotive itself.

The experience included a 15-minute interpretive talk about the loco followed by a walk through the cab and the tender; allowing visitors to follow in the footsteps of generations of enginemen who passed through on their journey at speed from King's Cross to Edinburgh.

After that, the locomotive joined the line's roster for the rest of its visit.

The railway's chairman Dr Matt Stroh said: "It showed the railway and our volunteers at their absolute best.

"We had about 17,000 visitors over the nine days, including 12,500 passengers who travelled on *Flying Scotsman*.

"The sense of achievement among the hundreds of volunteers who gave their time was palpable. Everyone worked so hard.

"We probably had over 100 volunteers rostered for each of the nine days *Flying Scotsman* was here. The feedback we received, which ranged from the chairman of Network Rail to the various other passengers I spoke to, was incredibly positive."

He said that the family from Australia included a young boy with autism who enjoyed a "journey of a lifetime" on the railway, and had been thrilled to meet driver Noel Hartley from the National Railway Museum.

The Old Hall in Haworth offered a supper to KWVR volunteers as a 'thank you' gesture for the extra trade the visit helped bring them. "I think that's symptomatic of what this event contributed to the local economy," said Matt.

Emphasising the now-long-proven value of heritage railways to a local economy, Matt added: "A lot of the passengers who came to travel on the *Flying Scotsman* stayed on the line and in the villages, because they really wanted to make a day of it, which was great.

"As a railway it'll be our 50th year next year. We've been asked how long it took us to prepare for *Flying Scotsman* and in a sense it has taken 49 years of preparation, because we'd not have got the locomotive here if we weren't good enough."

He added that the profits from the visit would be invested in future KWVR projects.

It was certainly a fitting celebration for the line's 150th birthday, the visit of

Unsung heroes: members of the KWVR Young Persons Group, pictured at Ingrow, play a vital part in the running of the railway and made a huge contribution to the smooth running of the visit of *Flying Scotsman*. CRAIG SZLATOSZLAVEK

No. 60103 bursts out of a steam-filled Mytholmes Tunnel with the 11.08am first Keighley departure of the day. ROBIN LUSH

the A3 lasting until four days before the actual anniversary on April 13.

To celebrate *Flying Scotsman*'s visit, Eagle Intermedia, the internet marketing consultancy firm, which runs the Bronte Country website, held a raffle for tickets to raise funds for the charity Bradford and Airedale Eyesight Trust. The raffle was won by Stockport resident, Gillian Mawson, a wartime historian and author of Guernsey Evacuees and Britain's Wartime Evacuees.

For her prize Mrs Mawson and her husband enjoyed afternoon tea in a carriage hauled by *Flying Scotsman* along the KWVR.

After its much-celebrated exploits on the line, Flying Scotsman travelled south over the national network for its appearance at the Bluebell Railway. However, the green-liveried legend had added its indelible mark to the plethora of those already rooted in the valley and its hillsides.

Dawn breaks over Haworth yard. After months of preparation and anticipation for the visit of *Flying Scotsman*, April 3, 2017 sees three steam locomotives prepared and ready for seven days of operation over the Worth valley branch. Left to right they are *Flying Scotsman*, WD 2-8-0 No. 90733 (to give assistance on the climb out of Keighley and up the Worth Valley at the rear of the train) and Midland 4F No. 43924. PAUL LIVSEY

Chapter 14

THE 21ST CENTURY RAILWAY CHILDREN

Yes, the Keighley & Worth Valley Railway is world famous as the setting for EMI's immortal big-screen version of Edith A Nesbit's novel The Railway Children. However, the heritage line is now also leading the way with a ground-breaking new visitor attraction, Rail Story, based around a coach which has been converted into a classroom to teach new generations of youngsters about Britain's rich railway heritage.

A survey among 500 parents and 500 children carried out by Situation Publishing found that three quarters of youngsters did not know who GWR engineer Isambard Kingdom was, and two thirds had never heard of *Rocket* inventor George Stephenson.

The study was carried out in support of a new travel book, Geek's Guide to Britain, and found that 73% of children – and almost half of adults questioned – drew a blank when asked about James Watt, who invented the steam engine.

If those figures are true, and remember the study was carried out with only a minuscule fraction of the population, it points towards a damning indictment of the teaching of history.

A rudimentary knowledge of the core part that railways played in the creation of the modern world should surely be a basic plank of education.

Richard Trevithick's invention of the self-propelled vehicle may have been a slow burner his day, but it sparked off a chain of events that would change the globe forever.

Railways facilitated the rapid mass movement of people and goods, the fellow products of the Industrial Revolution, in a way that was hitherto impossible in a short space of time.

They paved the way for the standardisation of time and the dawn of mass communication; the 19th-century forerunners of the internet.

A trunk railway had the power to shrink a continent, and bring long-distance travel within the reach of ordinary people.

The Rail Story learning coach in the former goods bay at Ingrow West. ROBIN JONES

The concept of the self-propelled vehicle later manifested itself in the motor car, the aeroplane and eventually the spaceship. In short, the steam railway was the most important invention since the wheel.

So how do the youngsters of today see Britain's world-changing market-leading railway history?

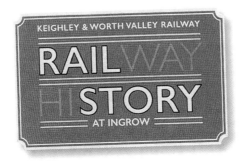

There are those whose grandparents were not even born when steam haulage ended on British Railways in 1968, and whose only experience of a steam locomotive would have come from Thomas the Tank Engine books or a trip on a Santa Special. When *Flying Scotsman* visited Birmingham's Tyseley Locomotive Works in 2016, Vintage Trains' chairman Michael Whitehouse commented that there were visitors with children who had never seen a steam locomotive before.

Many rail enthusiasts also find themselves in the same situation when it comes to traction engines. Born long after they had been superseded by tractors, for many, their only experience of them is as colourful steamy exhibits at country shows or occasional heritage railway visits; an enchanting novelty, but not workhorses. Children who are taken by their parents to a heritage railway must feel to a greater or larger extent much the same about steam locomotives, or even early diesels for that matter.

Yet railway history and heritage is far, far bigger than an entertaining afternoon out and engines with plastic faces. Understand how the railways changed human society forever, and you gain an essential insight into why our world is shaped as it is today.

Many heritage railways have embraced the immense potential of the education aspect of their operations to some extent. However, just as the KWVR led the revival movement somewhat in the wake of the resounding success of The Railway Children, showering it with relentless amounts of positive publicity, it has broken new ground with its latest Heritage Lottery Fund-backed venture – Rail Story.

THE *BAHAMAS* SPINOFF

As every organisation that has applied for Heritage Lottery Fund grant aid will know, the higher the educational value of a project, the better the chance of winning funding.

The Bahamas Locomotive Society needed funds for the overhaul of Jubilee 4-6-0 No. 45596 *Bahamas*, which had been absent from the main line since 1994. The society had developed a working partnership with the Vintage Carriages Trust and came up with the idea of enhancing the visitor experience at Ingrow station.

When applying for Lottery funding for *Bahamas*, it was decided to add a major educational element. Hence the 'Learning Coach', a facility designed to encourage students in science, technology and mathematics.

In March 2013, the Lottery awarded

Today's railway children attend a class in the Learning Coach. JOHN HILLIER

£776,000 for the twin project, which was to cost £90,000, and so *Bahamas* went off to Tyseley Locomotive Works for its first heavy overhaul since 1961.

The coach chosen for the project was 1924 Wolverton-built LMS corridor composite No. 8761, latterly DM395470. The Wolverton carriage and wagon workshops in Buckinghamshire were established in 1838 by the London & Birmingham Railway for the construction and repair of locomotives. In 1877 the locomotive work was transferred to Crewe and the workshops, then part of the London & North Western Railway, took on the repair of carriages and wagons. By 1907 it was the largest carriage building and repair works in the country employing around 4500 staff.

The amalgamation of the railway companies in 1923 and subsequent nationalisation in 1948 saw the works continue with its rolling stock function until 1962 when new construction

ceased and the works became a repair facility only. Part of the site continues in use for railway purposes.

When the workshops at Wolverton became part of the LMS in 1923, they came under the supervision of the Chief Mechanical Engineer's department, in which the carriage and wagon superintendent was Robert W Reid. Reid implemented a production-line method of carriage manufacture for a range of new standard carriage designs, to be built at Derby, Newton Heath near Manchester, and Wolverton.

What is now the Learning Coach was one of the first of the new designs. It was of the 57ft side-corridor composite type and built to diagram D1694. Such diagrams provided a schematic view of the vehicle and included important dimensions and features so as to be a means of ready reference to a variety of railway departments.

As a composite coach – that is one with both first- and third-class compartments – it was arranged with three 'firsts' and four 'thirds'. Each first-class compartment accommodated six seats and each third-class compartment accommodated eight.

A feature of the carriage design was that every compartment was accessible directly through an external door in addition to a sliding door from the side corridor. This concept was typical of the period until later variations replaced the individual external doors with large windows, so leaving access to the compartments only from the corridor. The operating department gave this type of coach design the generic code CPC.

Construction of these standard coaches followed that of the previous railway companies and comprised a wood-framed body mounted on a steel chassis. The framework, manufactured from teak, was clad externally with mahogany panels with the joints covered by beading of the same material. The roof was formed from wood boarding,

Jubilee 4-6-0 No. 45596 *Bahamas* outside publisher Mortons' offices in Horncastle in November 2013. Our publisher Mortons contributed IT equipment to the Rail Story project. ROBIN JONES

covered with canvas and suitably finished to make it weatherproof.

A total of 201 of these coaches was built to diagram D1694. The first 41 were ordered under Lot No. 30 and constructed at Wolverton. The Learning Coach was among the first 10 built (Lot 30A) and entered service in October 1924. It weighed 29 tons and carried the LMS number 8761. This number was changed to 3515 in 1933 as part of a renumbering scheme implemented to integrate newly built vehicles with those from the former companies.

From new, this type of carriage was utilised on many of the LMS Railway's West Coast Main Line long-distance trains. They were subsequently moved to lesser routes when improved steel-clad vehicles were introduced during the mid-1930s.

The colour of LMS coaching stock of this period was Crimson Lake, with the beading of the body panels lined with yellow and black to accentuate this constructional feature. The scheme was chosen by the railway's officers following an inspection of former Midland and LNWR vehicles at Euston station in April 1923. Subsequent overhauls and repainting usually occurred every six or seven years. It is likely that No. 8761 received only one repaint, and in a simplified manner, before the Second World War by which time it had received its new number of 3515. During the war some of these coaches were converted for use in ambulance trains and it has been suspected that the learning coach might have been among them. However, no evidence has been discovered to substantiate this consideration.

The war also inflicted excessive use on nearly all the railways' rolling stock and infrastructure. With minimum maintenance at this time, many vehicles such as these suffered external deterioration and so steel cladding came to be used to replace or part cover damaged wood panels.

Much of the beading was also removed, and usually in an ad hoc manner, which did little to improve their appearance.

Following the nationalisation of the railway companies in 1948 the descriptive code was changed from CPC to CK, but a significant visual change was the application of the new British Railways' two-tone livery of cream and crimson. Those allocated to the London Midland Region gained the prefix 'M' to their numbers.

The introduction of the new BR all-steel coaches in the mid-1950s heralded the demise of these old wood-bodied types. When M3515 was finally withdrawn from service in July 1958 it was one of five of the same type selected for conversion for use in breakdown trains.

The conversion was undertaken at its Wolverton birthplace. It was completed by the end of 1958 and was identified by its departmental number of DM395470, before its allocation to Southport in January 1959.

The conversion included the removal of all the first-class and one of the third-class compartments to provide an open space for the stowage of tools, jacks, and other breakdown equipment. Of the remaining three third-class compartments, one was enlarged and modified to become a kitchen, one assigned for the use of the breakdown crew, and one assigned for use by the District Locomotive Superintendent, who also had his own toilet. An additional toilet was provided for use by the rest of the breakdown crew.

When the Southport depot closed in 1966, the vehicle was moved to Northwich in Cheshire. Here it remained until, when due for scrap in 1981, it was gifted to the 8E Association, to enable this group of enthusiasts to use it as a base for the support and servicing they offered to visiting steam locomotives. It was formally handed over to the association in March 1982. The group removed some of its breakdown fixtures and fittings, gave it a repaint, fitted bunks and undertook other superficial work to make the vehicle suitable for their use.

Following the closure of the

THE SCIENCE CLUB

During 2017 a science club was formed under the banner of Science Stars with the aim of attracting children aged between eight and 12 on Saturday mornings throughout the summer.

The idea was to further some of the work provided during school visits to the railway, but more importantly to provide an enjoyable place where local children can feel comfortable and become familiar in a space they come to consider as theirs; one in which they may feel inclined to return when older and perhaps volunteer on.

The club, which took off in May that year, meets in the coach every other Saturday morning from 10am to noon.

The club also ran two-week-long summer schools, which proved popular.

Science Stars covers all areas of science and engineering.

The idea for the club is to bridge the gap between children growing out of programmes such as Thomas the Tank Engine and therefore losing interest in

Equipment for a science lesson laid out in the Learning Coach classroom. ROBIN JONES

railways and them being old enough to join the line's Young Persons' Group. The idea is that they will get used to coming to the railway on a Saturday morning (the same day the Young Persons' Group meet) and then when they turn 13 they can leave the science club and become a volunteer.

Debbie Cross, audience development coordinator, said: "It is all about giving them ownership of the railway when they are young to make sure we secure our future volunteers."

A young visitor to the Learning Coach meets Hudswell Clarke 0-4-0ST *Lord Mayor* in the Ingrow museum. JOHN HILLIER

Northwich depot in 1984 the van was no longer required and was offered for sale. A Bahamas Locomotive Society member purchased the van and had it moved to Dinting Railway Centre in 1985.

Here it worthily complemented the Craven 50-ton steam breakdown crane and became a store for lifting equipment and tools, when not otherwise used as a Santa's grotto!

Following the closure of Dinting Railway Centre in 1990 the van, together with the majority of the BLS collection, moved to the Keighley & Worth Valley Railway where it was placed into storage at Oakworth.

A CLASS CONVERSION

The idea of utilising the vehicle as an education facility depended upon its external refurbishment to ensure it would remain weatherproof and look attractive. Rail Restoration North East at Shildon was asked to provide a quotation for the work, and this figure was added to the Phase 2 bid of the HLF application. The announcement of the Lottery award allowed the van to move to Shildon in August 2013.

The van was visually restored to its riding and tool van appearance and returned to Ingrow in January 2014, having cost around £37,000.

Its conversion to departmental use in 1958 and subsequent life following railway service, had removed many of its original features. Society volunteers undertook the internal renovation and care was taken to examine the structure, components and fittings while the task was underway. This helped provide many clues to its former appearance and history.

Perhaps the most significant was, during the work at Shildon, when one of the original mahogany panels bearing the LMS identity was discovered beneath an area of the outer steel cladding. This was removed to become part of the current exhibition.

Its later departmental role was demonstrated by the survival of lettering denoting its allocation to Southport, and subsequent removal of a layer of paint revealed the remains of its prefix MPM (Motive Power Midland).

Internally, many of the detail wood components, such as the ventilator flaps on the doors, or the backs of panels, had been stamped or signed with the names of the craftsmen who had made the items at Wolverton in 1924. Names so noted include: G Dunkley, A Powell and E Barnard.

Notable among these is George Dunkley, whose name appears on the majority of the remaining panels fitted into the coach. Ancestral research indicates that George, who was born in 1881, would have been aged 41, lived in Newport Pagnell and was married with three children when he was helping

A DAY IN THE RAIL STORY EDUCATION CENTRE

Most of the Rail Story educational workshops follow the same itinerary. Here is an example of a typical school visit where a school has booked on to one of our workshops and has added a train ride on to its day.

10AM: School arrives at Rail Story education centre.
10.10-10.30AM: Welcome and introduction. Class is divided into two groups of 15.
10.30-11.45: Group 1 – Stay in learning coach and partake in paid workshop. Group 2 – Catch 10.30am train to Oxenhope and return at 11.30am.
11.45AM-NOON: Explore carriage works and engine shed museums. Prepare for lunch. Time available for Group 1 to purchase items from the shop if required.
NOON-12.25PM: Lunch is on one of the carriages in the carriage works or outside if the weather is accommodating.
12.25PM-2PM: Group 1 - Catch 12:30 train to Oxenhope and return at 2pm. Group 2 – Partake in paid workshop in the learning coach. Time available for Group 2 to purchase items from the shop if required.

School pupils learn about the exhibits in the nearby Vintage Carriages Trust museum.
JOHN HILLIER

2PM: Collect belongings from the learning coach and return to minibus to go back to school.

with the construction of this coach. He retired in 1947 and died in 1954.

Some of the features added during the 1958 conversion were removed and considered to have no suitable reapplication. Once recorded, objects such as sinks and mirrors from the toilets were passed on to similar organisations in exchange for items useful for this project.

One object recovered during the refurbishment was found to predate the vehicle's construction, and is more likely to be from the early Edwardian era. This is a ventilator flap fitted in one of the toilet cubicles installed during the conversion work in 1958. The flap is of LNWR manufacture and was the type usually fitted above each compartment door.

Although the coach interior had, over the years, received refinishing coats of varnish and paint, removal of some components revealed samples of the original red mahogany finish to the corridor and compartments and the medium-oak finish to the toilet cubicle.

Careful removal of layers of paint revealed signage from different eras. The toilet doors had both LMS and BR lettering to denote their purpose – BR-era transfers were discovered noting the risk of leaning from an open window, or the misdemeanour of pulling the

communication cord, and sign-written notices indicated the location for the storage of jacks in the tool space. One of the door hinges was stamped LNWR indicating how standard features crossed over into its successor company.

Concurrent with this 'house detective' approach to investigating the history of the coach, other research was undertaken in an attempt to establish further facts. A visit to the National Railway Museum's Search Engine archive at York found the original drawings for both the as-built arrangement and its conversion in 1958. The 'Order for New Stock', dated January 20, 1958, includes No. 3515 among the five noted for conversion, and details all the components used to complete the task.

Secondary sources, such as Essery and Jenkinson's book, *The LMS Coach*, and the *Railway Carriage* and *Wagon Handbook* by Sanders, have also been an important aid in comprehending the appearance of the coach, and the changes it underwent during its working life.

In order to recreate an appropriate appearance of the mahogany panelling, various books on wood finishing were consulted in order to understand the methods described in *The LMS Coach*. A variety of traditional and modern techniques were used to produce a result that appears sufficient to support the 'indicative' description.

As much as possible of the original material was utilised and stripped back to bare wood before refinishing. New wood (sapele rather than mahogany) was used only where rot or damage beyond effective repair prevented any alternative.

The finishing process incorporated three coats of water-based dye, one coat of grain filler, one coat of sanding sealer, one coat of spirit dye, and two or three of coats of satin polyurethane varnish. The satin finish was chosen specifically to 'tone down' the appearance and reduce any unforgiving blemishes in the original wood. The application of this finishing process was considered to be successful, but only as the project was

nearing completion!

In order to complete the task within the five-year time limit set by the Lottery it became essential to use contractors for some of work.

New wood panelling and other details, such as mouldings, were manufactured off-site to drawings,

and electrical contractors brought in to establish the basis of the electrical wiring and fitting of lights in the classroom.

One innovative solution to overcome non-availability of original material was that chosen for the compartment window blinds. A Wolverton drawing of the blinds in the NRM archive specified a blue and gold shell-pattern tapestry.

To have this manufactured for the quantity required would have been too expensive. The alternative was to have photographic images printed on to 'wind mesh'. Used commercially for outside signage, wind mesh is flexible, printable, and although it reduced the amount of daylight into the compartment it was found to be to a level that was acceptable. These blinds also had the advantage of recreating the idea used in

STEEL WHEELS AND FOUR-FOOTERS

One big theme highlighted in the Rail Story coach is the history of the interaction between animals and railways, ranging from cattle that were once transported by rail to horse-drawn tramways or horse shunting, and circuses that were moved by rail through to station cats and railway dogs.

Imprinted on the carriage's work tables are paintings of animals in railway settings, specially produced by artist John Wardle to highlight this central theme, which begins with the first railway motive power of them all.

Horse-drawn waggonways and tramways pre-empted the steam railways by several centuries. Indeed, the Rainhill Trials of 1829 were held by the Liverpool & Manchester Railway to determine whether to adopt steam

as the primary form of traction for the world's first inter-city line, or to play it safe and use horses in the time-honoured way. And all this 25 years after Richard Trevithick had given the world's first public demonstration of a steam railway locomotive!

Rocket inventor George Stephenson went back to horse traction when he designed the Whitby & Pickering Railway, which opened in 1836. His innovations did not immediately lead to the last bag of oats being eaten by any means!

In the 1920s, railways employed around 19,500 horses for cartage of goods onwards, about 10% of the entire UK horse population.

By 1930 the British railway companies owned 18,429 horses for shunting and road delivery services. By 1940 the number had fallen to 11,163, in 1950 to 4754 and in 1960 to less than 100.

The last horse-drawn passenger train service on an English railway was on the Port Carlisle branch of the North British

JOHN WARDLE

Dogs played their part on railways. A driver's dog is seen accompanying him on a trip. JOHN WARDLE

Railway in Cumbria. The last train ran on April 4, 1914 and the coach used on this service was later saved and in now on display at the National railway Museum in York. Railway horses were fed mixture of crushed oats and chaff, supplemented with bran, beans or maize. However, the stores where the grain was kept became boltholes for rats and mice and so station cats proved essential.

The last British Railways' horse was 24 year-old cross-breed Charlie, who began his career at Camden in 1949 and was used for shunting horseboxes at Newmarket from 1961 until March 1967.

Livestock was an extremely important commodity in the history of the UK rail network. For example, in 1930 the numbers carried by the LMS were: cattle – 1,870,601; calves – 188,544; sheep – 6,145,332; pigs – 722,076; horses – 24,377; miscellaneous – 2527 – a total tonnage of 1,252,520. Railways opened up rural backwaters and gave farmers a quick and efficient way of sending their livestock to market, rather than using drovers to herd then across countryside. In some cases, entire farms were moved across country by rail.

Very few railway stations and sheds did not have their own cat. An expert at keeping the rodent population down, it was often a case of a stray cat adopting a railway rather than vice versa.
JOHN WARDLE

THE FUTURE SHOWCASING THE PAST

Ingrow's railway museums – and indeed a ride over the five-mile branch line – are an additional attraction for people visiting the area, with society visitors increasing by a staggering 86% in 2015, while VCT recorded a 21% increase.

Holders of the line's rover tickets get free admission to Rail Story and for other visitors a joint ticket gives reduced price admission. Although a charge is made for visiting school parties or other similar activities, it was always intended that the exhibition was to be a free-to-access attraction for those visiting the railway. It is hoped that visitors would be willing to offer donations to help offset these costs.

Rail Story is open from 11am-4pm even when trains are not running.

The society, the VCT and KWVR also recognise that visitors need to spend longer at the Ingrow site as well as being able to learn about railways and rail travel, and major plans lie ahead.

A new amenities block with refreshment facilities, public visitor toilets, ticket office, and shops is in the pipeline, while new facilities for servicing steam locos at the northern end of the line anticipated.

Meanwhile, the Rail Story development will span many years, the aim being that by 2025 work will be complete and all will be ready to celebrate the bicentenary of public steam railways.

In the meantime, the provision of the learning coach has gone a long, long way, not only to fulfilling the wishes of the Lottery, but in plugging a hole that many believe exists in terms of education children about basic railway history and its importance to an understanding of the world they live in.

My view about the Learning Coach? Every heritage railway should have one!

*More details about Rail Story and the Learning Coach can be found at www. kwvr.co.uk/education

---

railway publicity pictures, whereby a landscape scene was photographically inserted into position on the initial print so as to obscure the usual background of railway sidings.

The subsequent copy created a more idyllic image for publicity purposes. The images chosen here for this application were considered more for their social history rather than any idyll. Unlike the platform-side window blinds, those for the corridor side are non-operational and dummy 'pulls' have been fitted.

The use of blue and gold colours for the original blinds gave consideration that a similar colour may have been used for the moquette upholstery of the seats, although no evidence has been found to substantiate this. In the event, and in view of the practicality of upholstering only two compartments, a sufficient quantity of moquette to a design used by the LMS, but of a later post-Second World War period, was obtained from the Severn Valley Railway. The re-upholstery of the seats was another task outsourced.

Of the other compartments, both of which had been modified during the 1958 conversion, that converted for use as a kitchen was stripped of all its original fittings and rebuilt for use as an office.

The compartment intended for use by the District Locomotive Superintendent had been altered to provide access to a separate toilet cubicle, and the seats had originated from a first-class compartment. The decision was made, therefore, not to restore this compartment but to renovate it in a sympathetic manner and utilise the space to further the educational role by incorporating digital and other media.

Sponsorship from publisher Mortons Media of Horncastle, Lincolnshire was forthcoming to help fund the equipment and the provision of access to the digital archive of *The Railway Magazine*, thus offering a useful research facility.

The classroom inside the Learning Coach. ROBIN JONES

The remaining two-thirds of the carriage acts as the classroom area for children and students.

A learning group of 30 children and six adults are the usual group size, with the party being split in half; one half use the classroom, while the others visit the Engine Shed and Carriage Works museum, before changing over.

However, its use is not limited to school parties. It is also available for other interest groups and already hosts some mutual improvement classes, once commonplace for training railwaymen in steam days and carrying on an old Dinting tradition, the original Derbyshire home of the society.

In addition to the partners at Ingrow, Helen Ashby, former head of knowledge and collections at the National Railway Museum, along with Anthony Coulls,

senior curator rail transport and technology at the York museum, are acting as museum mentors for the Bahamas Locomotive Society and Vintage Carriage Trust respectively.

In total the cost to convert the coach for its new educational role was approximately £69,000, £30,000 of which came from the Lottery award, with a further £7000 coming from specific donations or sponsorship. The remaining £32,000 was funded directly by owner the BLS.

The classroom was sufficiently ready to accept its first visiting school party during 2016. They were able to benefit from a range of subjects aligned with science and mathematics (the STEM topics) delivered by a small group of educational facilitators employed for this purpose.

Chapter 15

NOW FOR THE NEXT
50 YEARS
AND BEYOND

Keighley's heritage railway platform. ROBIN JONES

Having long established itself as one of the leading tourist attractions in the north of England, the Keighley & Worth Valley Railway is by no means content to rest on the groundbreaking successes of the past. Martin Shaw, strategy and development director of the Keighley & Worth Valley Railway Preservation Society, explains the vision for the future and how the Worth Valley branch will remain at the forefront of both the local tourism economy and the national railway heritage sector.

LEFT: Visiting LMS 'Black Five. No. 45305 steams into Haworth on December 28, 2014 amidst a wintry landscape that could have leapt straight from the pages of Wuthering Heights!

Fifty years of steady progress since the line reopened in 1968 has resulted in the Keighley & Worth Valley Railway being in a good place today.

It has a steam locomotive fleet which is the envy of many other heritage lines with no fewer than five locomotives fully operational and two more about to enter service again, its permanent way is in its best condition since the line's original opening almost exactly 150 years ago, it enjoys huge support for its exciting annual programme of enthusiast galas, specialist beer and music festivals, and family Santa Specials, and it currently has no debt but rather a six-figure sum in the bank.

Yet the railway, which its members reopened almost as a hobby 50 years ago, is evolving, like all its fellow heritage lines, into something more business-like.

The realisation of this has caused its board of directors to evolve a vision statement, which is that "we want our visitors and volunteers to enjoy the railway and its heritage while maintaining its long-term viability through continuing to develop the visitor experience."

Business speak perhaps, but necessary when you consider that the railway has just had to spend £175k replacing its Haworth locomotive shed roof, that its stunning steam locomotive fleet incurs annual restoration costs approaching £200,000 just to stand still, and that there are £500,000 of main line bridge repairs looming up just down the track!

Ivatt Class 4 2-6-0 No. 43106 visiting from the Severn Valley Railway powers out of Keighley with a demonstration freight special on February 2, 2012. The type was primarily designed for medium freight work but also widely used on secondary passenger services. A total of 162 were built between 1947-52, but only three were constructed by the LMS before Nationalisation in 1948. No. 43106, the sole survivor, a veteran of Midland & Great Northern Railway steam in East Anglia, dates from 1951. BRIAN SHARPE

The viability, or financial sustainability, of this heritage railway into the future is key, as the vision statement suggests. The KWVR just has to be around and steaming forwards in another half century's time. In order to achieve this, the railway has available to it two key resources – its volunteers and its visitors.

Its volunteers have been paramount to the success of its past 50 years and even today the railway has been fortunate in that, unlike some of its fellow preserved railways, the number of its volunteers has hardly wavered.

Understandably, however, the age of its volunteers has undoubtedly increased such that the railway's key volunteer challenge today is the passing down of skills and expertise from the original members to the incoming younger generation.

At the same time increasing regulations also challenge the railway's workforce such that it has proved necessary in more recent years to recruit full-time paid employees to assume some of the more routine responsibilities. The railway today still remains one of very few in the country not to have an employed general manager and yet its future plans might just have to see that change.

Any preserved railway's volunteers tend by nature to be enthusiasts and the railway has in hand several plans aimed at exciting and thus motivating them. To this end there are plans being considered both to convert two currently unrestored coaches into a replica LMS push-pull set that could be mated with the line's Ivatt 2-6-2T or 'Jinty' to produce an historical combination unique in the country. It is also hoped soon to complete the Keighley station resignalling scheme which will allow more flexible operation, possible even to the extent of a vintage train every weekend connecting to the exciting and new Rail Story exhibition at the line's Ingrow station.

The railway's visitors are of course its main source of revenue generation and their numbers have oscillated over the years, albeit more recently showing a very pleasing but steady trend of increases.

With the aim of increasing their numbers yet further much thought is being given to making the railway more of a half, or even full-day destination.

Alongside the Keighley resignalling project there are plans to reconstruct a canopy over Platform 3 (from where the vintage trains will start) and convert the ground floor of the original water tower

Lancashire & Yorkshire Railway Class 25 'Ironclad' 0-6-0 No. 957, one of the stars of EMI's movie version of The Railway Children, heads out of Keighley with a passenger train. The engine has also featured in BBC's Born and Bred and the remake of The Hound of the Baskervilles. BRIAN SHARPE

GNR 0-6-2T No. 1744, one of the first residents of the nascent Keighley & Worth Valley Railway returned for a guest visit on February 20, 2010 from its then Great Central Railway home. It is seen storming out of Keighley. BRIAN SHARPE

building into a state-of-the-art visitor information centre where interactive screens will allow visitors to plan their day on the KWVR.

At the other end of the line the Oxenhope facilities are overdue a planned revamp, which should include a new catering outlet, a kids' adventure playground, and an improved and more interesting presentation of the vast exhibition shed's content. In between the two termini, Ingrow already has

its stunning Rail Story museum and highly innovative learning coach – as highlighted in Chapter 13 – while Oakworth remains an Edwardian gem and one of the very few untouched goods yards anywhere in the UK preserved railway movement.

Combining this feature with the fame afforded to its attractive station by The Railway Children film, which seems as well known today as ever, has to be high on the list of future projects aimed at

giving the railway's visitors a real reason to disembark from the train at every one of its stations. With this aim in mind the new Oxenhope catering outlet is being designed to service new on-train dining services such that the railway's visitor of tomorrow will be able to take a meal while travelling between their preferred combination of those same station destinations.

Hopefully appealing to its volunteers and visitors alike are the railway's short-term plans to celebrate in style the half century of its reopening in June 2018. A gala programme of events has been booked for several days around the actual anniversary date with many locomotives that have served the preserved branch in the past seeing a return to the line. A famous visiting steam locomotive emulating the 2016 visit by *Flying Scotsman* – as covered in Chapter 12 – will haul special afternoon tea trains the length of the line. At the time of writing, February 2017, the intention has been to fully recreate the 1968 reopening special train on June 29, 2018 although for that to happen will require a steam locomotive restoration to conclude on schedule – a rare event in railway preservation circles today!

Whatever the details of that celebration prove to be the Keighley & Worth Valley Railway is proud of its past 50 years, in a good place today, and confident of its next half-century. Its future success might not, like any other business, be totally assured but the railway's exciting plans combined with its usual flexible approach should certainly enhance the likelihood of that success.

LMS Jubilee 4-6-0 No. 5960 *Leander*, a sister to *Bahamas*, powers through Mytholmes in February 2006. BRIAN SHARPE